The Process of
Paragraph Writing

Other Prentice Hall Regents books by Joy M. Reid:

Basic Writing
The Process of Composition
Teaching ESL Writing

The Process of Paragraph Writing

Second Edition

Joy M. Reid
University of Wyoming

Prentice Hall Regents
Englewood Cliffs, New Jersey 07632

Library of Congress Cataloging in Publication Data

REID, JOY M.
   The process of paragraph writing

   Includes index
   1. English language—Paragraphs.   2. English
language—Text-books for foreign-speakers.
I. Title.
PE1439.R45 1994   428.2'4   84-24962
ISBN 0-13-101205-3

Editorial Director: Arley Gray
Acquisitions Editor: Nancy Leonhardt
Director of Production and Manufacturing: David Riccardi
Electronic Production Coordinator: Molly Pike Riccardi
Creative Director: Paula Maylahn

Editorial Production/Design Manager: Dominick Mosco
Electronic/Production Supervision, Page Composition,
   and Interior Design: Noël Vreeland Carter
Electronic Art: Rolando Corujo and Noël Vreeland Carter
Cover Design Coordinator: Merle Krumper
Production Coordinator: Ray Keating

Cover Illustration: Wanda España

The author gratefully acknowledges the following publishers for permission to reprint copyrighted materials:
The Los Angeles Times for Heiman, Andrea. 1992. "Women in the Driver's Seat," Los Angeles Times, reprinted in the Fort Collins
Coloradoan, August 14, 1992, B1. Reprinted by permission.
Time Inc. for Anastasia Toufexis, Time, March 30, 1987. "Furry and Feather Therapists". Copyright 1987 Time Inc. Reprinted by
permission.

© 1994 by PRENTICE HALL REGENTS
Prentice-Hall, Inc.
A Simon & Schuster Company
Englewood Cliffs, New Jersey 07632

Printed in the United States of America

10 9 8 7 6 5 4 3

ISBN 101205-3

Prentice-Hall International (UK) Limited, *London*
Prentice-Hall of Australia Pty. Limited, *Sydney*
Prentice-Hall of Canada Inc. *Toronto*
Prentice-Hall Hispanoamericana, S.A., *Mexico*
Prentice-Hall of India Private Limited, *New Delhi*
Prentice-Hall of Japan, Inc. *Tokyo*
Simon & Schuster Asia Pte. Ltd., *Singapore*
Editora Prentice-Hall do Brasil, Ltda., *Rio de Janeiro*

Table of Contents

To the Teacher   ix
To the Student   xiii

Chapter 1 The Writer–Reader Connection   1

Academic Writing and Purposes for Writing   *2*
Academic Writing and Topic Choice   *3*
Writing for an Academic Audience   *4*
Journal Writing   *6*
Personal Letters   *7*
    Personal Letter: Thank-you Note   *8*
    Envelopes   *9*
Business Letters   *12*
    Business Letter Format   *12*
    Business Letter: Informing and Requesting   *13*
    Business Letter of Complaint   *17*
    Business Letter of Request   *18*
    Business Letter of Invitation   *19*
Sentence Combining   *21*
    Independent Clauses   *21*
    Combining Independent Clauses   *22*
    Dependent Clauses   *25*
    Combining Dependent Clauses   *26*
    Review of Sentence Combining Structures   *27*
Sentence Combining Exercise   *28*

Chapter 2 The Paragraph: An Introduction   29

Pre-Writing   *30*
    Choosing a Subject   *30*
    Narrowing a Subject to a Topic   *30*
    Review of Some Pre-Writing Strategies   *35*
The Topic Sentence   *36*
    Controlling Ideas   *38*
The Topic Sentence and Writing Strategies   *40*
Titles   *41*
Concluding Sentences   *42*
Sentence Combining Exercise   *52*

Chapter 3 Planning the Paragraph 55

Focus: Second Sentences *55*
    Connectors for Second Sentences *57*
    Second Sentence Guidelines *61*
Support in the Paragraphs *63*
    Facts *63*
    Examples *66*
    Physical Description *67*
    Personal Experience *69*
Using Multiple Supporting Techniques *71*
Paragraph Unity *75*
Paragraph Revisions *78*
Sentence Combining Exercise *79*

Chapter 4 Paragraph Organization: The Point Paragraph Outline 81

Paragraph Coherence *82*
    Scrambled Paragraphs *85*
The Point Paragraph Outline *86*
Planning the Point Paragraph Outline *87*
    Form: The Point Paragraph Outline *87*
        Point Paragraph Outline Guidelines *88*
Modifying the Topic Sentence *94*
    Guidelines for Modifying Topic Sentences *95*
Expanding the Point Paragraph Outline *102*
Sentence Combining Exercise *106*

Chapter 5 Explanation Paragraphs 109

Process Paragraphs *109*
Chronological Connectors *110*
Passive Voice *114*
    When to Use the Passive *114*
    Reducing Passive Voice Use *117*
Process Paragraph Problems *120*
Definition/Clarification Paragraphs *122*
Explanation Paragraph Connectors *125*
Sentence Combining Exercise *133*

Chapter 6 Comparison/Contrast Paragraphs 135

Organization of Comparison/Contrast Paragraphs *137*
    Discussion of Both Sub-Topics *137*
The Basic Comparison/Contrast Point Paragraph Outline *137*
    Discussion of Each Sub-Topic Separately *138*
The Alternative Comparison/Contrast Point Paragraph Outline *138*
Comparison/Contrast Connectors *143*
    Overall Organization of Comparison/Contrast Paragraphs *150*
    Using Parallel Structures in Comparison/Contrast Paragraphs *153*
Sentence Combining Exercise *154*

Chapter 7 Cause-Effect Paragraphs   157

Organization of Cause-Effect Paragraphs   *158*
Cause-Effect Connectors   *162*
Developing Academic Cause-Effect Paragraphs   *170*
   Interviews   *170*
       Reporting the Results of an Interview   *172*
   Surveys   *175*
Sentence Combining Exercise   *181*

Chapter 8 Multiple Paragraphs   183

Developing Multiple Paragraphs   *183*
Expanding a Rough Draft   *186*
The Essay   *189*
Sentence Combining Exercise   *199*

Chapter 9 Using Secondary Sources   201

Academic Writing Tasks   *202*
Academic Libraries   *202*
Organization of U. S. Academic Libraries   *204*
   The Card Catalog   *205*
   The Computerized Card Catalog   *209*
   The General Reference Section   *211*
       The Library of Congress (LC) System   *211*
       Locating LC Materials in the Library   *214*
Finding and Using Magazine Articles   *215*
   Using Periodical Indexing Journals   *215*
   Computerized Indexing Journals   *221*
   Identifying Magazine (Journal, Periodical) Articles   *224*
   Locating Periodicals   *225*

Chapter 10 Summary Writing   229

Writing Summaries   *230*
Academic Summaries   *233*
Organization of Summaries   *237*
Citation of Articles   *245*
Sentence Combining Assignment   *247*

Appendices   249

Appendix A: Diagnosing Your Language Strengths and Weaknesses   *249*
Punctuation   *250*
   Periods   *250*
   Question Marks   *250*
   Commas   *251*
   Apostrophes   *253*
   Colons   *254*
   The Hyphen   *255*

Appendix B: Taking an Essay Examination or a Short-Answer Test *257*
Analyzing the Question *257*
    Identifying the Focus *258*
    Planning Your Time *259*
    Organizing Material for the Response *260*
20 Test-Taking Guidelines *261*

Index   263

GUIDELINES

Audience Analysis Guidelines	*inside front cover*
Paragraph Planning Guidelines	*inside front cover*
Pre-Writing Strategies Review	*35*
Second Sentence Guidelines	*61*
Point Paragraph Outline Guidelines	*88*
Guidelines for Modifying Topic Sentences	*95*
Paragraph Revision Guidelines	*inside back cover*

TO THE TEACHER

The Process of Paragraph Writing is a text designed for intermediate English as a Second Language (ESL) writing students. The rationale for the text derives from the following assumptions:

1. Students from different language or cultural backgrounds have writing strategies and objectives that differ from U.S. strategies and objectives (Leki, 1991; Kaplan, 1987; 1988; 1990; Purves, 1988). They often generate and present written material that is inappropriate for U.S. academic readers because they do not understand (or they lack experience with) the patterns that produce the "certain flow of information that any [U.S.] reader conditioned by literary custom expects to hear" (Jacobs, 1981, p. 245).

2. Writing academic discourse is essentially learned behavior for an audience that is absent (Emig, 1977; Kroll, 1991). ESL students, even more than native English-speaking students (NESs), must therefore be taught "the styles of thinking and ordering that dominate [U.S.] academic discourse" (Shaughnessy, 1977, p. 239).

3. There are many processes involved in writing. In general, these can be classified into pre-writing, writing, and revising. However, within these broad categories, the art and science of composing and producing a paragraph consists of a series of complex, recursive, and often uniquely individual steps (Perl, 1980; Raimes, 1987).

4. Because of the complexity and individuality of the composing processes in writing, students must have opportunities to examine, analyze, and practice a variety of possible strategies as they work with their own writing (McGroarty, 1992; Oxford, 1990; Reid, 1993).

5. Recent research has demonstrated the cognitive links between writing and reading (Blanton, 1992; Carrell, 1987; Carson and Leki, 1992; Carson et al., 1990; Johns, 1991). Reading provides students with stimuli for topics, activates the schema (that is, the background knowledge) of the students about a topic, and shows them the value of audience in writing. The writing–reading connection is, therefore, essential to a successful writing classroom.

6. Students learn to write by writing. In addition to formal academic tasks, students increase fluency and accuracy by frequent informal writing in journals (Peyton, 1990; Peyton and Reed, 1991).

7. Sequencing assignments, so that students gather information, write, discuss their writing, return to that writing, and improve that writing, allows students to improve their skills by spiralling increasingly difficult concepts (Leki, 1991–1992; Reid, 1989, 1993).

8. Students learn from classmates (and from the writing of classmates) as much as they learn from the teacher. To that end, collaboration, in the forms of pair and group work, peer feedback and review, and collaborative writing, is the foundation of this textbook (Christison, 1990; Scarcella & Oxford, 1992).

9. ESL writing teachers serve as facilitators, mediators, and cultural informants. They are an integral part of the classroom community whose primary responsibility is to serve as resources for the students. In that capacity, teachers prepare students for writing, establish the community of the classroom, and intervene in student writing through class discussion, conferencing, and responding to writing. (Goldstein and Conrad, 1990; Reid, 1993).

10. Because a classroom textbook should focus solely on the needs of the students a complete **teacher's manual** is available at no cost from Prentice Hall Regents, Englewood Cliffs, New Jersey 07632.

The Process of Paragraph Writing fulfills these goals by:
- concentrating on writing rather than on the theories of writing
- giving students a step-by-step approach to the various processes involved in writing a paragraph, including the skills of:

- identifying and/or analyzing audiences
- choosing and focusing a topic
- generating ideas through pre-writing
- organizing available material into appropriate formats for the U.S. academic writing

- using student samples about relevant topics that are written in structures and vocabulary that students understand, enjoy, and are able to imitate

- focusing on the importance of classroom community in collaborative exercises and multiple opportunities for small-group work

- providing a series of "guidelines" that function as the framework for writing

- offering a limited sentence structure and grammar review (and diagnostic exercises) that covers the most commonly made ESL writing errors

The Second Edition

Much research and teaching has occurred in the field of ESL writing since the first edition of **The Process of Paragraph Writing** was written in 1984. I have tried to incorporate some of what I have learned during those years. First, I have de-emphasized the importance of grammar in writing by (a) placing the diagnostic and grammar exercises in an appendix, (b) interweaving the sentence structure exercises with student writing, and (c) putting additional language-based exercises in the teacher's manual for use in individual remediation. Second, as my own ESL writing classes have become more community-based and student-centered, I have developed exercises, writing assignments, and an approach to teaching that reflects that philosophy; in this textbook, I have tried to build a classroom community through collaborative and cooperative group work. Third, my work in the writing-reading connection is reflected in the focus in **The Process of Paragraph Writing** on the identification and analysis of the reader by the writer. Moreover, while students had many opportunities to read (student samples) in the first edition, I have added a chapter on summary writing that integrates the writing-reading connection as it teaches an essential academic skill. Finally, I have tried to sequence the activities in all of the chapters so that students have many opportunities to return to their writing, and I have worked particularly on the multiple paragraph chapter and the secondary sources chapter to give students a wider range of writing and reading tasks, both in and outside of the text.

Acknowledgments

First, my heartfelt appreciation to Peggy Lindstrom, whose generosity and friendship, master-teaching, and insights made the first edition of **The Process of Paragraph Writing possible.** For help on the first edition, sincere thanks also to Maryann O'Brien, Linda Stratton, Leslie Noone, Jim Griswold, and Jeff Kaplan for their suggestions and contributions; to Peter Voeller, Doug Larson, Maggie McCaffrey, and Katie Knox for class testing the materials; to the many students in the Intensive English Program at Colorado State University for the writing samples that fill this book; and to the following reviewers for their careful evaluation of the original manuscript, and for their helpful suggestions: Irwin Feigenbaum; John N. Fleming; Sharon Grisdale; Alexandra Krapels; and Katherine Larson.

For the second edition, more thanks: to Anne Riddick and Nancy Leonhardt at Prentice Hall Regents for their continuing encouragement and support; to those teachers who have used the first edition, especially those who sent suggestions for this edition; to students at the University of Wyoming, at universities I visited in Hungary, Russia, Siberia, Ukraine, and Egypt, and at several universities and intensive language programs in the United States, who willingly gave their permission to use their writing in this book; and to my family: my husband, Steve, whose composition textbooks have inspired me, my daughter Shelley, who has begun to teach ESL writing, and Michael, who steadfastly majored in botany so we would have something else to talk about at family dinners.

References

Blanton, L. L. (1992). Text and context: Changing roles of readings for writers. Paper presented at the International TESOL Convention, Vancouver, B.C. (March).

Carrell, P. L. (1987). Text as interaction: Some implications of text analysis and reading research for ESL composition. In U. Connor and R. B. Kaplan (Eds.), *Writing Across Languages: Analysis of L2 Text* (pp. 47–56). Reading, MA: Addison-Wesley.

Carson, J. E. and Leki, I. (1992). Reading in the Writing Classroom: Second Language Perspectives. Boston: Heinle and Heinle

Carson, J. E., Carrell, P. L., Silberstein, S., Kroll, B., and Kuehn, P. A. (1990). Reading-writing relationships in first and second language. *TESOL Quarterly*, 24, 245–266.

Christison, M. A. (1990). Cooperative learning in the ESL classroom. *English Teaching Forum, 28* (4), 6–9.

Emig, J. (1977). Writing as a mode of learning. *College Composition and Communication, 28*, 122–128.

Goldstein, L. M. and Conrad, S. M. (1990). Student input and negotiation of meaning in ESL writing conferences. *TESOL Quarterly, 24* (3), 441–460.

Jacobs, S. 1981, Rhetorical information as predication. *TESOL Quarterly, 15* (3), 242–248.

Johns, A. M. (1991). Insights into the reading-writing relationship. Paper presented at the California TESOL Conference (CATESOL), Santa Clara (April).

Kaplan, R. B. (1987). Cultural thought patterns revisited. In U. Connor and R. B. Kaplan (Eds.), *Writing Across Languages: Analysis of L2 Texts* (pp. 9–22). Reading, MA: Addison-Wesley.

Kaplan, R. B. (1988). Contrastive rhetoric and second language learning: Notes towards a theory of contrastive rhetoric. In A. Purves (Ed.), *Writing Across Languages and Cultures: Issues in Contrastive Rhetoric* (pp. 275–304). Newbury Park, CA: Sage Publishers.

Kaplan, R. B. (1990). Writing in a multilingual/multicultural context: What's contrastive rhetoric all about? *Writing Instructor, 10*(1), 7–17.

Kroll, B. (1991). Teaching writing in the ESL context. In M. Celce-Murcia (Ed.), *Teaching English as a Second or Foreign Language* (pp. 245-263). New York: Newbury House/Harper Collins.

Leki, I. (1991). Twenty-five years of contrastive rhetoric: Text analysis and writing pedagogies. *TESOL Quarterly, 25* (1), 123–143.

Leki, I. (1991–1992). Building experience through sequenced writing assignments. *TESOL Journal, 1* (2), 19–23.

McGroarty, M. (1992). Cooperative Learning: The benefits for content-area teaching. In P. Richard-Amato and M. Snow (Eds.), *The Multicultural Classroom: Readings for Content-Area Teachers* (pp. 58–69). New York: Longman.

Oxford, R. L. (1990). *Language Learning Strategies: What Every Teacher Should Know.* New York: Newbury House/Harper and Row.

Perl, S. (1980). Understanding composing. *College Composition and Communication, 31,* 363–369.

Peyton, J. K. (Ed.). (1990). *Students and Teachers Writing Together.* Alexandria, VA: TESOL.

Peyton, J. K., and Reed, L. (Eds.). (1991). *Dialogue Journal Writing with Nonnative English Speakers: A Handbook for Teachers.* Alexandria, VA: TESOL.

Purves, A. (Ed.). (1988). *Writing Across Languages and Cultures: Issues in Contrastive Rhetoric.* Newbury Park, CA: Sage.

Raimes, A. (1987). Language proficiency, writing ability and composing strategies: A study of ESL college student writers. *Language Learning, 37* (3), 439–468.

Reid, J. (1989). ESL expectations in higher education: The expectations of the academic audience. In D. Johnson and D. Roens (Eds.), *Richness in Writing: Empowering ESL Students* (pp. 220–234). New York: Longman.

Reid, J. (1993). Teaching ESL Writing. Englewood Cliffs, NJ: Prentice Hall Regents.

Scarcella, R. and Oxford, R. (1992). *The Tapestry of Language Learning: The Individual in the Communicative Classroom.* Boston: Heinle and Heinle.

Shaughnessy, M. (1977). *Errors and Expectations: A Guide for the Teacher of Basic Writing.* New York: Oxford University Press.

TO THE STUDENT

The information in this book will help you write
- the kinds of paragraphs that U.S. college and university students write
- the kinds of paragraphs that U.S. college and university professors expect to read

All inexperienced writers, both native speakers of English and English as a Second Language (ESL) students, have problems as they try to find ways to communicate their ideas successfully. ESL writers have an additional problem: They do not fully understand the expectations of the U.S. academic audience.

This book will help you answer the following key questions about planning, writing, and revising U.S. academic tasks.

KEY QUESTIONS: PLANNING

ASSIGNMENT

What is the assignment?

What is the purpose of the assignment?

How long will the assignment be?

Is the subject provided? If so, what must you write about?

Are you going to choose your own subject?

TOPIC SELECTION

What are you going to write about?

What do you know about your subject?

Which key words or terms are associated with your subject?

Why have you chosen this subject?

What do you know about your subject?

What do you need to find out?

What do you want to communicate about your subject?

AUDIENCE

Who is the audience?

Age? Interests? Education? Other background information?

What does your audience already know about your subject?

What do you know about your subject that will interest your audience?

What is your communication purpose for this piece of writing?

TOPIC NARROWING

How can you narrow your topic to a subject?

What part(s) of the subject are you most interested in?

What part(s) of the subject do you know a lot about?

What is the main idea you want to communicate?

PRE-WRITING STRATEGIES

How can you generate ideas about your subject?

listing?	clustering?	treeing?
freewriting?	brainstorming?	flow-charting?

PURPOSE AND AUDIENCE

What is the purpose for your writing?

Do you want to inform your audience? Of what?

Do you want to persuade your audience? Of what?
Do you want to entertain your audience?
What do you want your audience to learn/discover while reading?
In what ways do you want your audience to change as a result of reading?
How do you expect your audience to feel after reading?
What do you expect your audience to do after reading?
What do you expect your audience to think after reading?

KEY QUESTIONS: DRAFTING AND REVISION

INFORMATION GATHERING

What information do you already have about your topic?
How can you find additional information?

interview an authority?	design and give a survey?
use the library?	read about the topic?

How can you explain, define, and/or support your topic?
What facts can you use?
Do you know of any examples?
Can you use physical description?
Do you have any relevant personal experience?
What specific details will:

support your main idea?
provide adequate evidence for your main idea?

ORGANIZATION

What is the most effective way(s) to arrange your available material?
Will you communicate with your audience by

describing a process?
explaining your topic?
comparing and/or contrasting your main idea with another idea?
discussing the causes and/or effects of your topic?
investigating a question?
evaluating your topic?
identifying and solving a problem?

How have you organized each paragraph?
Have you written a clear *topic sentence* with *controlling ideas*?
Are the points in each paragraph directly related to the controlling ideas in your topic sentence?
Do you have enough specific detail to support the points you have made?
Is there a clear concluding sentence?

REVISION FOCUS

What revisions will improve your writing?

refocus the main idea?	revise the topic sentence?
add examples or detail?	strengthen evidence?
rewrite the concluding sentence(s)?	

Is the purpose of your writing still clear and relevant?
Are you still responding to the assignment?
Has the focus changed since you began planning?
Are you still fulfilling the needs and expectations of your audience?
Does the title accurately reflect the content of your writing and the interest of your audience?

EDITING

Is the language in your writing formal or informal? Why?
Is the vocabulary appropriate for your audience?
Have you varied your sentence structure for emphasis and audience interest?
Have you used appropriate connectors?
Are the mechanics in your writing correct? Check:

punctuation	capitalization	spelling

Is the grammar correct? Check:

word order	subject-verb agreement	word use
run-on sentences	sentence fragments	

The Process of
Paragraph Writing

1

The Writer-Reader Connection

The hardest part of writing is to decide what to write about. But even after I make up my mind about my topic, it is still hard to write because I am worried that it may not be so interesting for my reader. Then I overcome this problem by deciding to just write until I run out of what to say.

Ahmed Mohamed Ali
(Somalia)

In the past, writing and reading were considered separate skills: the writer wrote a message, and later, the reader extracted the message. The writer was an active composer whose message was more important than the reader; the reader was a passive receiver who could understand the message if she or he were clever enough. The relationship between writer and reader was thought to be like this:

WRITER ——————▶ TEXT (message) ——————▶ reader

However, researchers have found that the relationship between writers and readers is quite different. Both writing and reading are active, complex skills, and the more writers know about their readers, the more successful their writing will be. That is, writers are responsible for considering the needs and expectations of their readers. In the same way, the more readers know about the writer and the topic of the text, the easier and more successful the reading will be.

Both writers and readers bring their life experiences to their task; that is, as writers begin to write, they use their background knowledge to help them, and as readers begin to read, their background knowledge helps them comprehend the text. On the following page is a diagram of the relationship between writer, text, and reader, as the reader begins to read.

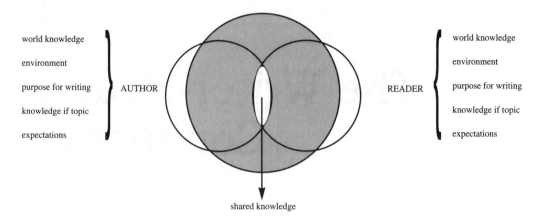

world knowledge

environment

purpose for writing   AUTHOR

knowledge if topic

expectations

world knowledge

environment

purpose for writing

knowledge if topic

expectations

READER

shared knowledge

Figure A. Reader-Writer Relationships

As the reader reads, the outside circles move closer and closer, and the area of "shared knowledge" increases. Based on this writer-reader relationship, there are three basic rules for successful academic writing:

1. **Identify a purpose for writing**. Only then can you communicate your ideas.

2. **Write about what you know**. If you are familiar with your topic, it will be easier to write.

3. **Always write for an audience.** If you can identify for whom you are writing, the purpose of the paragraph will become clearer and your communication with that audience will be more successful.

Academic Writing and Purposes for Writing

People have many different reasons for writing: One person might write a grocery list, another a poem; still another may write a letter to a friend or a research paper for an academic class. These kinds of writing have different purposes and different audiences, so the language, the organization, and the focus in the writing will be different for each. If, for example, you write a grocery list for yourself, the list will probably contain less information and different information than it would if a friend was going to grocery shop for you.

The purposes for academic writing differ from most other kinds of writing. For example, when you write (a) a letter to your parents, (b) directions to your house for a friend who is coming to visit, or (c) a poem, your purposes are to inform, explain, or amuse your audience. You are communicating ideas that will teach or entertain the reader; most often, you are a kind of expert who is offering knowledge to specific readers. In contrast, often the main purpose of an academic writing assignment is to **demonstrate knowledge** to the professor that you have learned as a result of the class. It is probable that the professor, who has assigned the writing task, has designed that task as a kind of test. The professor is the expert; she or he expects to learn whether or not you have understood material presented in class, reading for the course, and class discussions. In addition, the professor may expect you to demonstrate your ability to read additional material, summarize and synthesize that material, and present your ideas in appropriate ways.

Exercise A

Read the two academic writing assignments below. Identify the purpose(s) for each assignment. Which assignment would be easier for you to complete? Why? Then answer the questions that follow each academic assignment.

1. Undergraduate Political Science class

   Write a letter to your local state legislator. Your letter should be about a current political issue. The letter should contain an opinion on the issue, solid reasons backing that position, and a request for a response. To prepare to write the letter, read several articles on the topic you wish to write about. This will add to your own political literacy and help you communicate effectively. Your letter should be typewritten and addressed correctly.

   A. Circle the key words in this assignment—that is, the words that signal what the assignment is.

   B. What will the audience (that is, the state legislator) expect from your letter? How could you fulfill those expectations?

   C. What main idea would you choose to communicate in your letter?

   D. How might you find supporting detail for your opinion?

2. Undergraduate class in Women and Third World Development

   Write a short critical paper on the following assignment: Is the role of women in Third World development an equity issue or a productivity issue? Use the readings assigned for the class as well as your personal experience and other reading to respond to the question.

   A. Circle the **key words** in this assignment—that is, the words that signal what the assignment is.

   B. How long should this assignment be? What specific questions might you ask the professor about length?

   C. What do you know about this topic ? What don't you know?

   D. How might you find out the information you need?

Academic Writing and Topic Choice

Research has shown that in most academic classes, writing tasks are assigned. That is, students do not choose their topics; instead, they are assigned by the professor. However, in most classes, students are given a choice of topics. It is therefore important that students learn to analyze writing assignments in order to choose topics that they know about.

Exercise B

Read the two academic writing assignments below. Then decide which of the assignments you would feel more comfortable writing about. What questions could you ask the designer of each of these assignments (that is, the instructor) that would help you fulfill the expectations of your academic audience?

1. Undergraduate Ethics Essay Competition (Topic: Euthanasia: Mercy or Murder?)

   Your mother is terminally ill with bone cancer. Both she and your father are living with you in your home. Despite your mother's chronic pain and suffering, your father would do anything to prolong her life, but her physicians have told you that she will probably live only six months to a year. You have received instructions from the doctors about your mother's care, including giving her a powerful painkilling medication. Too many pills could be fatal. You are greatly anguished by her suffering, and you consider giving her a lethal dose of the painkillers.

   Write an essay considering the arguments for and against euthanasia, based on this situation. You are to be a moral <u>judge</u>, making an intelligent decision based on the available information. Do not focus on the correctness of any particular religious view. Rather, your essay will be judged on your ability to examine the relevant evidence and to explain how that evidence supports a given conclusion.

2. Undergraduate course on Adult Education

   Identify something that you want to learn about this semester (for example, diamond mining, ski diving, snakes, etc.). The assignment involves three things. First, write a plan by which you will learn this new thing. Second, keep a diary as you go about the process of learning. This diary should include insights you get about the nature of learning as well as specific thoughts regarding your own learning. Third, write a descriptive statement (of whatever length) that summarizes how you believe you learn best when you have something you want to learn about.

Writing for an Academic Audience

Understanding the connection between writer and audience is essential for good writing. The reader(s) for your writing will determine what you say and how you say it. In personal writing, for example, your vocabulary, your ideas, and even your sentence structures will be less formal than those elements will be in academic writing. Moreover, if you write about the same topic for different audiences, the elements of your writing will differ, depending on that audience.

Exercise C

The three paragraphs below about trees are written for three different audiences. The first is written for elementary school children, the second for secondary school students, and the third for a university professor. Read each paragraph, and notice

- the amount of information communicated
- the kind of information communicated
- the vocabulary
- the length of the sentences.

Then answer the questions that follow the paragraphs.

maple

I

There are two kinds of trees. One kind is called the coniferous (con-í-fér-óus) tree. The other kind is called the deciduous (de-cí-du-óus) tree. The coniferous tree has narrow leaves that look like green needles. These leaves do not fall off in the winter time. They are green all year, so these trees are often called "evergreens." The deciduous tree is quite different. It has wide green leaves. In the fall, the leaves turn many different colors: red, gold, and orange. Then the leaves die and fall of the tree. The deciduous tree looks very beautiful in the fall, but the coniferous tree looks very nice all year.

Sabine Luttege
(Germany)

II

Whether a tree is coniferous or deciduous, whether it bears fruit or not, whether it grows in the tropics or in the temperate zone, every tree has three parts: the roots, the trunk, and the crown. The roots, the part of the tree underground, hold the tree firmly against windstorms and provide the tree with food gathered from the soil. The trunk, which is the most important woody part of the tree, is the body of the tree; it carries the food from the roots to the branches. The crown of the tree consists of the branches, the leaves, and the fruit of the tree. The leaves use the food sent from the trunk for many purposes, one of which is a process that is particularly useful to humans. In this process, called photosynthesis, the leaves absorb carbon dioxide from the atmosphere and give oxygen to the atmosphere. This single process is essential to human life because humans breathe oxygen in order to exist.

Kamil Al-Makossi
(Iraq)

III

The root system of the tree has three important functions. First, the root system provides mechanical support for the aerial parts of the tree and anchors the tree against windstorms. Second, the youngest rootlets in particular absorb water and dissolved minerals from the soil; these materials move through the older roots into the trunk and ultimately reach the upper region and the leaves. In the leaves, the materials are used in various cellular processes, including photosynthesis, and a large proportion of the water is lost to the air by transpiration. Second, food accumulated in root cells during dormant periods provide energy and material for the rapid flush of new growth during the spring. Finally, the roots of many trees such as the cherry, aspen, beech, and sassafras are important in vegetative reproduction. These species produce suckers, or adventitious stems, that may develop to tree size.

Yoshimine Kato
(Japan)

1. The verb "to be" is used most often in the first paragraph. Why?

2. Determine the average sentence length in paragraphs I and II by counting the total number of words in each paragraph and dividing that number by the total number of sentences in each paragraph. Why is there a difference between the average sentence length in the two paragraphs?

3. How does the vocabulary in each of the paragraphs differ? Use specific examples to support your answer.

4. The information given in paragraph I is about all trees; the information in paragraph II is about the three parts of every tree; in paragraph III, the information is about only a single part of every tree. Why is there such a difference? What conclusions can you draw from this narrowing of the topic for each audience?

Journal Writing

Some writing is more formal than others. For example, if you write two letters, one to your mother and another to the president of a university, the information, the language, and the focus of the letters will almost certainly be different. Personal writing—writing letters to friends, writing in diaries or journals—is often less formal than academic writing.

For many writing students, one way to improve writing is to write, informally, every day. Practice in writing can give you confidence and make writing easier, particularly if the focus of some of your writing is **fluency** (that is, writing with ease). Writing in a journal offers the chance to write without worrying about organization or grammatical accuracy. The purpose of journal writing is to put ideas into written form, not to worry about errors. Writing daily in a journal will give you the opportunity to write about what interests you and to express your thoughts and opinions about a variety of topics. In addition, journals can be used to gather information for writing essays, for summarizing ideas that you have learned about writing, and for evaluating the processes of writing that you are experiencing.

While your writing teacher may read all or parts of your journal in order to give you credit for your work, the audience for a journal can be whomever you choose: yourself, a real or imaginary friend (some students begin their journal entries "Dear Journal"), your teacher, or a professional acquaintance.

The goals of journal writing in this course are:

• to write every day

• to think about your journal entry before you write

- to communicate your thoughts in writing
- to improve your English fluency through practice.

Your journal for this class will probably be a notebook. Each day, put the date in the margin (May 31, 1995 or 5-31-95), and write a paragraph or two. Your journal entries can be of your own choosing (about your family, current events, feelings and impressions, or opinions/evaluations) or they can be assigned. Journal assignments like the one below ask you to write about writing.

Journal Assignment

Write for five minutes about the kinds of writing you do in your own language. What purposes do you have for writing? Who are the audiences for your writing? Describe two pieces of writing you have completed in your native language.

Personal Letters

Another way to improve your writing is to write informal and formal letters. Letter and note writing in the United States is part of the culture. Furthermore, letters and notes are written for many reasons and for various audiences. A personal letter is one written to a friend or acquaintance to communicate across the miles. Shorter letters, called notes, are commonly used

- to send an invitation (for dinner, a party, etc.)
- to say thank you (for a gift, a special dinner, etc.)
- to express congratulations (for an award, a graduation, the birth of a baby, etc.)
- to show sympathy (for a death, illness, or accident)

The form of a personal letter or note is informal, but even informal letters have a form that includes the address (which is sometimes eliminated in a very personal note or letter), the date, the salutation (or greeting), the body of the note itself, and the closing. Informal notes are often handwritten, and they follow the general format on the next page:

Personal Letter: Thank-You Note

your address ⟶ 1424 Fairview
Denville, N. J. 08542

the date ⟶ September 24, 1983

Dear Dr. Habib, ⟵ the salutation

Thank you for your assistance yesterday. I have completed the application and mailed it.
I very much appreciate the time and trouble you took.

the closing ⟶ Sincerely,

your name ⟶ Betty Brown

Note the following about personal letters:

- the margin at the left side of the letter (about 1/2 inch)
- the address and closing are placed the same distance from the right margin
- commas are used between the day and the year in the address, but not at the end of each line of the address;
- commas are also used after the salutation (or greeting), and after the closing

Envelopes

Envelopes in the U.S. have the following format:

Writing Assignment 1

In your journal, write a letter of thanks to someone who has done something for you. Your audience is the person to whom you are writing. Follow the general format given above.

Exercise D

Read the personal letters below. Then answer the questions that follow each.

I

October 23, 1995

Dead Mom and Dad,

I arrived here last week. The trip was terrible. Dr. Stevens says that my leg will be better soon. My roommate is very strange. The police say my money is gone forever. Please send $1500 to my address right away. Thanks.

Your loving son,

Mark

1. This is the first letter Mark's parents received after he left for college. What do you think his parents will think about this letter?

2. Where will his parents send the money?

3. What other information might his parents like to know?

4. What advice can you give Mark about writing letters?

II

2411 Louisiana #7
Santa Barbara, CA 93106
September 11, 1994

Dear Hector,

    I am pleased to let you know that I had a pleasant journey here. I enjoyed my trip by airplane because the Boeing 747 was very comfortable and the stewardesses were so willing to be of service. I also enjoyed looking at beautiful and colorful landscapes during my flight. We looked at the Bahama Islands which are composed of a large chain of islands, the Mexican Gulf, and other interesting points.

    Now I have found an apartment and I am getting acquainted with my new lifestyle. In addition, I have settled into my program of study here at the university. I have even found some old friends and have met some new ones.

    Greetings to your wife and children.

With my best wishes,

Julio Samboy

1. What does this personal letter tell you about the relationship between Hector and Julio? That is, what is the writer-reader connection in this letter?

2. What is Julio's reason for writing this letter?

3. What do you learn about Julio in this letter?

4. How will Hector feel when he reads this letter? What will he do?

III

1113 W. Plum   104E
Rockaway Valley, PA 70456
January 27, 1995

Dear Safi,

It gives me a good feeling when I write to you. How are you and how are things going? Is everything ok? How is your family?

I'd like to tell you that over Christmas vacation I went to Los Angeles, California, and I spent some very nice days there. The climate is fair. There is no wind, no snow, and the sun shines all day long. The streets are clean. You don't see trash everywhere. In front of every entrance you find a trash basket.

There are many highways. Oh, I'm sorry, they don't call them highways as they do in Boonton. They call them freeways.

I'd like you to see Los Angeles at night. If you do you're going to be crazy about it. At first I thought I was in Paradise. I found myself on brightly lit streets. The shops had been decorated for the holiday and everything was sparkling.

I hope you understand my feelings because imagining it isn't like reality. Los Angeles is the only city I've visited in the U.S.A. that I like a lot.

That's all this time. If I visit another city, I'll tell you about it the next time.

after letter
Post Script

Yours,
Mahmoud Ghazzaoui
Mahmoud Ghazzaoui

P.S. Please say hello to everyone around you.

1. What can you guess about Mahmoud? His age? Interests?
2. What was his purpose in writing this letter?
3. What does the P.S. mean?
4. What additional information would you like to read about in this letter?

Writing Assignment 2

Write a letter to a friend in which you describe a recent trip you have taken. Focus on one place (one city, one resort) and describe your reactions to it.

Peer Feedback: In a small group of classmates, read several letters that are not your own. At the end of each letter, write one question you would like the author to answer in the letter. Then discuss your questions with your classmates.

Revision: Using the questions written by your classmates, improve your letter. Then rewrite your letter. Address an envelope and mail the letter to your friend.

Business Letters

In business and professional situations, letters are used to
- make requests (for goods, for admission, for information, etc.)
- make complaints (about poor service, a flawed consumer product, etc.)
- give information (to a supervisor or teacher, to a business associate, etc.)
- make recommendations (by sharing opinions, solving problems, etc.)

Following is the basic form for the business letter. A business letter written by a university professor to a colleague follows.

Business Letter Format

Your address
Your City, state, and zip code
Today's date

Full name of the person receiving the letter
The person's street address
The person's city, state, and zip code

Dear _____ : The person's shortened name (Mr. X, Ms. Y)

Your letter

Sincerely,

Your signature   *John A. Smith*

Your typed name   John A. Smith

JS/mk } Letter for John Smith typed by Mary Knowles

Encl. } Something is enclosed with the letter

Business Letter: Informing and Requesting

Electrical Engineering Department
Georgetown University
Washington D.C. 20007
August 1, 1994

Professor Howard A. Mohr
Engineering Department
Michigan State University
Lansing, MI 49423

Dear Professor Mohr:

The DISEM (Digital Systems Educational Materials) project has been funded by the National Science Foundation to study the current status of digital systems education, to develop prototype materials, and to suggest methods for developing an instructional system to improve digital systems education at the national level.

For your information, a copy of the first project newsletter is enclosed. The newsletter provides an overview of the project and describes the progress to date. Please show the newsletter to faculty in your department who might be interested in the project. We welcome suggestions about or contributions to the newsletter.

Sincerely yours,

Thomas A. Brubaker

Thomas A. Brubaker
Project Director

Enclosure
TAB/mt

Exercise E

Below are three letters requesting information about admission to a university. Each has a slightly different goal and a different audience. Read the letters. Then answer the questions that follow each.

I

4547 Shoreline Drive
San Diego, CA 90178
March 30, 1995

Mr. Dennis Dreher
Foreign Student Advisor
Florida State University
Tallahassee, FL 32306

Dear Mr. Dreher:

I am interested in finding out more about the graduate program in agricultural economics at Florida State University. Would you please send me a catalog of classes and any other relevant information?

I am currently enrolled at the American Language Institute at San Diego State University. I have just received a TOEFL score of 580, so I am interested in beginning my course work as an undergraduate at Florida State as soon as possible. Would it be possible to begin in June? If not, could I begin in September?

Thank you in advance for your help.

Sincerely yours,

Samer El-Hammouri

Samer El-Hammouri

1. What is the purpose of this letter? What does Samer hope to do?
2. Who is the audience?
3. How might Mr. Dreher respond?

II

915 James Court, #2
Oakville, Ohio 46819
June 12, 1994

Admissions Office
Kansas State University
Manhattan, KS 66502

Dear Admissions Officer:

I am interested in beginning graduate study in the field of plant pathology at Kansas State University in September of this year.

Attached are my transcripts, a complete application form, and additional information concerning my previous studies and my experience.

Please send me a university catalog and schedule and any information you have concerning financial aid for graduate students in my field. In addition, please send me any other information you consider pertinent.

Thank you for your consideration.

Sincerely,

Mohamed El-Ghouri

Mohamed El-Ghouri

Enclosures

1. How does the audience in this letter differ from the audience in the previous letter?

2. How does the purpose differ?

3. This letter has a more formal tone than the previous one. How can you tell?

III

218 N. Wood St.
Portland, OR 97207
July 16, 1994

Chair, Department of Textiles and Clothing
Oklahoma City University
Oklahoma City, OK 73106

Dear Chair:

I would like to apply to the graduate school of your university for admission. Besides admission, I also hope to obtain a teaching or research assistantship in your department.

I received my bachelor's degree from National Taiwan Normal University in June, 1989. During my academic years, the courses I took related to textiles and clothing were psychology, general chemistry, organic chemistry, sewing, applied coloring, clothing and textiles, and home economics education.

In 1989, having finished my courses, I was employed by Taipei Soan Shan Junior High School as a teacher for four years. The experience in teaching has offered me many opportunities to put much of the knowledge I gained in school to practical use, and at the same time it intensified my interest in the study of textiles and clothing. Since that time I have been attending the English language program at Portland State University. I will finish the program next month and will take the TOEFL at that time.

Please send me the application form for a graduate assistantship. If further information is required for this request, please let me know at your earliest convenience. Your assistance is highly appreciated. I look forward to hearing from you soon.

Sincerely, yours,

Suh-Ju Shen

Suh-Ju Shen

1. The purpose of this letter is more complicated than the previous letters' purposes. What are the author's objectives?
2. How might the reader of this letter react?
3. Is the letter writer successful in persuading the Chair of her qualifications? Why or why not?

Writing Assignment 3

In your journal, write the draft of a letter to a college or university requesting information concerning admission procedures and information about your major field. Use the correct business letter format.

> **Peer Feedback:** In a group of 3-4 classmates, read each letter that is not your own. Underline any problem you find in format or grammar. Then discuss these problems with your classmates.

> **Revision:** Using the comments of your classmates, make improvements in your letter. Then rewrite the letter.

Exercise F

You may have to write other kinds of business letters while you are studying in a U.S. college or university. Below are formal letters of complaint, request, and invitation. Notice that each letter is short and direct. The reason for writing the letter is given immediately. Then a fuller explanation follows in the second short paragraph. Finally, each letter ends with a short concluding sentence/paragraph. Read each letter; then answer the questions that follow.

Business Letter of Complaint

500 W. Prospect
Fort Collins, CO 80521
January 29, 1994

Editor
The Coloradoan
1212 Riverside Ave.
Fort Collins, CO 80526

Dear Editor:

Please cancel my subscription to your newspaper, *The Coloradoan*, and refund my money.

The reason I do not wish to continue receiving *The Coloradoan* is that the delivery of the newspaper is very late. I telephoned your Circulation Editor, Karl Madsen, two weeks ago about this problem, and he stated that the problem would be solved. However, the newspaper has continued to be delivered too late for me to read it.

Enclosed are the coupon and the receipt of payment for six weeks of my subscription. Please send me a refund check for $14.50.

Respectfully yours,
Octavio Mijangos
Octavio Mijangos

Encls: Handy coupon, Receipt

1. What is Octavio's purpose in writing this letter?
2. Do you think he will be successful? Why or why not?
3. How will the editor of The Coloradoan probably react after reading this letter?

Business Letter of Request

Box 226
Austin, MN 55603
December 17, 1994

Travel Bureau
99 Washington Ave.
Albany, NY 12245

Sir or Madam:

    Would you please send me the maps and pamphlets describing interesting places in New York? I hope to visit your state next summer, so all the materials you can send me will be helpful. For example, will there be any special festivals during July?
    Thank you in advance for your kind attention.

Yours truly,

Ms. Maria Santiago Ramos

Ms. Maria Santiago Ramos

1. Why is the salutation (greeting) "Sir or Madam"? Is the identity of the person who will read this letter important?
2. What is Maria's purpose in writing? Do you think she will achieve her purpose? Why or why not?
3. In both of the letters above, what is the tone of the letter: angry? courteous? aggressive? Why, do you think, is the tone similar in both letters?

Business Letter of Invitation

10510 S. Millard
Chicago, IL 60655
Feb. 1, 1995

Dr. Kimberly Brown
Department of History
Loyola University
Chicago, IL 60652

Dear Dr. Brown:

On Monday night, I attended your lecture at the Chicago Public Library about your trip to India. It was very interesting. I especially enjoyed seeing the beautiful silk dresses and slides of the people with whom you worked.

I am a student in the Intensive English Program at Loyola University. In my advanced listening class, we have been studying about other peoples and cultures. My teacher in that class, Professor Carolyn Young, asked me to write you. We would be very glad if you would come to talk with us about your trip.

Please let me know by Monday, February 25th, if you will come to visit our class. My telephone number is 555-3903.

Sincerely yours,

Diomande V/Famboude

Diomande V/Famboude

1. What is the purpose of this letter?
2. What questions might Professor Brown have about the letter?
3. What additional information might have been included in the letter?

Writing Assignment 4

Each address below represents the tourist bureau in one of the United States. In your journal, write a rough draft of a business letter to one of them, asking for information you might need for a successful tourist visit to that state.

New Mexico. Tourist Division, 113 Washington Ave., Santa Fe, NM 87503

New York. Travel Bureau, 99 Washington Ave., Albany, NY 12245

North Carolina. Travel Development Section, Raliegh NC, 27611

North Dakota. Travel Division, Capitol Grounds, Bismarck, ND 58505

Ohio. Travel and Tourist Bureau, 30 East Broad Street, Columbus, OH 43215

Oklahoma. Tourism and Recreation Dept., 500 Will Rogers Blvd., Oklahoma City, OK 73105

Oregon. Travel Information Section, Room 105, State Highway Bldg., Salem, OR 97310

Pennsylvania. Bureau of Travel Development, 431 South Office Bldg., Harrisburg, PA 17120

Rhode Island. Dept. of Economic Development and Tourism, One Wybosset Hill, Providence, RI 02903

South Carolina. Division of Travel and Tourism, Box 113, 1205 Pendleton Street, Columbia, SC 29201

South Dakota. Dept. of Tourism, State Office Building Number Two, Pierre, SD 57501

Tennessee. Tourism Development, 1028 Andrew Jackson State Office Bldg., Nashville, TN 37219

Texas. Travel and Information Division, Austin, TX 78701

Utah. Travel Dept., Council Hall, Capitol Hill, Salt Lake City, UT 84114

Vermont. Information-Travel Development, 61 Elm Street, Montpelier, VT 05602

Virginia. State Travel Service, Six North Sixth Street, Richmond, VA 23219

Washington. Travel Development Division, 101 General Administration Bldg., Olympia, WA 98504

West Virginia. Travel Development Division, Room B-553, 1900 Washington St. East, Charleston, WV 25305

Wisconsin. Vacation and Travel Service, Box 450, Madison WI 53701

Wyoming. The Wyoming Travel Commission, 2320 Capitol Avenue, Cheyenne, WY 82001

Peer Feedback: In a small group of classmates, discuss what states you have decided to visit and the reasons why. Then read the letters that are not your own. Underline any problem you find in the format or grammar. Discuss the problems you have found with each of the authors.

Revision: Using the comments and marks of your classmates, make necessary changes in your letter. Then rewrite the letter, address and stamp the envelope, and mail the letter to the appropriate tourist bureau.

Sentence Combining

In English, as in your native language, there are many ways to communicate thoughts. Academic writing requires that you use different kinds of sentences to communicate different kinds of information. For example, often:

- short, simple sentences are used for emphasis
- medium-length sentences are used to explain ideas
- longer sentences are used for descriptions and to show relationships among ideas

Learning to use different sentence structures can help make your writing clearer for your reader. Combining short, simple sentences can make your academic writing more successful.

Written English consists of **clauses**. A clause is a group of words with a subject (S) and a verb (V)—and <u>perhaps</u> a complement (C). The complement is a group of words that follow the verb. If a group of words does not have a subject, it is not a clause; if a group of words does not have a verb, it is not a clause.

Examples:

(S)   (V)   (C)

<u>**Jedda is**</u> (the largest city in Saudi Arabia)   (clause)

On the Red Sea.   (no subject, no verb—not a clause)

<u>**It is**</u> (a beautiful, modern city).   (clause)

The population of Jedda.   (no verb—not a clause)

Is about one million people.   (no subject—not a clause)

In written English, there are two kinds of clauses:

Independent Clauses   (**IC**)
Dependent Clauses   (**DC**)

Independent Clauses

An independent clause (**IC**) is a group of words with a subject and a verb (and perhaps a complement) that can stand by itself. It is complete. It is a <u>strong</u> clause.

Exercise G

Each of the clauses below is an independent clause. Identify the subject (S) and the verb (V) in each independent clause. The first sentence has been completed.

(**S**)   (**V**)   (**C**)

1. **The weather in Jedda is** (hot and humid most of the year).

2. Jedda is protected by the sea.

3. The sea reduces the number of sand storms.

4. Most of the people go to the sea every other day.

5. Jedda is developing very quickly.

6. This development can be seen from the tall buildings all over the city.

7. The people in Jedda are very nice and helpful.

8. The city has many shops.

9. Some of the shops open at 8:00 or 9:00 a.m.

10. Many places are open for twenty-four hours each day.

Maatoug Al-Arawi
(Saudi Arabia)

Each of the sentences above is <u>one</u> independent clause. Each is a complete, simple sentence. However, many sentences in English contain more than one independent clause. In each sentence below, two independent clauses have been joined together (that is, "combined").

1. **São Paulo is** (a large city in my country); **it is** (located in southeastern Brazil).

2. **Everyone in São Paulo works** (hard), but **they** also **enjoy** (living there).

3. **The city has** (many elegant restaurants and museums), so **the people** always **have** (places to go).

4. **São Paulo has** (many beautiful beaches), and **you can meet** (your friends there).

5. **This city has** (many industries); **it is** (an important business city).

6. **Tourists in São Paulo have** (a good time); moreover, **they appreciate** (the technology as well as the night life).

Maria Santoro
(Brazil)

Combining Independent Clauses

There are two ways to combine (that is, to join) independent clauses (IC) in written English. The first is to join the clauses with a comma and a **"short word."** These "short words" (also called coordinate conjunctions)* are signs to the reader. They signal the relationship between the independent clauses.

---

* Other coordinate conjunctions, used less frequently in English, are *or, nor, for,* and *yet* .

IC, and IC   **, and** → signals that additional information is coming

IC, but IC   **, but** → signals that contrasting information is coming

IC, so IC   **, so** → signals that an effect following a cause is coming

Exercise H

Each of the sentences below has two ICs. Identify the subject (S) and the verb (V) in each IC. Circle the comma and the short word that join the two ICs. Identify the relationship between the two ICs: additional information, contrasting information, or cause-effect information.

1. Warsaw is the largest city in Poland, and it is also very old.

2. There are many historical buildings in Warsaw, and there are many old monuments.

3. Warsaw is an old city, but the people are very young.

4. The city was bombed during the war, so many people died.

5. Then my county, Poland, rebuilt Warsaw, and now many industries and offices exist in the city.

6. Embassies from every country in the world are in Warsaw, so it is an international city.

7. Warsaw is the capital of Poland, and it is the center of culture.

Ewa Nowoskawska
(Poland)

Exercise I

Read the following sentences. Identify the subject (S), the verb (V), and the complement (C) in each IC. Combine the two ICs with a comma plus a short word. Identify the relationship between the ICs. Sometimes two relationships are possible.

<u>*NOTE*</u>: *do not capitalize the first word of the second IC when you combine the clauses.*

1. Seoul is the largest city in Korea.

   It is the capital of my country.

2. Nine million people live in Seoul.

   The density of the population is great.

3. Thirty percent of the population of Korea live in Seoul.

   The land area of the city is small.

4. Therefore we don't have very many buildings.

   Some of them are sixty stories tall.

5. Seoul is a beautiful city built in the mountains.

   Its people appreciate its long history.

6. The city is very clean.

   The people are very kind to others.

7. The weather in Seoul is warm and rainy in the summer.

   It is cold and snowy in the winter.

Kyu Yong Lee
(Korea)

Another way to combine ICs is to use a semicolon. If the ideas in two ICs are related, they may be joined by a semicolon (;)

Examples:

In my country, Taiwan, I like watching television; I enjoy watching the news, sports, and dramas.

Television programs increase my knowledge and common sense; they also make me laugh and cry.

If you use a semi-colon to join two ICs, you may also use a "**long word**." These "long words" signal the reader about the relationship between the two ICs. The use of these "long words" (also called conjunctive adverbs) is optional; use them if you think they make the sentence clearer for the reader.

<u>NOTE</u>: "long words" come after the semi-colon, and they are followed by a comma.

IC; moreover, IC   (signals that additional information is coming)

IC: furthermore, IC   (signals that additional information is coming)

IC; however, IC   (signals that contrasting information if coming)

IC; therefore, IC   (signals an effect that follows a cause is coming)

IC; consequently, IC   (signals an effect that follows a cause is coming)

Examples:

In Taiwan, almost every family has a television set; **therefore,** each individual watches at least three hours of television every day.

I have watched many television programs on U.S. television; **however,** I can't understand the language.

Exercise J

Read the sentences below. Identify the subject (S), the verb (V), and the complement (C) in each clause. Put a semicolon between the two ICs. For three of the combined sentences, add a "long word" after the semicolon. Identify the relationship between the ICs: additional, contrasting, or cause-effect information. Sometimes two relationships are possible. Put a comma after each long word.

1. I like television.

   It communicates the technology of the world to the people.

2. In addition, television teaches people about their environment.

   It also shows them how to stay healthy.

3. Television also helps to raise children.

   It teaches them vocabulary and facts.

4. Television transmits information.

   It entertains people.

5. Most important, television gives education without the presence of professors.

   It is the cheapest method of acquiring new knowledge of the world.

Hailu Kenno
(Ethiopia)

Writing Assignment 5

In your journal, write 10 **pairs** of ICs about why you like (or dislike) television. Trade sentences with a partner. Identify the subject (S), verb (V), and complement (C) in each of your partner's sentences. Then combine the pairs of your partner's sentences. Use a comma and a short word in five combined sentences. Use a semicolon (and in some cases a long word) for the other five pairs of sentences.

Dependent Clauses

In written English, a dependent clause (**DC**) is a group of words with a subject and a verb (and perhaps a complement) that cannot stand by itself. It is a <u>weak</u> clause. In other words, a DC is not a complete sentence.

Examples:

   <u>before</u> Steve leaves for Alaska

   <u>even though</u> the policeman didn't give him a ticket

   <u>until</u> Jose returns from Washington

   <u>if</u> Luis and Marta don't pass the TOEFL

   <u>while</u> they were at the movies

Written English contains many dependent clauses. These clauses make part of a combined sentence less important than (that is, subordinate to) the other part of the sentence (the IC).

Combining Dependent Clauses

A dependent clause <u>must</u> be combined with an independent clause. The DC may come first in the sentence, or it may come last.

Example:

DC, IC   or   IC DC

<u>When I was on the airplane</u>, I saw New York City beneath me.

I saw New York City beneath me <u>when I was on the airplane</u>.

NOTE: When the DC comes first in the sentence, it is followed by a comma. When the IC comes first in the sentence, there is no punctuation.

A dependent clause begins with words called "**subordinating words**." These words make a strong clause (an IC) weak (notice that if you remove the underlined words in the "Examples" on the previous page, the clause becomes independent). Subordinating words, like short words and long words, give the reader a signal about the relationship between two clauses (contrasting information or cause-effect information). However, often the relationship is a time relationship.

While DC, IC	When DC, IC	Time signal for the reader
Before DC, IC	After DC, IC	Time signal for the reader
Until DC, IC	During DC, IC	Time signal for the reader
Because DC, IC		Cause of an effect is coming
Since DC, IC		Cause of an effect is coming
Although DC, IC		Contrasting information is coming
Even though DC, IC		Contrasting information is coming

Exercise K

Read the pairs of sentences below. Combine the pairs; you may change the order of the sentences if necessary. Use a subordinating word in each sentence that signals the reader about the relationship between the DC and the IC. There may be more than one appropriate relationship.

1. I hate the idea of writing.
   It takes too much time.

2. I attend classes all day.
   I have to go shopping.

3. The word 'writing" appears in my mind.
   It becomes pressing.

4. I prefer writing late at night.
   Nobody bothers me.

5. I change into old cozy clothes to write.
   That makes me feel more comfortable.

Natalia Papsuyera
(Ukraine)

Review of Sentence Combining Structures

Clauses can frequently be combined in more than one way:

IC, and / but / so   IC
IC; IC
IC; moreover, / furthermore, / however, / therefore, / consequently,   IC

DC, IC
IC DC

Exercise L

Read the pairs of sentences below. Combine each set of clauses in at least two ways. Use appropriate short words, long words, and/or subordinating words to signal the relationships between the combined clauses.

1. I have had two interesting jobs in my career.
   I was a teaching assistant in the Nantong Medical College for three years, and then was a doctor in the Aimon County Hospital for three years.

2. In the hospital, I examined patients and diagnosed their illnesses.
   I prescribed drugs and treatment for them.

3. I was a teacher in the college.
   I taught students and helped them with research.

4. I was working in the hospital.
   I did research with heart disease.

5. At the college, my research work was in microbiology and immunology.
   I devoted myself to the study of the mechanism of immunity and the growth of bacteria.

6. My schedules were quite different in these two jobs.
   The work at the college was less demanding.

7. In the hospital, I worked Monday through Saturday for twelve hours each day.
   I often worked during the evenings.

8. At the college I worked only eight hours every day.
   I had summer and winter vacations.

Haiying Nui
(People's Republic of China)

Sentence Combining Exercise

At the end of each chapter in this book, you will have the opportunity to practice your sentence combining skills. Below are three jokes. Usually, jokes are very short, with no extra words. However, each joke below has many short, choppy sentences, and some information is repeated. Combine the sentences so that the jokes flow more smoothly. You may eliminate some words if necessary. Use appropriate connectors to help your reader.

I

One day, there was a mother rat. There was her son. They were searching. They were searching for food. They were in the kitchen. They met the cat. The mother rat barked. She barked like a dog. She barked at the cat. The cat got scared. The cat ran away. The mother rat spoke. She spoke to her son. She said, "See? Now you can understand the importance of a second language!"

Tai-Lysh Hwang
(Taiwan)

II

There was a lady. She had a pig. The pig had legs. The legs were artificial. A man sees the lady. He sees the pig. He asks a question. He says, "Why does this pig have artificial legs?" The lady answers. She says, "This pig is cute. He is so cute that I am eating him. I am eating him little by little!"

Kyung-Chon Chan
(Japan)

III

Last year I took a trip. I was in a park. The park was Yellowstone National Park. I asked a question. I asked a girl if she had ever been in Mexico. She answered me. She said that she hadn't. But she told me something. She said that she would like to go to Latin America. Then I spoke to her. I told her that I invited her to Mexico. She answered. She said "Someday." But I thought she said "Sunday." So I was surprised. Then I spoke to her. I told her, "All right, next Sunday." She said, "No! No! I said someday," Then everybody laughed. They laughed loudly.

Celedonio Bravo
(Mexico)

2

THE PARAGRAPH: AN INTRODUCTION

When I hotly plunge into writing, nothing bothers me. I'm always thinking what to write, what words are better—I try to follow grammar rules, but in general that ends in failure.

Igor Ivanov
(Siberia)

In American academic writing, **a paragraph is a series of sentences about one idea called the topic.** A paragraph usually consists of four to eight sentences about a single topic. Usually, a paragraph begins with a general sentence that introduces the topic. This sentence is called the **topic sentence**, and it contains the main idea in the paragraph. The topic sentence tells the reader what the paragraph is going to be about.

The topic sentence contains words that need to be explained, described, and supported in the sentences that follow in the paragraph. These words are called **controlling ideas** because they control the information that is given in the paragraph. The sentence that ends the paragraph is called the **concluding sentence**.

A paragraph begins with an indentation (——➤). The topic sentence, with its controlling ideas, usually is the first sentence in the paragraph. Generally, then, an academic paragraph will look like this:

Title

——➤Topic Sentence with controlling ideas   .
Several sentences that **explain**,
_____**describe**,_____
_____**and/or support**_____
the controlling ideas in the topic sentence.
Concluding Sentence   .

Pre-Writing

"Pre-" means before; pre-writing means the work done by the writer before the paragraph is actually written. Pre-writing strategies include the decisions you make and the steps you take (whether written or not) before you write a draft of your paragraph. The following pages demonstrate several forms of written pre-writing.

Before you begin, you will make three major decisions:

1. choose a subject that you know about and are interested in

2. choose an audience: elementary school children? a university professor?

3. decide on a purpose: what, exactly, do you want to communicate?[*]

Choosing a Subject

Suppose, for example, you decide you would like to write about your arrival in the U.S. As you begin to make decisions about what you want to communicate to your reader, you would find that this subject could be used for several paragraphs. You might pre-write by making a list of those possibilities:

Listing

My arrival in the U.S.

My brother meeting me	Alone at JFK airport
Problems with customs	What I was a afraid of
First impressions of the U.S.	My first U.S. meal

As you continue to select ideas for your paragraph before you draft that paragraph, you will be using **pre-writing strategies**. The order of your pre-writing strategies (that is, the decision you make first, second, etc.) and the number of pre-writing steps you take will depend on (a) the topic, (b) the audience, (c) the available material, and (d) your individual writing strategies. The decisions and steps may not be linear (that is, a straight line); instead, they will probably overlap. You will probably be making several decisions about your paragraph at nearly the same time during your pre-writing process.

Narrowing the Subject to a Topic

A subject is a broad area of information. Books are written about subjects. However, in order to write a single paragraph about a subject, you must narrow that subject to a topic. That is, you must move from a general subject to a more specific topic. Audiences are more interested in details about a narrow topic than in general statements about a broad subject. Therefore, narrowing a subject to a topic is essential for good writing.

---

[*]Most academic writing you do will begin with an assigned task. A professor will design a writing assignment and the purpose of the assignment will be stated. Moreover, that professor will be your primary audience. Then you must develop strategies to help you analyze the assignment and the expectations of the professor. See Chapter 1 for more information about these strategies.

For example, as you think about your arrival in the U.S., you might discover that the subject is like a cake: it can be cut into many "pieces"—or topics for paragraphs. You might also find that some of the pieces would work better than others because your audience might be more interested in that topic, or you have more detail about that topic. As you continue to think about the ideas, information, or example that you could use in this paragraph, you might write your thoughts in a variety of ways; one, called "clustering," is below.

Clustering

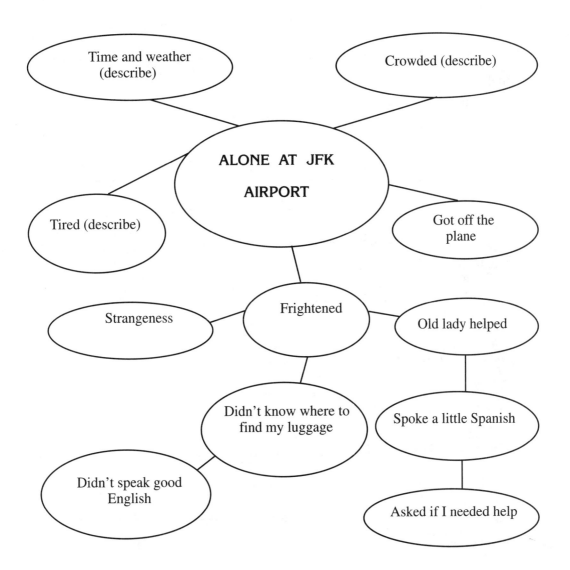

Exercise A

Another way to pre-write is to use "trees." Think about each of the broad subjects below. Then, in the "branches" of the trees below, write three narrowed (that is, more specific) topics that could be used as topics for three different paragraphs.

SUBJECTS   **TOPICS**

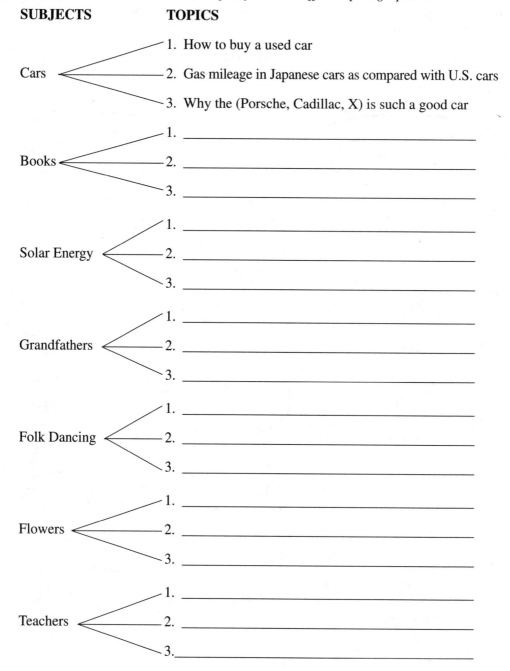

Cars
1. How to buy a used car
2. Gas mileage in Japanese cars as compared with U.S. cars
3. Why the (Porsche, Cadillac, X) is such a good car

Books
1. _____
2. _____
3. _____

Solar Energy
1. _____
2. _____
3. _____

Grandfathers
1. _____
2. _____
3. _____

Folk Dancing
1. _____
2. _____
3. _____

Flowers
1. _____
2. _____
3. _____

Teachers
1. _____
2. _____
3._____

Exercise B

Sometimes a topic is still too general for a single paragraph. Choose one of the topics from three of the sets you wrote in Exercise A above. Then, using the "tree" pre-writing below, write three more specific topics for each.

GENERAL TOPICS **MORE SPECIFIC TOPICS**

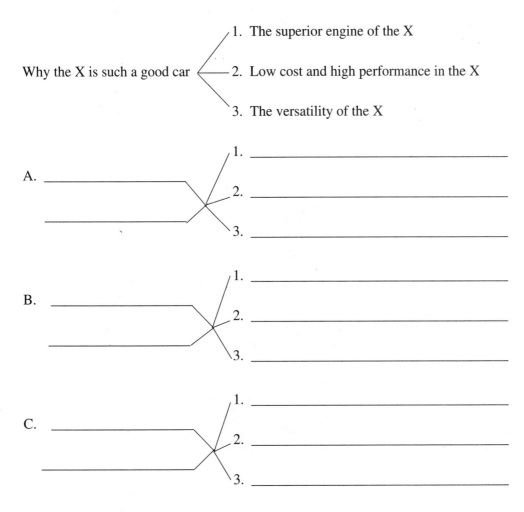

Why the X is such a good car

1. The superior engine of the X

2. Low cost and high performance in the X

3. The versatility of the X

A.

1. _____
2. _____
3. _____

B.

1. _____
2. _____
3. _____

C.

1. _____
2. _____
3. _____

In another form of pre-writing, called "brainstorming" or "freewriting," writers write everything that comes into their minds about a topic without stopping. They allow the "storm" in their brains to flow onto the paper without worrying about organization or grammar. When they have finished brainstorming (typically in five or ten minutes), they reread their writing and select ideas that are best suited to their writing. Below is an example of brainstorming (about negative feelings about writing):

Brainstorming

I hate writing in both languages, English and Russian. I have to write in English more because

I have to prepare all my other classes

I write my American friends

When I'm writing letters, it takes me a long time to find right words which are adequate for my feelings—often I don't find them and don't like sentences I write. Once I was writing an article (in English) for a newspaper, it took me 2 months to write it. I don't think that writing in my native language is easier for me.

I think motivation is important in teaching writing. If students understand that writing is a necessary thing to know, then the teacher only has to make students be interested in her subject. One way of motivation (as I see it) is opening of many joint-ventures, and people who know foreign languages and can write better are welcome to get a job. And business in this country is very popular now.

Nadya Maltseva
(Ukraine)

Still another form of pre-writing is called "looping." Writers freewrite steadily for five minutes, not lifting their pens from the paper. At the end of the freewriting period, they read what they have written, then choose the idea they think is the most interesting and begin a new period of freewriting, using that idea in the first sentence and focusing on that idea for the next five minutes of freewriting. The process can occur several times, with each new period of freewriting "looped" into the freewriting above it. Below is a shortened example of looping.

Looping

The critical period for ducks and geese: how important it is for geese to have certain experiences during the first 24 hours. They follow the first moving object they see after they are hatched. Usually this is the mother, but if not, they follow something else. For example, research with geese has shown goslings who have followed chickens, bouncing footballs, or even humans. The geese acted as if they thought the human was their mother and that they (the geese) were humans. The strongest time is between 16 to 24 hours after the baby goose is hatched.

← first free-writing

The research involved studies about what researchers call "imprinting": that is, the innate characteristic of the gosling to follow, as their mother, the first moving object they see after hatching. The investigators designed their research so that they kept goose eggs in the dark until after they (the eggs) hatched. The goslings were not allowed to see the world until two or three days later. The researchers found that the goslings' who had been deprived of light for more than two days did not imprint. However, about 48 hours after hatching, a

← second free-writing

second surge occurs in the goslings, and once again they imprint on the first moving object they see.

Anne Lene
(Norway)

Journal Assignment

Below are several sayings from different cultures. Choose two sayings that are not from your culture. Write about what you think those two sayings mean. Do you have a similar saying in your language?

SAYINGS: Even a bitter plant attracts some insects. (Japan)

Love enters through the kitchen. (Venezuela)

A lily cannot cover a dead elephant. (Thailand)

No wall can totally shield from the wind. (China)

Tell me who you walk with, and I'll tell you who

you are. (Brazil)

If a dog bites you, don't bite him back. (Lebanon)[*]

Review of Some Pre-Writing Strategies

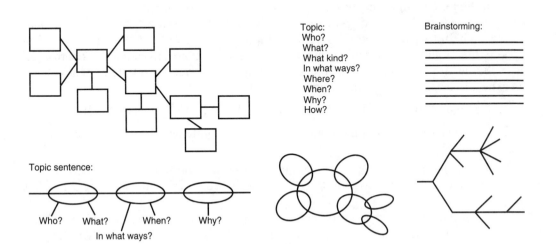

Topic sentence:

Who? What? When? Why?

In what ways?

Topic:
Who?
What?
What kind?
In what ways?
Where?
When?
Why?
How?

Brainstorming:

---

[*] Sayings courtesy of Julia Williamson, "Proverbs of the World—Customs and Culture," Tennessee TESOL Convention, May 1991

The Topic Sentence

In most academic writing, the first sentence of each paragraph is the topic sentence. **The topic sentence is the most general, most important sentence in the paragraph.** It:

- introduces the reader to the topic of the paragraph
- states the main idea of the paragraph
- focuses the paragraph

Finally, the topic sentence contains **controlling ideas** that need to be explained, described, and supported in the paragraph that follows. That is, these controlling ideas are words about which readers can ask questions that they expect will be answered in the paragraph. Consequently, the topic sentence is not simply a statement of fact; simple facts cannot be developed into full paragraphs. The following are examples of statements of fact that cannot be topic sentences of paragraphs:

1. Christmas is celebrated on December 25th.

2. Abraham Lincoln was President of the U.S. during the Civil War.

3. The San Francisco 49ers won the Super Bowl in 1992.

In contrast, the controlling ideas are words or phrases about which questions can be asked and answered. Usually, a topic sentence can be:

- a statement of intent
- a statement of opinion
- a statement that is a combination of intent and opinion

A statement of opinion makes a judgment. Words like *interesting, bad, exciting, best, terrifying, difficult*, etc. give the writer's subjective opinion (that is, a personal feeling or belief of the writer). The paragraph that follows a statement of opinion supports the opinion of the topic sentence as it answers questions about the controlling ideas. Below are examples of statements of opinion, followed by questions that readers can expect to be answered in the paragraph:

1. Computers make some jobs easier. (How? What jobs? In what ways?)

2. The most exciting pastime I have is climbing mountains. (Why? In what ways is it exciting?)

3. The main cause of misunderstanding between me and my close relatives is that, unlike me, they are too serious. (How does this cause misunderstandings? In what ways?)

A statement of intent is an objective sentence that tells the reader what will be objectively explained in the paragraph that follows. In these paragraphs, the writers give information about their topics and answer their readers' questions about those topics. The following are statements of intent with appropriate questions that readers might expect to be answered in the paragraphs that follow.

1. The pesticide DBCP has several side effects. (What are they? What do they look like?)

2. There are three steps in processing canned peaches. (What are they? Which comes first? Second? Third?)

3. The word "routine" can be defined either positively or negatively. (How is it defined positively? Negatively? In what ways is it positive? Negative?)

Often, topic sentences combine both opinion and intent. In these paragraphs, writers give support for their opinions as they give information about their topics and answer their readers' questions about the topic. Below are examples of combination opinion/intent statements, followed by questions that need to be answered in the paragraphs that follow.

1. One-parent families can be as strong as two-parent families. (How? In what ways? Why?)

2. Violence on television reflects life (How? In what ways? What is the relationship between life and television?)

3. There are three reasons I hate to write in English. (What are they? Why?)

Exercise C

Read the topic sentences below. Identify them as either a statement of opinion, a statement of intent, or a combination of the two.

STATEMENT OF ...

1. A pharmacist has two major responsibilities: to prepare drugs accurately and to check their effectiveness. _____

2. Women in the C.I.S. have more problems than men. _____

3. Living in Florida is better than living in New York. _____

4. The burial ceremony in Indonesia has three rituals. _____

5. Raising the drinking age to 21 will save many lives. _____

6. Photosynthesis is a chronological process. _____

7. Making *hayacas*, a traditional dish, is complicated. _____

8. There are two ways to lose weight. _____

9. Learning to use the university library is necessary. _____

10. Doctor's wives lead unusual lives. _____

Journal Assignment

Which of the ten sentences in Exercise C interests you most? Choose one of the sentences and, using one of the pre-writing strategies you have studied in this chapter, pre-write for ten minutes as though you were going to write a paragraph about that topic sentence.

Controlling Ideas

Controlling ideas are words or phrases in a topic sentence that need further explanation. For writing students who have difficulty finding adequate detail for their paragraphs, asking questions about controlling ideas can help provide the reader with interesting and valuable information. Asking and answering questions is another form of pre-writing, another way to gather information for writing. For example, read the following short paragraph:

> In Saudi Arabia, parents have separate responsibilities for raising their children. It is the father's duty to financially support his family and to make family decisions The mother in Saudi Arabia must care for the children and give them her love and guidance.

By answering the following questions, the author was able to expand (that is, to develop) his paragraph and make it more interesting for the reader:

1. *How* does the father support the family?
2. *What* decisions does he make?
3. *In what ways* does the mother care for the children?
4. *What kind* of guidance does she give them?
5. *Are there other* responsibilities that each parent has?

Here is the revised paragraph:

> In Saudi Arabia, parents have separate responsibilities for raising their children. The father, for example, has the duty to provide complete financial support for his family. **He therefore works at a job to earn money, and he buys the clothing and food for his family. He also has the authority to make all decisions concerning his children: what schools they should attend, what friends they should have, and whom they should marry.** The mother's most important responsibility for her children is to stay home and take care of them. **She cares for their everyday needs, like cleaning the house and preparing meals for them, and she provides love and friendship for them. She also teaches her children moral virtues such as friendship, generosity, and courtesy.** With the authority of the father and the love of their mother, the children grow to maturity.

Ahmed Al-Himadi
(Saudi Arabia)

Below is another topic sentence with controlling ideas (circled) that need to be explained, defined, and/or supported for the audience.

Topic Sentence of Intent:

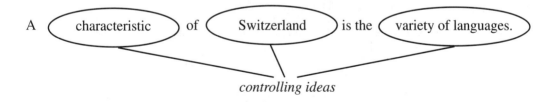

controlling ideas

The following questions could be answered in the paragraph that follows the topic sentence:

Which languages?   *How many?*

In what part of the country is each language spoken?   *Why?*

How many people speak each language?

As you read the paragraph developed from the sentence above, find the answers to the questions. Then do the exercise at the end of the paragraph.

A characteristic of Switzerland is the variety of languages. There are four linguistic sectors: French, German, Italian, and Rheto-Roman (or Romanche). The west part of Switzerland speaks French. In that area, the provincial dialect doesn't predominate; it is spoken only in a few regions of the mountains like Valais (in the Southwest), Fribourg, and Jura (in the northwest). Still, only 18% of the Swiss population speak French, not a majority of the Swiss people The southern part of my country, especially Tessin and Grisons (southeast), speaks Italian. However, the people speak this official language only for outside contacts; among themselves, the inhabitants speak their local dialects. It is not the same for the "Rheto-Roman" (some people of Grisons) who speak and write their local dialect as the official language: "Romanche." But only 1% of the Swiss population speaks this language, which is a mixture of German, Italian, and Latin. The biggest variety of languages is in the German part of Switzerland (the central and northern parts of my country). In that area, every canton has its own dialect, and very often, the real German people can't understand a word of the "Swiss German" because there are a lot of different pronunciations. For example, my grandmother was a native of the canton of Bern (which speaks a kind of German). She wasn't able to understand the German language of the canton of Basel, which is right next door! [Today, about 65% of the Swiss population speaks German. For that reason, students in the French and Italian parts of Switzerland learn German as a second language.]

Annick Burkhalter
(Switzerland)

Exercise D

1. What is the topic of this paragraph? Why did the author write this paragraph?

2. What would be an appropriate title for this paragraph?

3. Who is the audience for this paragraph? How do you know?

4. Could the bracketed [ ] last sentence of this paragraph become a topic sentence for another paragraph?

Writing Assignment 1

The paragraph above describes a characteristic of the author's country. Write a paragraph similar to the one above. Describe a characteristic of your country. You might describe one idea about the geography of your country (for example, a single river, the best place to vacation), the religions in your country, or the peoples in your country. For this assignment, your audience will be a classmate: Select one person in your class who is not from your country, and write your paragraph for that person.

> **Pre-writing and Drafting:** In your pre-writing for this assignment, answer as many of the following questions as possible in your journal:

Who?	What?	When?	What kinds of?
Where?	Why?	How?	In what ways?

Then formulate a possible topic sentence for your paragraph and write a first draft (called a **rough draft**) of your paragraph in your journal.

> **Peer Feedback:** Exchange rough drafts with the classmate you selected as your audience for this paragraph. As you read your classmate's paragraph, at the end of that paragraph:

- write the questions the author answered in the paragraph

- write what you found most interesting about the paragraph

- write one detail you remembered after you read the paragraph

Return the paragraph to your classmate and discuss each other's comments.

> **Revision:** Make any changes that will improve your paragraph. Then write the final draft of the paragraph.

The Topic Sentence and Writing Strategies

Constructing a topic sentence for a paragraph can occur at any time during your writing processes. For example, some writers prefer to write the body (that is, the middle) of the paragraph before they decide what the topic sentence will say. These writers "discover" their topic sentences as they write. Often these writers prefer to brainstorm or cluster as their pre-writing, and to then select the ideas they wish to communicate. For these writers, beginning with a topic sentence can limit their ability to develop a complete paragraph; for them, beginning in the middle is a more successful writing strategy.

Other writers construct topic sentences after thinking about their topics. Often their pre-writing techniques involve listing or answering questions. Beginning with a topic sentence, these writers develop their ideas directly from the controlling ideas in the topic sentence. These writers often find beginning in the middle difficult because their paragraphs seem unfocused. For them, beginning with the topic sentence is essential even though they may modify that topic sentence during their writing process.

Many writers have multiple strategies available for gathering information and writing paragraphs. For these writers, the writing process depends on the task, the audience, and the available material. Sometimes brainstorming is effective, and other times listing is more successful; sometimes they begin in the middle, and sometimes at the beginning. Developing such multiple strategies can prove beneficial for all students, though of course each student will have "favorite" strategies.

As you write your paragraph assignments, experiment with several of the pre-writing techniques demonstrated in this chapter, and observe which of these processes are easier (or more successful) for you. You may find that one strategy works well every time, or you may discover that you change your writing strategies to fit the assignment.

Writing Assignment 2

Write a paragraph describing one language spoken in your country. Describe three differences between that language and English. Give specific examples of each difference. Your audience for this paragraph is a U.S. university student who is planning to study your native language.

> **Pre-writing and Drafting:** Try two kinds of pre-writing for this assignment. First, do some "clustering" in your journal. Write your language in the middle of the page and circle it; then begin writing related words and ideas about your language in connected circles. Second, try "brainstorming": write without stopping for five minutes without worrying about organization or grammar. Then evaluate your information. What ideas will interest your audience? Which other details might be interesting? What ideas should probably not be part of this paragraph? Select the most important ideas and begin drafting the paragraph.
>
> **Peer Feedback:** In a small group of classmates, read several rough drafts. At the end of each draft, write one question that you would like the author to answer in that paragraph.
>
> **Revision:** Using the questions written by your classmates, make improvements in your draft. Then write the final draft.

Titles

The title of a paragraph, essay, or novel is the reader's first introduction to the text that follows. Generally, titles are not complete sentences. Instead, they state the topic of the text; often the selected topic for a paragraph can function as its title.

NOTE: The major words in titles are usually capitalized; sometimes the entire title is capitalized.

Examples:

My Hobby   HOW TO WRITE A PARAGRAPH

Soccer vs. Football   THE GEZIRA SCHEME

Greenhouse Gardens   THE PROCESS OF PHOTOSYNTHESIS

Concluding Sentences

The concluding sentence at the end of an academic paragraph usually uses one or more of the following techniques:

1. *summarizes* the material in the paragraph

2. *offers a solution* to the problem stated in the paragraph

3. *predicts* a situation that will result or occur from the statements made in the paragraph

4. *makes a recommendation* concerning material presented in the paragraph

5. *states a conclusion* to information given in the paragraph

Exercise E

Read the paragraphs below. Then do the exercise that follows each paragraph.

I

The Cold Front

Several signs can be observed before and during the passage of a cold front. The first sign of changing weather is the wind that starts to blow from the southwest. Normally, it brings into the area warm and wet air that makes us feel uncomfortable. At the same time, the air pressure decreases gradually as the cold front approaches. Next, in the northwestern sky we can see the penetration of high level clouds named "cirrus" clouds, followed by other middle level clouds called "autocumulus" clouds; these will be followed by thunderstorms that will drop snow or rain. This is the passage of the cold front itself. At this time, the temperature, which rose with the initial southwest winds, begins to decrease rapidly. Thus, the name describes what happens: a *cold* front.

Luis Teixeira
(Brazil)

1. Underline the topic sentence and circle the controlling ideas.

2. Does the title adequately introduce the reader to the paragraph?

3. Describe the audience for this paragraph: age, education, interests, etc.

4. Which concluding technique(s) is/are used in this paragraph?

II

OM' KALTHOOM

Om' Kalthoom, who was the most famous singer in the Arab world, had a lovely voice that always made me feel very emotional. Her voice changed with the kind of song she sang. It could be very strong in pitch, or it could be quiet and soft, depending on the music and the words. Sometimes the songs were very harmonious like the sea waves on a quiet day. Other times her voice was as comfortable as a gentle breeze or as fiery as the summer sun. Her melodious voice captured the hearts of her audience; when she sang, the people who listened laughed or cried with her songs. Even now, many years after I heard her sing, Om' Kalthoom is still an unforgettable singer. When I listen to a recording of her voice, I always go deeply into the world of emotions.

Abdullah Amirah
(Saudi Arabia)

1. Is the topic sentence for this paragraph a statement of opinion, intent, or a combination of the two? How do you know?

2. How does the audience for this paragraph differ from the audience for the previous paragraph? How do you know?

3. Describe one detail you remember after reading the paragraph (don't look!).

III

It's my opinion that women's hair and clothing styles have always reflected the age in which people lived. For example, medieval society squeezed women into fanciful and often ridiculous clothes, preventing them from moving easily. In the same way, medieval prejudices fettered women's thought and movements. In the eighteenth century, women used to wear large wigs, and they didn't take them off or wash them. When one woman finally removed her wig, it turned out that a family of mice were living in it! In the 20th century, women have put on trousers and mini-skirts. These clothes reflect the time of emancipation, and even women who look ugly in these fashions feel comfortable.

Maria Agaltsova
(Russia)

1. How does the second sentence help the reader focus on the paragraph?

2. Write a title for this paragraph.

3. Write a concluding sentence for this paragraph.

Writing Assignment 3

Write a clear topic sentence and a paragraph describing one attitude of people in the U.S. that surprised you when you arrived. You might choose the attitude toward "being on time," the attitudes toward pets (cats and dogs), the attitudes toward leisure time, or any other attitude you have encountered. Your audience for this paragraph is a class of U. S. students who know little about other cultures. Your purpose in writing this paragraph is to inform these students about attitudes they may not know they have.

> **Pre-writing and Drafting:** In your journal, pre-write to develop your ideas for this paragraph. After you have written a rough draft of your paragraph, read it again. Does the topic sentence still give the main idea for the paragraph, or should you revise the topic sentence?

> **Peer Feedback:** In a small group of classmates, read paragraphs that are not your own. At the end of each paragraph, write a complete sentence that begins with "The most interesting part of this paragraph is ..." Then discuss the parts you liked in each paragraph with the author.

> **Revision:** In your journal, write about one thing that you discovered during the peer feedback workshop that you will be able to use to improve your paragraph. Then make the necessary changes in your paragraph, and write a final draft.

Exercise F

Read the following three topic sentences and paragraphs. Circle the controlling ideas in each topic sentence. Identify each topic sentence as a statement of opinion, a statement of intent, or a combination of both. Then write questions that might be answered in the paragraph that will follow each topic sentence. Finally, answer the questions that follow each paragraph.

I

Topic Sentence: **The vacation that I took in San Diego at Thanksgiving was enjoyable.**

Statement of _____

Questions: _____

_____

MY TRIP TO SAN DIEGO

The vacation that I took in San Diego at Thanksgiving was enjoyable. When I first arrived, I visited the museum. I saw American Indian costumes, paintings of the war between the Indians and the Mexicans, and weapons used by both the Indians and the Mexicans. Next I visited the zoo. I saw many kinds of animals and birds like deer, elephants, monkeys, foxes, and snakes. It was fun to see their movements and their colors. I watched not only the animals but also the other people who were visiting the zoo; how nice it was to see so many people enjoying themselves as I was! Finally I returned to my hotel; that evening I watched television until I fell asleep, completely tired and relaxed. The next day I took a bus tour of the city and looked at the high buildings, the open markets, and the many restaurants. That evening I returned to the airport, and while I waited for my plane I watched the people saying hello and goodbye. Finally I climbed onto my plane, sat down, and felt very happy; my trip had been peaceful and interesting, and it had left me with a pleasant feeling.

Mohammed Al-Kelbi
Saudi Arabia

1. Does the topic sentence in the paragraph adequately tell the reader what the paragraph will be about?

2. Did you find the answers to your questions?

3. What additional information would you like to have read in this paragraph?

4. What concluding technique(s) does the author use to end the paragraph?

II

Topic Sentence: **Explorers investigating a large area located in the south of Venezuela called that area "The Lost World" because of what they found there.**

Statement of _____

Questions: _____

_____

THE LOST WORLD

Explorers investigating a large area located in the south of Venezuela called that area "The Lost World" because of what they found there. The area is one of the oldest undeveloped regions in the world. The landscape is beautiful and impressive because it is a combination of tropical forests, many large rivers, and high mountains with flat tops. It is a sparsely inhabited area, populated even today by primitive Indian tribes who have named the characteristic mountains *tepuy*. Plants and insects have been found in "the Lost World" which exist only in that area and, in some cases, only on a specific *tepuy*. Another unusual geographic site that is part of this area is "Angel Falls," the highest waterfall in the world (almost 3,200 feet high) which was named after the first man to fly over the falls.

Ahmed Irazabal
(Venezuela)

1. Does the topic sentence tell the reader what the paragraph will be about?

2. What was the author's purpose in writing this paragraph? What did he want to communicate to his audience?

3. How do the vocabulary and sentence structure in this paragraph differ from those in the previous paragraph? Why do they differ?

4. Write a concluding sentence for this paragraph. Which concluding technique(s) did you use?

III

Topic Sentence: **Continued progress in advanced technology is not necessary.**

Statement of _____

Questions: _____

Advanced Technology: STOP!

Continued progress in advanced technology is not necessary. Already the technical progress in our world has caused severe pollution in the air and in the water. Although the technical progress in previous years has been helpful, recent technology has significantly increased pollution. Another reason to stop technical progress is that many inventions which were developed for good causes are not also used for powerful weapons or have been found to have serious side effects. For example, pesticide put inside particle board to prevent termites has now been found to be toxic to human life. [Technology does not always bring good effects.] For example, computers do much work faster than man, but then man loses his job to a machine. Because no man can guarantee that technology will have only good effects and will be used only for the benefit of man, we should suspend the continued development of technology.

Maliwan Peyayopanakul
(Thailand)

1. What was the author's purpose in writing this paragraph? Did she succeed? Why or why not?

2. What support for the main points of the paragraph are given?

3. What additional information would you like to have read in the paragraph?

4. Would the bracketed sentence [ ] be a better topic sentence for this paragraph? Why or why not?

Peer Feedback: Exchange paragraphs with a classmate. At the end of the

Writing Assignment 4

Write a paragraph about a vacation trip you have taken. Tell your audience (your classmates) why you would like to return to this place (or why you would not like to return).

> **Pre-writing and Drafting:** For this paragraph, gather details that use your senses by using the "clustering" (see the example below) strategy in your journal. Then, in your journal, begin drafting your paragraph, including a title and a clear topic sentence with controlling ideas.

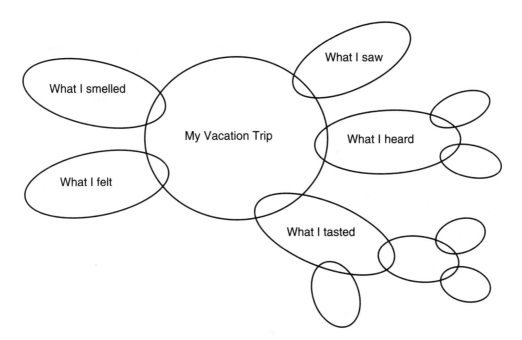

paragraph, answer the following questions:

- What senses did the writer use? Write what the writer

  saw: _____

  heard: _____

  felt: _____

  smelled: _____

  tasted: _____

- What additional information could the author have used? What questions would you ask the author about the paragraph? Write those questions.

Revision: After discussing the questions your partner asked, make changes in your paragraph to improve it. Then write the final draft.

Exercise G

Read the topic sentences below. Circle the controlling ideas. Then write questions that might be answered in the paragraph that follows the topic sentence. Identify each as a statement of opinion, a statement of intent, or a combination of both.

1. The capital of Ecuador is small, but it is a popular place.

   Statement of _____

   Questions: _____

   _____

2. When I was young, I was afraid of ghosts; my brothers knew it, and so they played a frightening joke on me.

   Statement of _____

   Questions: _____

   _____

3. ESL students write more successfully when they are interested in the topic.

   Statement of _____

   Questions: _____

   _____

4. When I was an officer candidate in the Japanese navy, I had a terrible experience during swimming practice.

   Statement of _____

   Questions: _____

   _____

Writing Assignment 5

Write a paragraph about a personal experience that made you sad, afraid, or angry.

Pre-writing and Drafting: For your pre-writing, write your proposed topic sentence in your journal and circle the controlling ideas. Write questions about the controlling ideas that you might answer in the paragraph following the topic sentence. Then answer the questions as you write a rough draft of the paragraph.

Peer Feedback: When you have finished writing a draft of your paragraph, exchange paragraphs with a classmate. As you read your partner's paper:

- underline the topic sentence and circle the controlling ideas

- put an asterisk (*) in the margin where the best detail occurs in the paragraph

- at the end of the paragraph, write two questions that will help the author improve the detail in the paragraph

- discuss possible revisions for your paragraph with your partner

Revision: Using the advice of your partner, change your paragraph to make it better. Then write the final draft.

Exercise H

Each of the paragraphs below has no topic sentence. In small groups, read each paragraph. Then discuss possible topic sentences, and decide what the topic sentence for each paragraph might be. Write the topic sentence, and circle the controlling ideas. Then, as a group, answer the questions that follow each paragraph.

I

_____

_____

_____. I paid little attention to the early writing classes in the Intensive English Program because I was too busy concentrating on passing the TOEFL test, which is the only way to successfully gain admission to most U.S. universities. Although I scored 510 on the TOEFL, I have realized that I made a big mistake in my study plan, because even though I have passed the TOEFL, I can't write in English. In other words, because I had ignored the early writing classes by not doing my homework, by not writing paragraphs, and by not following the basic rules of writing, I am not able to write the required papers in my university classes. After realizing how important the writing class is, I have attended it this semester, and in my academic work I hope to take advantage of what I am learning.

1. Write a title for this paragraph.

2. Who is the audience for this paragraph?

3. What is the purpose of the paragraph?

II

_____

_____

_____. We have classes in three different buildings, and they are not very close together. In fact, it takes ten minutes to walk from one class to another. When there is snow or ice on the ground, we are often late for classes because we have to walk so far. In addition, the Language Laboratory is in one building, the office is in another, and the classrooms are in three other buildings. Therefore, we must always walk in order to attend to any aspect of learning English. We spend most of our time rushing between buildings, and there is never time to talk with our teachers or our friends. To solve this problem, I recommend that the administration of this program schedule all our classes in one building.

1. Write a title for this paragraph.
2. Who is the audience, and what is the purpose of this paragraph?
3. Do you think this is a successful paragraph?   Why or why not?

III

The Student Health Center

_____

_____. If you are sick, you can see a doctor or a nurse without paying a fee. If you get hurt, the Student Health Center will send an ambulance to pick you up and take you to the Center for treatment. If you have an injury, you can receive physical therapy with a trained technician without cost, and if you have a psychological problem, you can see a psychiatrist. There is also a pharmacy in the Student Health Center where you can get prescriptions filled more cheaply than in a regular pharmacy. For these reasons, having student health insurance that allows you to use the Student Health Center is a good idea.

1. Does the title accurately introduce the paragraph?
2. How does the detail strengthen this paragraph?
3. What concluding technique(s) does the writer use?

IV

Spelling in English

_____

_____. For example, many words contain letters that are not pronounced. In the word "knife," the "k" is not pronounced. Also, the word "light" has five letters but only three sounds: "lit." Other words in English are pronounced the same, but they are spelled differently. For instance, "to," "too," and "two" are all pronounced the same way. "Claws" and "clause" are also pronounced exactly the same, but each has a very different meaning. In addition, English spelling has so many exceptions (words that do not follow the regular spelling rules). For example, one rule states that "i" comes before "e" except after "c" *except* in words like "n<u>ei</u>ghbor" and "w<u>ei</u>gh" and "l<u>ei</u>sure" and "for<u>ei</u>gner." Because of all the exceptions and strange rules, spelling is one of the frustrating skills to learn in English.

1. Did you write a statement of opinion, a statement of intent, or a combination of the two for the topic sentence for this paragraph? Why?

2. What is the purpose of this paragraph? Does the writer communicate successfully?

3. How might the reader react to this paragraph? Be specific.

4. Which of the paragraphs in this exercise was the most interesting for you? Why?

Exercise I

Write topic sentences, and narrow the following subjects to topics that might function as a title for a paragraph. Then write a possible topic sentence for each topic.

1. Soccer

    Narrowed topic: _____

    Possible topic sentence: _____

    _____

2. The TOEFL examination

    Narrowed topic: _____

    Possible topic sentence: _____

    _____

3. American food

Narrowed topic: _____

Possible topic sentence: _____

_____

4. Education

Narrowed topic: _____

Possible topic sentence: _____

_____

5. Motorcycles

Narrowed topic: _____

Possible topic sentence: _____

_____

Writing Assignment 6

Choose one topic sentence from the ones your wrote for the previous exercise. Develop a paragraph from that topic sentence.

> **Pre-writing and Drafting:** In your journal, try <u>looping</u> to focus your paragraph: Write steadily for five minutes; then read what you have written, and choose the best idea. Begin the next loop with that idea, and again write for five minutes, not worrying about organization or grammar. Reread what you have written and select another good idea; begin the next loop with that idea and write for five minutes about it. As you draft your paragraph, select details from your looping to strengthen your ideas.

> **Peer Feedback:** Exchange rough drafts with a classmate. Help your classmate by offering suggestions for additional detail that will make the paragraph more interesting. Also, underline any grammar problem you find: subject-verb agreement, word order, sentence structure, spelling, punctuation, capitalization, and word use.

> **Revision:** Using the help from your partner, make changes in your draft. Then write the final draft of your paragraph.

Sentence Combining Exercise

In the jokes below, some of the sentences are short and choppy, and some information is repeated. Combine the sentences so that the jokes are shorter and that they flow more smoothly. You may eliminate some words if necessary.

I

Many years ago, a man spoke. He spoke to his servant. He said, "I want you to go to the market. I want you to buy two pounds of pork. This is a $50 bill. It is the smallest that I have. Be sure to bring the change back to me." The servant did as he was told. However, he spent the whole amount. He bought almost half a pig. The butcher was happy. He was very happy. He spoke. He said, "You bought so much pork. I will give you a gift. I will give you a pair of pig's ears. You are a very good customer." The servant was very happy. He delivered the pork. He delivered it to his master's kitchen. But he left the pig's ears. He left them in his own pocket. He thought the ears should belong to him. He thought they should not belong to his master.

His master spoke. "Where is my change?" the master asked. The servant replied. He said, "I spent the whole $50 for the pork. There was no change." His master shouted. He shouted in great anger. "I don't think you can hear very well. Why don't you wash your ears? The servant was obedient. He obediently took the ears from his pocket. He washed them.

Han Wen Shao
(People's Republic of China)

II

An American visited Taiwan. He was young. It was southern Taiwan. It was a rural area. Then he felt a pain. The pain was in his stomach. He looked in a field. The field was full of rice. He saw a latrine. He went to the latrine. He went in. He was in a hurry. He didn't do something. What he didn't do was lock the door. Moments later, a lady came. She was old. She wanted to go in. She opened the door. She saw the young man. She was angry. She said to him, "Mna Arl Moh Sah." That means, "Why didn't you lock the door?" The young man misunderstood. He thought she had said something else. He thought she had said, "I'm sorry." So he was surprised. First, he was surprised that a country woman could speak English. Second, he was surprised that Chinese were so polite.

Jinlai Shyu
(People's Republic of China)

3

Planning the Paragraph

I have trouble writing because I am always told to write about things I don't like to write about. The topics don't interest me, and they are brand new for me.

Chris Fogstad
Norway

Making decisions is at the heart of planning paragraphs. Writers must decide about topics, purposes, and audiences. Then there are decisions about organization and presentation of ideas, topic sentences, and details. And there are decisions concerning language structures and vocabulary. Finally, there are decisions about modifying and revising the paragraph. Successful decision making occurs when the writer knows about the processes of writing and has developed appropriate decision-making strategies.

Academic writing assignments require students to analyze tasks and audience expectations. The purpose of most academic writing is to explain material to a specific audience and/or to persuade a specific audience that a judgment is valid. To achieve these objectives, a paragraph must be focused, supported, and unified.

Focus: Second Sentences

While the topic sentence is the most important and most general sentence in a paragraph, the second sentence of an academic paragraph is also important because it focuses the topic sentence and directs the reader. The function of the second sentence in academic paragraphs is to help the reader anticipate (that is, predict) the organization of the paragraph that will follow. Often the second sentence of a paragraph begins with a connecting word that signals the reader about the organization of the paragraph that will follow. If the second sentence is inappropriate, it misdirects and confuses the reader. Therefore, constructing appropriate second sentences helps the writer focus successfully.

Exercise A

Below is a topic sentence that begins a paragraph of narration—that is, the paragraph tells a story. Following the topic sentence is a series of second sentences (written by native English speakers) that help the reader anticipate the organization of the paragraph. The second sentences are classified by the function each second sentence serves. In each case, the second sentence fulfills the expectations of a typical U.S. audience. Read the topic sentences and the second sentences. Then answer the questions that follow.

Title: My Most Embarrassing Moment

TOPIC SENTENCE: **My most embarrassing moment happened in an airport.**

Native English speakers' second sentences do one of the following:

1. *Immediately begin the narrative*
   A. When I started to grab my suitcase off the luggage carousel, it opened, and my underwear flew everywhere.
   B. I thought my luggage had been stolen, so I yelled at an airport employee.
   C. I bent over to pick up my bag and heard the rip of the rear seam.

2. *Frame the narrative (that is, set the scene) before beginning the story*
   A. It happened when I boarded the wrong flight.
   B. I was carrying a large bag of Christmas gifts, and one of the gifts was a toy gun.
   C. I was just exiting the plane when the dreaded moment occurred.

3. *Frame and begin the narrative*
   A. I was waiting for my flight to Minnesota when this Holy Krishna approached me.
   B. Just as I was preparing to board the plane, the strap on my carry-on tripped me and I fell face down on the ramp.
   C. I was on my way to get on my flight, but I couldn't get through the metal detector.

4. Following are three second sentences for this paragraph that are *inappropriate*; they misdirect the reader. Discuss the problems that each of these second sentences present to the reader:
   A. Embarrassment is an ugly feeling.
   B. Usually, I love to fly.
   C. Fortunately, all the people around were strangers and most probably I'll never see them again.

Write a new second sentence for this paragraph. What function does it fulfill? In what ways does it help the reader anticipate the paragraph that will follow?
What do you think the purpose of the topic for this paragraph might be?

Connectors for Second Sentences

Introductory words that indicate the relationship between one sentence and the sentence that follows help the reader understand the paragraph. These words connect the ideas between one sentence and another. Below are examples of connectors that are often used with second sentences. These connectors show readers the relationship between the topic sentence and the second sentence.

Connector		Relationship
1. First, second, third		process of chronology (time)
2. When…	Since…	framing with time (narration)
Once…	Just last week…	
3. For example,		illustration
4. One reason	Another reason	cause-effect, reasons

Exercise B

Below is a topic sentence of explanation. Following the topic sentence is a series of second sentences (written by native English speakers) that help the reader anticipate the organization of the paragraph. The second sentences are classified by the function each second sentence serves. In each case, the second sentence fulfills the expectations of a typical U.S. audience. Read the topic sentences and the second sentences. Then answer the questions that follow.

Title: Burials in Indonesia

TOPIC SENTENCE: **The burial ceremony in Indonesia has three rituals.**

Native English speakers' second sentences do one of the following:

1. *Begin explaining the first ritual*   (The first…)
   A. The first is the most bizarre.
   B. First the relatives must attend a ceremony while wearing black clothes.
   C. The first of the three involves beads and handmade headpieces.

2. *Introduce all three rituals*   (First, …second, …, and third …)
   A. First is the prayer, second is the entrance in the ground, and third is the dirt throwing.
   B. First the victim is killed, their praises are sung, and then they are thrown into the volcano.
   C. First the family will pray for the dead, second they will carry him to the burial location, and third he will be burned.

3. *Focus on the order or importance of the three rituals.*
   A. I will discuss each ritual in the order they occur.
   B. It is important to know each ritual and how they relate.
   C. All three have different religious connotations.

1. The native English speakers who wrote the second sentences in this exercise knew nothing about Indonesian culture. Which of their sentences seems most clear and interesting?

2. Write an original second sentence for the topic sentence. Use an appropriate connector. Then discuss your second sentence with a small group of classmates. Which of your classmates' second sentences was the most interesting? The clearest? Why?

3. Following are three second sentences for this paragraph that are inappropriate; they misdirect the reader. Discuss the problems that each of these second sentences present to the reader:

   A. Rituals are critical to the cultural survival of the tribe.

   B. Both of them are hereditary.

   C. Japan has similar rituals.

Exercise C

Below is a topic sentence of causes/reasons. Following the topic sentence is a series of second sentences (written by native English speakers) that help the reader anticipate the organization of the paragraph. The second sentences are classified by the function each second sentence serves. In each case, the second sentence fulfills the expectations of a typical U.S. audience. Read the topic sentences and the second sentences. Then answer the questions that follow.

Title: Milk

TOPIC SENTENCE: **Milk is one of the most important sources of nutrition for humans.**

Native English speakers' second sentences do one of the following:

1. *Introduce the first reason.*

   A. We need milk for strong bones and teeth.

   B. Calcium is the principle element found in milk.

   C. From infancy, we are fed milk to make us strong.

2. *Introduce two or more reasons.*

   A. It provides daily amounts of vitamins and minerals.

   B. It contains calcium and proteins that help develop human bones and muscles.

   C. It provides calcium, vitamin C, and vitamin D as well as a high percentage of protein.

1. Following are three second sentences for this paragraph that are inappropriate; they misdirect the reader. In a small group of classmates, discuss the problems that each of these second sentences present to the reader:

   A. Nutrition is an extremely important issue for physical training.

   B. Milk is very good for you.

   C. Humans like milk.

   D. Buy milk in our store and you'll be healthy.

2. Why is it more difficult to write an "original" second sentence for this topic sentence?

3. With a small group of peers, identify the audience for the paragraph that will follow about milk. What does the audience know? What are the ages, interests, and education of this audience? How do you know?

Inappropriate Second Sentences

Characteristics that make ESL second sentences inappropriate include:

1. **selection of an inappropriate word in the topic sentence as the main idea for the second sentence** (that changes the direction of the paragraph and confuses the reader).

   – control.

   Example: This chart explains how the use of four sources of fuels that generate electricity in the U.S. has changed since 1973. The electricity is much more expensive than other fuels.

   Solution: determine the controlling ideas in the topic sentence, and ask questions about those controlling ideas.

2. **writing a sentence that is more general than the topic sentence.**

   Example: My most embarrassing moment happened in an airport. Airports can be fun.

   Solution: make the second sentence more specific than the topic sentence.

3. **writing a sentence that contradicts the topic sentence.**

   Example: Burning fields for shift cultivation is a simple process. Yet it is an air pollution process as well.

   Solution: consider the purpose and the audience for the paragraph; use the controlling ideas in the topic sentence as your guide.

4. **repetition or restatement of the topic sentence.**

   Example: Going to the movies is a nice way to spend leisure time. After work, the movies is a good place to go.

   Solution: save the restatement for the concluding sentence in the paragraph.

5. **writing a second sentence that is unrelated to the topic sentence.**

   Example: Swimming is my favorite sport. I also enjoy many other activities.

   Solution: consider your audience and use the controlling ideas to formulate the second sentence.

Exercise D

Below are topic sentences followed by inappropriate second sentences. With a small group of classmates, read each topic sentence and circle the controlling ideas. Using the characteristics of inappropriate sentences listed above, analyze why each second sentence is inappropriate. Then decide on an appropriate second sentence for each topic sentence.

Title: Stress in the Workplace

1. According to a recent study, many workers and employees suffer from stress disorders at the workplace. <u>Most workers and employees have stress disorders.</u>

Problem: _____

Appropriate second sentence: _____

_____

2. There are many different reasons for work stress. Therefore, relaxation seems a reducing factor for productivity in the workplace.

Problem: _____

Appropriate second sentence: _____

_____

3. The intensity of work-stress was really low in the past. All workers and employees who complain of stress desire to get rid of it.

Problem: _____

Appropriate second sentence: _____

_____

4. Bosses and managers should avoid giving much stress to their workers. But they must be sure to fulfill the objectives of the business.

Problem: _____5.___ *for example.* _____

Appropriate second sentence: ___*because they are feeling*___

But they is very impotant for successful. solved problems

5. There are several symptoms of work-related stress. Any of these symptoms can lower productivity in the workplace.

Problem: _____

Appropriate second sentence: _____

Second Sentence Guidelines

1. **Think about your purpose.** Circle the controlling ideas in the topic sentence. Then ask what questions you expect to answer about those controlling ideas in the paragraph that follows the topic sentence.

   Example: Cambodian New Year is the most exciting day in my country. The preparations begin months in advance. (What preparations? How are they exciting? Why begin so early?)

2. **Think about your audience.** As the audience reads the topic sentence, what questions will the reader(s) expect to be answered?

   Example: Acapulco is known as the best city in Mexico for vacations. There are three reasons for its popularity. (What are the reasons? What is there about each characteristic that makes Acapulco "best"?)

3. **Use appropriate connecting words and phrases** that provide direction for the reader.

   Example: Spelling is one of the most frustrating skills to learn in English. **First,** there is no clear rule how to spell certain words, so that you've got to memorize the right order of the letters. **For example, ...**

4. **Make the second sentence more specific than the first sentence.**

   Example: In Saudi Arabia, parents have responsibilities for raising their children. The mother's responsibility is to care for the children when they are young.

5. **Save the restatement of the topic sentence for the concluding sentence in the paragraph.**

   Example: Getting a driver's license is very important for me. One reason is that I need a car to get to school ..., ...; If I didn't have a driver's license, I would be in great trouble.

Exercise E

Read the topic sentences below. Circle the controlling ideas in each topic sentence. Then write an appropriate second sentence for each topic sentence. When you have finished, share your second sentences with a small group of classmates. Be prepared to explain why you chose each of your second sentences.

1. My first meal in the U.S. was wonderful (or terrible).

   _____

   _____ .

2. The university administration often treats students as though they are irresponsible.

   _____

   _____ .

3. There are three ways I prepare for the TOEFL examination.

   _____

   _____ .

4. Young people from Egypt travel abroad for several reasons.

   _____

   _____ .

5. The weather in my hometown is…

   _____

   _____ .

Writing Assignment 1

Choose one of the topic sentences (and your original second sentence) from Exercise D or Exercise E (above).

Pre-writing and Drafting: In your journal, use two pre-writing strategies to generate ideas for the paragraph that will follow. Then write the draft of the paragraph in your journal.

Peer Feedback: In a small group of classmates, read the paragraphs that are not your own. For each paragraph:

- circle the controlling ideas in the topic sentence
- underline the connecting word in the second sentence that directs the reader
- in the margin, label the way the second sentence helps the reader
- Then discuss with your peers any questions or suggestions you have about their paragraph.

Revision: Using the advice of your peers, revise and write the final draft of your paragraph.

Support in the Paragraph

In order to communicate successfully, a paragraph must be about a single idea. In order for the paragraph to be complete, the topic sentence must be supported: That is, the controlling ideas in the topic sentence must be **explained, described and/or proven with specific supporting detail.**

The four basic techniques of support are **facts, examples, physical description**, and/or **personal experience**. One or more techniques of support must be used in any paragraph that you construct.

FACTS

The use of factual evidence in academic writing is expected by the U.S. audience. Any piece of information that can be easily verified can serve as factual support. Included are numbers (percentages, number of miles, etc.) and statistics as well as facts that can be found in books, newspapers, and magazines.

Exercise F

The two paragraphs and the letter to the editor below contain supporting factual material such as numbers, statistics, and verifiable facts. Read the paragraphs and answer the questions that follow each.

I
Milk: The Perfect Food

Milk is one of the most important sources of nutrition for human beings and animals. It is the first food provided for newborn babies because milk contains a large variety of nutritional constituents, and at the same time it is easily digestible. Milk is about 13% solids, and the solids contain 3.3% protein, *facts* 5% carbohydrates, 4% fat, and many vitamins and minerals. Moreover, milk protein contains all of the essential amino acids like casein and lactobacillus. Lactose is the principal carbohydrate of milk, and milk is the only source of lactose in nature. Milk also contains all of the known vitamins: A, B, D, E, and K. For all of these reasons, milk consumption is the keystone of human beings and animals.

Samir Atrash

(Libya)

1. What is the purpose, and who is the audience for this paragraph? How do you know?

2. In what way(s) does the second sentence help focus the paragraph?

3. Underline the easily verifiable facts in this paragraph.

4. Underline with wavy lines (~~) the numbers and statistics used as evidence in this paragraph.

II
The Geography of Saudi Arabia

Saudi Arabia is a large country with many interesting geographical areas. First, the Kingdom of Saudi occupies nearly 80% of the total area of the Arabian Peninsula and has a population of about 7,000,000. On the west coast of Saudi Arabia, there is the Red Sea; to the east is the Arabian Gulf, the State of Bahrain, the United Arab Emirates, the State of Qatar, and the State of Kuwait. To the south there is North Yemen, South Yemen, and the Sultanate of Oman; to the north is Iraq and Jordan. Saudi Arabia covers an area of 2,240,000 square kilometers (1,400,000 square miles), about six times the area of the whole British Isles and four times the area of France. Most of the Kingdom's area is deserts, but the highest parts of the country are in the west and the southwest where mountains rise 10,000 feet. Near the water, there is fertile land, but in the north, arid sandy deserts extend for 900 miles to reach the borders of Iraq and Jordan. In the southeast of the Kingdom lies "the Empty Quarter" (Al-Ruh Al-Khali), a desolate area without plant or animal life.

Jamal Al-Kahtani
(Saudi Arabia)

1. Circle the controlling ideas in the topic sentence.

2. How does the second sentence help to focus the paragraph that follows?

3. Underline the easily verifiable facts in this paragraph.

4. Write a suitable concluding sentence for the paragraph.

III

1344 Fairview Drive
Pocatello, Idaho
March 29, 1995

Time Magazine
Time and Life Building
Rockefeller Center
New York, New York 10020

Dear Sir:

For the average citizen, the salary paid a college football coach seems very high. However, I have recently learned that the salary is only a small part of the coach's income. According to a recent article in *Sports Illustrated,* the former coach at Georgia Tech earned $40,000 a year, but he listed his annual additional income, called "perks" (that is, perquisites or added benefits) as the following:

TV show	$ 34,677
Radio show	5,000
Salary for administrative assistant	21,000
Salary for secretary	12,500

Home mortgage allowance	9,187
Tickets, private stadium booths	7,660
On-campus football camp	7,500
Membership and entertainment	
Capital City Club	7,050
Cherokee Town Club	4,654
East Lake Country Club	970
Gifts from alumni	5,335
Use of Cadillac	5,000
Coca-Cola promotions	4,809
Speaking appearances	4,700
Training-table meals	3,250
Expenses for meetings	2,100
Life insurance premiums	1,815
Gas and oil	1,800
General expense money	1,200
Car-insurance premium	1,166
Health club membership	880
Tennis club membership	667
Hawks, Braves, Flames tickets	620
Falcons, four season tickets	600
Tech season football tickets	560
Tech season basketball tickets	336
Tech football away tickets	160
Holiday Inn lodgings	400
Pocket money road games	375
Parking	38
Tech baseball admission	15
	$146,024

The former coach stated that since two-thirds of his "perks" were non-taxable, his actual income would have been $497,000.

I know that college football is a popular national sport, but in this age of inflation in the U. S., for a college football coach to be paid 20 times more than the average mailman, ten times as much as most college presidents, and five times as much as the President of the United States, is an insult to the American people.

Sincerely,

Peter Voeller

Peter Voeller

(U.S.)

1. <u>Underline</u> the topic sentence in the first paragraph of the letter. How does the last sentence in the letter restate the topic sentence?

2. Who is the audience for this letter?

3. Underline with wavy lines (~~) the non-numerical, easily verifiable facts in this letter.

4. What is the purpose? Do you think the audience will be persuaded? Why or why not?

Writing Assignment 2

Read a newspaper (or a magazine) from your school or city. Choose an article about a problem or issue that interests you. Then write a letter to the editor of the newspaper (or magazine) in which you give your opinion about the problem or issue. Use easily verifiable facts, numbers, and/or statistics to support your opinion. You might also include the attitude that many people in your country have toward the problem or the issue. The purpose of this letter to the editor is to persuade the readers of the newspaper (or magazine) that your opinion is valid.

> **Pre-writing and Drafting:** In your journal, use two pre-writing strategies to generate ideas about the problem or the issue you have chosen. Begin drafting the letter, following the format for the business letter in the letter to the editor above.
>
> **Peer Feedback:** With two or three classmates in a small group, read letters that are not your own. Then, as a group, choose one letter to revise and mail to the editor of the newspaper (or magazine).
>
> **Revision:** Work together to suggest revisions to the draft. Then write the final draft of the letter, sign your names, and mail the letter to the editor.

EXAMPLES

Another technique of support is the use of examples. Examples can explain or define a controlling idea, or they can prove an idea or a point made in the topic sentence. Sometimes a series of short examples is effective evidence for a topic sentence. Other times, a single extended example can serve as solid support in a paragraph.

Exercise G

Below are two paragraphs that use the technique of examples as support. Read the paragraphs and answer the questions that follow.

I
Indonesia's Transmigration Program

In Indonesia, the government has been concentrating on a transmigration program. Transmigration is the process of moving people from one island to another in order to improve living conditions. For example, one island, like Java, may be very crowded, while other islands are nearly empty because there are still a lot of jungles and open land that have never been cultivated. Another example is in some of the villages, where the land can no longer be used because of a lack of water. The government has been transferring many people from those islands and villages to other islands, and the people receive free land to begin their lives again. For instance, on one of those islands the government is building a giant dam to supply water for irrigation for the surrounding area. By transmigration, those people will have a good water supply from the new dam; consequently, they will be able to produce food and increase their crops.

Endah Frey
(Indonesia)

1. Circle the controlling ideas in the topic sentence.

2. What is the function of the second sentence in this paragraph?

3. Put an asterisk (*) in the margin where examples occur in the paragraph.

4. Is the language in this paragraph formal or informal? Give examples to support your opinion.

II
Television Advertising

Advertisements are one of the most frustrating parts of watching television. In the first place, the advertisements waste time. For instance, about 15 minutes is lost by watching the advertisements during a single news program. In the same way, the watcher wastes his time watching advertisements during a good movie. In the second place, the advertisements interrupt the viewer. For example, the viewer may forget the situation or show during the advertisement. Even worse, during a good movie, the watcher loses his feelings when the ad comes on, and that has bad psychological influences. In the third place, the advertisements make many products look more appealing than they really are. For example, an expensive car is made to seem luxurious, or a bad product like deodorant is made to look very good by showing a beautiful amazing lady taking a shower. Accordingly, the television viewer must be aware and critical of the advertisements in order to endure them.

Rafia Majeed

(Iraq)

1. Is the topic sentence in this paragraph a statement of opinion, a statement of intent, or a combination of the two? How do you know?

2. Put an asterisk (*) in the margin where examples occur in the paragraph.

3. How might the author add details to the paragraph? What questions might you ask that could also be answered in the paragraph.

4. What concluding techniques are used in the paragraph?

PHYSICAL DESCRIPTION

Still another way to support a topic sentence is by using physical description, that is, words and phrases that appeal to the five senses:
- sight
- hearing
- smell
- touch
- taste

Physical description support is often used to explain or describe controlling ideas in the topic sentence.

Exercise H

The paragraphs below use physical description to support their topic sentences. Read the paragraphs, and then answer the questions that follow.

I

My Old House

I like to remember my old house from San Luis Potosi, in Mexico, because there I enjoyed my infancy and adolescence. Although it is a small house, for me it always seems that it was bigger, mainly the patio where I played soccer with my cousins and friends. On the patio there was a small pool where we played with small boats of paper. I remember each corner of my old house, but mainly my favorite place was the window of the living room. From this window I could see the rain in the summertime, and I could feel the tranquillity and freshness of the streets. Moreover, from this window, I could admire the stars in the dark sky. For all these reasons, my old house occupies a special place in my mind.

Armando Valencia

(Mexico)

1. With a small group of classmates, underline the words or phrases in the paragraph that appeal to one or more of the five senses.

2. The topic sentence in this paragraph does not accurately reflect the supporting information in the paragraph. With your small group, construct a clearer topic sentence for this paragraph.

3. Is the topic sentence one of opinion, intent, or a combination of the two? How do you know?

4. What is the purpose of this paragraph? Use examples to support your opinion.

II

JAVA WEDDING

On the wedding day in Java, flowers and plants play an important part in the traditional ceremony. At the entrance to the house, many plants set on the left and right of the doorway symbolize the hopes of the people for the young couple who will soon be married there. A banana trunk laden with ripe "King" bananas represents God's blessing on the bride and groom and is a symbol for a life as prosperous as that of a king and queen. Sugar cane, because it tastes sweet, traditionally means that the couple will have a sweet life. The leaves of sedge-grass, kemming and klwirh, which are placed together, have a meaning of rejecting danger and driving out the evil spirit. Huge fig trees are characterized by their many large leaves which give much shade in my hot country; the fig tree, therefore, means that God will protect and bless the bride and groom so they will always have peace and a safe life. In Indonesia the people use the coconut tree for many purposes; by including the coconut fruit at the doorway, the people hope that the bride and the groom will grow like a coconut tree and be just as useful to society. Finally, the young coconut leaves symbolize the hope that the couple will always look young and fresh, and remind them that they will always have special places in the hearts of people.

Endah Frey
(Indonesia)

1. Underline the words or phrases in the paragraph that appeal to one or more of the five senses.

2. Which of the five senses is used most frequently in both of the paragraphs above? Why?

3. Write an appropriate concluding sentence for the paragraph.

4. What concluding technique did you use?

Writing Assignment 3

The paragraph above describes a small part of the wedding day in the author's country (that is, the flowers and plants). It uses physical description to support the topic sentence. Write a paragraph about a wedding day in your country. Try to narrow your topic so that your paragraph will concentrate on the detail. You might describe the clothing, or the flowers, or the people who attend the ceremony, or the decorations, or a part of the ceremony. Your audience for this paragraph will be a native speaker of English who knows nothing about the wedding ceremony in your country. Then use the supporting technique of physical description to write a draft of your paragraph.

Pre-writing and Drafting: Use one of the pre-writing strategies you studied in the previous chapter to develop material for your paragraph. Use words and phrases that appeal to one or more of the five senses.

Peer Feedback: exchange paragraphs with a classmate. Read your partner's paragraph and

- underline the topic sentence and circle the controlling ideas
- underline with wavy lines (~~) the words or phrases that appeal to the senses
- at the end of the paragraph, write two questions that will help your partner add more physical description to her/his paragraph
- discuss possible revisions of the paragraph with your partner

Revision: using the advice of your partner, make necessary changes in your paragraph draft. Then write the final draft of your paragraph.

PERSONAL EXPERIENCE

The final technique of support is personal experience. While personal experience is not often used in formal academic papers, it can serve as a valuable support tool in paragraphs, particularly when an ESL student can connect personal experience about an academic topic from her/his own country. Sometimes a paragraph will contain a series of small personal experiences. Other times a paragraph will have a single, extended personal experience to support the controlling ideas in the topic sentence.

Exercise I

In the paragraphs below, the authors discuss topics by using experiences from their personal lives. Read the paragraphs and answer the questions that follow.

I
EELS

I am afraid to eat food cooked with eel. In Thailand, eel is a kind of expensive and well-known fish. This fish is about 1 1/2–2 feet long, usually yellowish dark brown and snake-like. It lives in fresh water, but unlike most fish, it has no scales. Instead its skin is mucus-like, so in preparing to cook it, we have to rub its body with sand or with the leaves of the "khoy" tree (*Strebus aspen*) to remove the mucus. Once when I was young, my aunt asked me to prepare the fish. First I beat their heads with a stick and rubbed their skins with khoy leaves; then I cut their heads off and put them in a large bowl to wash. When I poured the water into the bowl, the headless, pinkish white eels began to twist and swing left and right. After that day I never ate eel again.

Arthorn Boonsaner
(Thailand)

1. With a small group of classmates, decide who the audience is for this paragraph: Thais, eel fishermen, or classmates of the author? How do you know? How would the other audiences react to this paragraph?

2. The second sentence of this paragraph does not help the reader. With your classmates, replace the second sentence in this paragraph. How does your new second sentence help the reader?

3. Does the author of this paragraph use enough specific detail from his personal experience to explain his dislike? What detail(s) do you and your classmates remember *without looking again at the paragraph?*

4. Has the author of this paragraph persuaded you and your classmates? Why or why not?

II

Sometimes enemies become friends. For example, when I was younger, I was beaten very often by a boy who was much stronger than I. I wished to take revenge upon him; that was on my mind for a very long time. But it was a problem for me because of my being unaware of the way to do it. I practiced a lot of wrestling, but it didn't help me because I was afraid of him. Usually he started a fight by accusing me of something. I felt confused when he did that, and he knew that I couldn't stop being afraid. One day he hid one of his gloves and said that I had taken it. He tried to kick me in the stomach, but I twisted my body and made a counter-kick in his knee. He gave a very loud scream of pain.

Then he dropped on his knee, saying that he was wrong. I know it was cruel of me to act like this. But now we are friends, and I discovered that people sometimes have to fight or quarrel before becoming friends.

Yuri Pirogov

(Siberia)

1. This paragraph uses a single, extended example to support the topic sentence. Is it a persuasive example? Why or why not? Use details from the paragraph to support your opinion.

2. How does the second sentence help the reader to focus the paragraph?

3. What senses are used in this paragraph: taste, smell, feeling, hearing, seeing? Use details from the paragraph to support your answer.

4. Write a title for this paragraph.

Using Multiple Supporting Techniques

Often a topic sentence will be supported by more than one technique of support. For example, a personal experience will contain physical description, or an example will contain some facts. Multiple forms of support are often more interesting for an audience and provide stronger evidence for the controlling ideas in a topic sentence.

Exercise J

The paragraphs below use various techniques of support (facts, examples, physical description, and/or personal experience) to support their topic sentences. Read the paragraphs, identify the techniques of support in each, and answer the questions that follow.

I
University Costs

The international student needs much money to study at a university in the U.S. The cost can be divided into three categories. First is the price of house rent; that expense differs according to the kind of house. For example, a single basement room with a small kitchen at one end and a bed at the other costs at least $200 a month, but an apartment with a separate bedroom and kitchen costs at least $350 a month. The second expense is the cost of food; this cost is also various for each person. I spend at least $300 per month, so my daily cost for food is about $10. The final expense is the cost of tuition. This cost is especially high. I need $2000 per semester for tuition at this university because I am an "out-of-state" student. And that doesn't even count the expenses for books, clothing, and other expenses. Therefore, I need at least $4000 for each semester.

Hiro Yabuki

(Japan)

Techniques of Support: _____

1. Circle the controlling ideas in the topic sentence.

2. What function does the second sentence in the paragraph fulfill?

3. What questions do you expect to be answered in the paragraph that follows?

4. Are those questions answered?

II
Pronunciation in English

Although my first language, Spanish, has many aspects which are similar to English, for me it has been very difficult to achieve good pronunciation of words in English due to the number of sounds that it has. In Spanish we have five vowels and five basic sounds. But in English the vowel "a" alone has, I think, five or six sounds. Sometimes two words have a very small difference, but their meanings are completely different. This particular situation can take away sense from a conversation and sometimes makes it funny. An example of that happened to me. I wanted to buy a half-pound of Muenster cheese in slices, but my pronunciation of "Muenster" was "monster." The salesperson began to smile because she couldn't imagine how to get a "monster in slices!"

Ahmed Irazabal
(Venezuela)

Techniques of Support: _____

1. What is the most effective technique of support used in this paragraph? Why?

2. What additional detail could this author use in this paragraph? Be specific.

3. What is the purpose of this paragraph: to inform, to persuade, and/or to entertain?

4. Write a concluding sentence for this paragraph.

III
LEAD POISONING

The terms "lead absorption" and "lead poisoning" are not used consistently everywhere, so it is convenient to define their use. Lead may enter the body through the respiratory tract through inhalation of vapor or particulate matter or through ingestion. Lead absorption is the process whereby an individual takes up lead from the environment by whatever means, and at whatever stage he is in his development. Lead poisoning may be metabolic or clinical. Metabolic poisoning may be said to be present when it is possible to detect alterations in metabolism which are the result of lead absorption. Clinical lead poisoning is diagnosed when the absorbed lead produces signs which are evident to the patient or his doctor: nervous, excitable jerking of the muscles, delirium, stupor, diarrhea, and finally collapse. Plumbism, Saturnism, and lead intoxication are all terms which are used as synonyms for clinical lead poisoning.

Julio Ferrer
(Mexico)

Techniques of Support: _____

1. Is the topic sentence in this paragraph a topic sentence of opinion, intent, or a combination of the two?

2. Who is the audience for this paragraph? How do you know?

3. How do the language and sentence structure in this paragraph differ from the language and sentence structure in two previous paragraphs? Be specific.

4. What is the most effective technique of support in this paragraph? Support your opinion.

IV
The Cold Summer

In 1989, when I first entered Moscow Airport from my country, I felt for the first time in my life that I had been carried to an unknown place. After finishing the control procedures at the airport, I took a taxi to the downtown area. The road, lined with its bare and yellow trees, contrasted with what I had just left in Sudan. I had left my town in the middle of summer, where everything was green and lovely. Sitting in the taxi, the bleak, gray city passed in front of me as if I was watching a movie. I was so completely absorbed in my thinking that when the driver said something to me I couldn't understand a single word. But I did understand that he probably meant that I had reached my terminal point. I took my luggage from the taxi and found myself in front of a huge gray building. I entered the building and went through a narrow semi-dark corridor until I reached the Foreign Student Office. There they gave me a key for my room. The room was small, damp, and painted gray. After I rested for a while, I opened the window to look at the street outside. The weather was cold and dark, the sky covered with dark clouds. I realized then that I had left the clear sky and twinkling stars of my country behind.

Hashim Elobeid
(Sudan)

Techniques of Support: _____

1. With a small group of classmates, modify and then rewrite the topic sentence for this paragraph so that it relates more directly to the paragraph.

2. Discuss with your classmates the purpose of this paragraph.

3. What is the most successful technique of support used in this paragraph? Underline the most memorable details in the paragraph.

4. As the reader, how did you feel when you finished reading the paragraph? Why?

Journal Assignment

In your opinion, which of the four paragraphs above is the most successful and effective? Write a paragraph evaluating the strengths of that paragraph, beginning with "I liked X because..."

Exercise K

Below are three incomplete topic sentences.

1. Finish each topic sentence.

2. Circle the controlling ideas in each topic sentence.

3. Identify the topic sentence as a statement of opinion, intent, or a combination of the two.

4. Then consider your audience. What details will interest them? Ask questions that you (and your readers) might ask and that you might answer in the paragraphs that follow.

5. Construct a second sentence for each topic sentence. Use an appropriate connector that will help your reader anticipate the paragraph that will follows.

6. Indicate what technique(s) of support you might use to support each topic sentence and to interest your audience.

I. My greatest problem living in the U. S. is _____

_____. Statement of _____

Second Sentence _____

_____

Techniques of Support: _____

II. Handicapped people in my country_____

_____. Statement of _____

Second Sentence _____

_____

Techniques of Support: _____

III. If I had two weeks vacation, I would go to _____

_____ Statement of _____

Second Sentence _____

_____

Techniques of Support: _____

Writing Assignment 4

Choose one of the topic sentences (and its accompanying second sentence) from the exercise above, and then choose a specific audience for the paragraph you will write. Write a paragraph using the techniques of support you indicated.

> **Pre-writing and Drafting:** In your journal, use one or more of the pre-writing strategies to generate details for the paragraph. Then write a rough draft of the paragraph.
>
> **Peer Feedback:** When you have finished your first draft, exchange paragraphs with a classmate. Read your partner's paragraph; then
>
> • circle the controlling ideas in the topic sentence
>
> • at the end of the paragraph draft, write questions that <u>were answered</u> in the paragraph
>
> • then write one question you would like the writer to answer in the final draft of the paragraph
>
> • underline any grammar or sentence structure problems you find in the paragraph
>
> • discuss the question you wrote and the problems you found with your partner
>
> **Revision:** using the advice of your partner, as well as the Guidelines for Revision (on the inside back cover of this book), make any changes that you think will improve your paragraph. Then write the final draft of the paragraph.

Paragraph Unity

A paragraph is a group of sentences about a single idea. While the topic sentence introduces the audience to the topic, the second sentence signals the reader about the organization of the paragraph that will follow. The remaining sentences in the paragraph should support the controlling ideas in the topic sentence, and the last sentence concludes the paragraph. If all the sentences in the paragraph are about a single idea, and if the sentences are closely related, the paragraph will probably be unified. Any sentence that does not support the topic sentence is irrelevant; that is, it does not relate. That sentence should be modified or removed from the paragraph.

Exercise L

In the paragraphs below, some sentences are irrelevant. They destroy the <u>unity</u> of the paragraphs. Draw a line through those sentences. Some of the paragraphs contain only one irrelevant sentence; others have two sentences that should be eliminated. After you have crossed out the irrelevant sentences, answer the questions that follow each paragraph.

I

_____

Acapulco is traditionally the best city in Mexico for vacations. The tourist can have fun all day long in this city. In the morning he can go to the beach and swim in the ocean. In the afternoon there are many museums and shops to keep the visitor busy. Bolivia also has some nice cities to visit. In the evenings, the vacationer can enjoy the many restaurants, theatres, and discos in Acapulco. After partying and dancing until dawn, the visitor can go to a beautiful hotel for a long rest.

Alejandro Maiz
(Mexico)

1. Write a title for this paragraph.

2. Is the topic sentence a statement of intent, opinion, or a combination of both?

3. What questions might you ask the author to answer with more specific detail?

II
A Holiday in My Country

One of the biggest holidays in the Armenian culture is Jrorhnek on the sixth of January. We Armenians believe that Jesus Christ was baptized on this day, and so we celebrate this event every year. The Armenian religion is Greek Orthodox, and so we do not celebrate Christmas, but instead of Christmas we celebrate the sixth of January. The Armenian people gather together with their families on Jrorhnek night; they decorate their houses and their dinner tables, and they eat special food. The next week everyone returns to work as usual. They are happy, and they give gifts to one another. _____

_____

Rima Kodadian
(Iran)

1. How does the second sentence focus this paragraph for the reader?

2. What techniques of support are used in this paragraph?

3. Write a concluding sentence for this paragraph.

III
The Celebration of the New Year

If you go to Cambodia during the New Year, you will get excited together with all of the people of the country. The month after harvesting, in the middle of April, is Cambodian New Year. All the public offices, schools, factories, and shopping stores close for three days. There are six main holidays each year in Cambodia. In front of the Royal Temple, in all the city parks and on the big plaza, there are crowded ceremonies to celebrate these significant days. You can join the traditional dances, classical operas, and different, interesting kinds of games. Even though we feel tired at the end of the holidays, we believe that New Year will bring happiness and hope to us.

Long Nguon
(Cambodia)

1. With a small group of classmates, modify or rewrite the topic sentence for this paragraph.

2. Circle the controlling ideas in the new topic sentence.

3. Ask questions about the controlling ideas; are they answered in the paragraph?

IV
INDEPENDENCE DAY!

Independence Day, the twentieth of July, is the most important day in Colombia. We celebrate Independence Day each year with a military parade down the main street of every major city: Bogota (the capital of Colombia), Medellin, and Cali. Every person in the cities, and many people from the country who visit the cities during the holiday, dress in fine clothes, and they go to see the parades. The soldiers put on their best parade uniforms, and they march about 10 kilometers. After that, the President speaks in the Principal Room of the Congress Building to the Colombian people, the Senate, and the Lower House. My brother says this is his favorite holiday. It is an obligation for the Colombians to put out the Colombian flag on this day. If they don't, they have to pay a fine. The Colombian people enjoy this holiday very much because it symbolizes freedom.

Juan Muñoz
(Colombia)

1. Circle the controlling ideas in the topic sentence of this paragraph.

2. What is the purpose of this paragraph? Who is the audience?

3. What techniques of support are used in this paragraph?

Journal Assignment

Which of the paragraphs above was the most interesting or valuable for you? Write a paragraph in your journal evaluating the strengths of that paragraph. Use specific examples from the paragraph to support your opinion.

Paragraph Revision

Successful writing requires many decisions and many steps. One important step is revision: re (again) + vise (look) = look again.

Looking again at your writing may result in changes that will improve your paragraph. Having friends, classmates, or your teacher look at your writing may result in good advice that will improve your writing. For these reasons, most experienced writers often write several drafts of a writing task before they are satisfied with their work.

Revision is an important part of learning to write well because it allows writers to
- discover new and better ways to present and support ideas
- consider and reconsider the purpose and audience for the writing task
- identify strengths and weaknesses in the writing
- solve problems (organizational, grammatical, mechanical) in the writing

The revision process has several steps; these steps may occur during the composing process and/or after the paragraph is completed. Similarly, the revision process has many individual strategies. For example, some writers prefer to write their rough drafts without worrying about organization or grammar. Then, after spending time revising, these writers rewrite the paragraphs. Other writers revise as they write, going back over each phrase or sentence, correcting and changing words and phrases. Still others "pre-revise" in their minds before they write; the result is sometimes a rough draft that needs only a few revisions. Of course, revision strategies may differ from writing task to writing task.

As you write the rough drafts of your paragraphs, observe your revising strategies. Remember that no matter how complete and correct your rough draft is, looking again will give you a valuable opportunity to learn about your writing and to improve it.

Writing Assignment 4

Choose <u>two</u> of the following subjects (or select another subject). Narrow the subjects to topics. Then develop and write a paragraph for each topic.

- the value of quiet (or noise)
- taking vitamin pills
- hamburgers
- ghosts
- police
- dreams

    Pre-Writing and Drafting: In your journal, use the Paragraph Planning Guidelines (on the inside front cover of this book) to develop the rough drafts of paragraphs about those two topics.

Peer Feedback: With a small group of peers, read several paragraph drafts that are not your own. As you read each draft, help the author by

- putting an asterisk (*) in the margin where you find excellent supporting detail
- asking two questions (or making two suggestions) at the end of the draft
- making one suggestion about sentence combining
- marking any grammar errors that you find

Then discuss your suggestions and marks with the author of each paragraph.

Revision: Using the advice of your classmates and the Paragraph Revision Guidelines (on the inside back cover of this book), revise the drafts of your paragraphs, and write a final draft of each. (Remember: your individual steps may occur in a different order, and some steps may occur simultaneously.) Finally, in your journal, write a paragraph describing and evaluating the best paragraph draft your read in your group. Discuss why the paragraph was successful, and use detail that you remember from the paragraph to support your opinions.

Sentence Combining Exercise

The jokes below have many short, choppy sentences, and some information is repeated. Combine the sentences to make the jokes flow more smoothly.

I

There was a man. He was Somalian. He was cowardly. He was called Al Shiddad. He tried to walk from his house. He tried to walk to his neighbor's house. It was at night. When he was in the village, he was in the center. He saw something. It was a tree. He thought that the tree was something. He thought it was an animal. He thought the animal was harmful. He stood. He stood at that spot. He stood there until morning. In the morning, he recognized it. He recognized what he had been afraid of all night. He recognized the tree. He reached this conclusion. He spoke. He said, "I thought that you were a harmful animal, but you were a tree. What I will never do again is take walks at night."

A. A. Ismail
(Somalia)

II

One day a man went someplace. He went to the restaurant. He spent money. He bought pies. He bought five of them. He ate them. But he still felt hungry. He bought another pie. He ate it. Then he felt very full. Suddenly he was angry. He shouted. He shouted at the waiter. He said, "This pie was useful. It made me full. Why didn't you bring it to me first?"

even do

Yuan Ren
(People's Republic of China)

4

Paragraph Organization: The Point Paragraph Outline

I think writing is the most difficult skill in learning English. I still think in Chinese first, then translate it into English. The sentence patterns are always Chinese styles. And because I cannot always use simple sentences in writing papers, I think writing is even more difficult than speaking.

Mei-Ya Lu
(Republic of China)

Most academic writing you will do will be objective. You will be explaining, evaluating, and/or supporting material for your audience and persuading your audience that your information and/or opinions are valid. For academic writing, you will also be demonstrating your ability to gather, organize, and present knowledge about a topic for a professor/teacher.

In order to communicate effectively, you must be aware of the forms the academic audience expects. Basically, **the paragraph form for academic written English moves from a general statement (or topic sentence) to specific data that explains, describes, or supports (that is, proves or gives evidence about) the general statement.** Elementary school children in the U.S. learn that the paragraph has three parts: the introduction (tell your audience what you're going to tell them); the body (show your audience what you have to tell them); and the conclusion (tell your audience what you have told them). Secondary school students are taught the "hamburger" paragraph: the top bun (the topic sentence/introduction); the meat (the body/middle of the paragraph); and the bottom bun (the concluding sentence).

This chapter will teach you to arrange material that you have gathered into a paragraph form that your academic reader will expect. First, you will study the element of coherence in paragraphs; then you will learn a special form of organization called the point paragraph outline.

Paragraph Coherence

Even when a paragraph is unified, and the topic sentence is well supported, the paragraph can still "sound" choppy (that is, rough or interrupted) unless the writer uses coherence devices to make the paragraph smoother. **Coherence means "to stick together."** In writing, it means that one thought flows smoothly into the next, that a thought is connected to the one that comes before it.

One way to achieve coherence is with the use of **connectors**: words or phrases that link one sentence to another. Connectors are often called transitions, that is, words or phrases that help the reader go from one sentence to another. In the same way that the second sentence of a paragraph helps a reader anticipate what the paragraph will be about, using connectors between sentences helps the reader make the connection between sentences. Some basic connectors that are used with techniques of support in the middle of paragraphs are:

Facts	**Examples**
In fact,	For example,
That is, (i.e.,)	For instance,
As a matter of fact,	Furthermore,
Besides that,	Moreover,
	Specifically,

Physical Description	**Personal Experience**
On the right,	First (second, next,
Next to X,	then, finally)
At the top,	Before (during, after,
Between X and Y,	when, while)

Exercise A

Read the following paragraphs. Underline the connectors, and answer the questions that follow.

I

My greatest problem living in the U.S. is the food. For example, when I want to have a meal, sometimes I can't find what I like to eat because I am not used to American food. In addition, often American food contains pork, but I am not supposed to eat pork because my religion and my customs are different. I must be very careful in the grocery store to check the ingredients of whatever I buy, and when I eat in a restaurant, I must always ask whether or not something contains pork. For example, McDonald's hamburger buns are made with pork fat; therefore, I cannot even order a "Big Mac"!

Abdurrahman Juhani
(Saudi Arabia)

1. With a small group of classmates, decide on a title for this paragraph.
2. In your small group, identify the technique(s) of support used in this paragraph.
3. Work with your peers to insert a sentence <u>after</u> the second sentence that gives further detail about the second sentence.
4. With your small group, write a concluding sentence for this paragraph.

II

Why is the TOEFL Exam Difficult?

For the majority of foreign students, it is usually hard to get the required score on the TOEFL exam. From my experience, I also found it hard, and I can give reasons for that. First of all, you may have very good English, yet you may still not get the required scores because the most important fact about taking the TOEFL is to know how to deal with the test itself and how to make the most of the assigned time. For example, the first time I took that exam I didn't watch the time, and I was, therefore, too late to finish the grammar section. In my attempt to be quick on the next section, I answered the tenth question in the place of the ninth, and I didn't realize until I came to the last questions that all my answers were in the wrong spaces. Before I could make the necessary changes, the time was over. In addition, the TOEFL is full of tricks, and usually it concentrates on certain subjects or points that foreign students usually don't know. So in order to get the required score, one should be aware of these facts and should practice as much as one can with the test samples.

Hassen Hassen
(Libya)

1. With a small group of classmates, circle the controlling ideas in the topic sentence. Then draw lines from those controlling ideas to the details in the paragraph that support them.

2. With your group of classmates, discuss how the second sentence in this paper focuses the rest of the paragraph for the reader.

3. Decide with your group what techniques of support are used successfully in this paragraph. Be specific.

4. With your group, write one or two additional sentences just before the concluding sentence that gives detail about the "full of tricks" sentence.

III

When I first came to the United States, I was amazed to find out the real meaning of "pulling your leg." There was a time when my friends were making fun of me. They told me that if I wanted the person I loved to think of me, I should call out his name a few times before I went to sleep. Next, I should try to imagine his face. If I could see him clearly, it meant that he was not thinking of me at all, and vice-versa. Because they said that people had tried this experiment before, I believed them. Later, they told me that they were only "pulling my leg." At that moment, I did not know the meaning of that idiom, and I was too shy to ask. But I thought that it was an insult or a term used to make a person feel bad, and I felt sad that my friends had insulted me. The following day, I talked to an American friend about the slang term that bothered me a lot. I was surprised that it means someone is playing a joke on another person. I should have known, with all the laughter that followed when my friends used that term.

Hasni Mohd Salleh
(Malaysia)

1. Who is the audience for this paragraph? How do you know?

2. What is the purpose of the paragraph. Use detail from the paragraph to support your opinion.

3. Write a title for this paragraph.

4. What concluding techniques are used in this paragraph?

Writing Assignment 1

Your friend is coming to the U.S. from your country. Write him a **personal letter** about one serious problem you had during your first month in the U.S. Then, in the next paragraph, advise your friend about how to avoid that problem. Choose your details and your techniques of support carefully so that your friend (your audience) will understand both the problem and the solution.

Pre-writing and Drafting: In your journal, use two pre-writing strategies (brainstorming, listing, flow-charting, clustering, etc.) to help generate ideas about your topic. Consider your audience and purpose as you begin to construct your topic sentence, your second sentence, and your supporting details. Use the Paragraph Writing Guidelines (on the inside front cover of this book) to write a rough draft of your paragraph.

Peer Feedback: In a small group of classmates, read several letters that are not your own. Ask your group to help you by becoming your audience. They can ask questions and offer suggestions about your paragraph, and you should help them in similar ways.

Revision: Using the advice from your group, revise your rough draft. Then write the final draft of your letter.

Scrambled Paragraphs

If a paragraph is unified, coherent, and well supported, the sentences in the paragraph could be mixed up (that is, "scrambled"), and then reassembled by a reader who is not the author of the paragraph. The steps in reassembling a scrambled paragraph are:
- read the scrambled sentences
- identify the most general, most important sentence that introduces the paragraph (that is, the topic sentence)
- find the second sentence that helps the reader anticipate what the paragraph will be about
- look for connectors that indicate the places of the middle supporting sentences in the body of the paragraph
- locate the concluding sentence of the paragraph

Exercise B

In the paragraphs below, the sentences have been scrambled. Locate and underline the topic sentence for each paragraph. Then, working with classmates in a small group, use the guidelines for reassembling scrambled sentences to <u>re-number</u> the sentences in the paragraph in a logical order. After that, work with your group to answer the questions that follow each paragraph.

I

_____

_____Finally, rivers give us fish to eat and water to drink, and they are homes for many kinds of plant and animal life. ____ We also use river water for power to make electricity. ____ They provide beauty and coolness to the scenery. Rivers play a very important part in our lives. ____ In the summer we swim in rivers, and in the winter we skate on them. ____ Furthermore, we irrigate crops with river water. ____ For these reasons, rivers are an important part of our earth's ecology.

1. Write a title for this paragraph.

2. What techniques of support are used in this paragraph?

3. Underline the connectors in the paragraph.

II

_____

_____ First, if money is lost or stolen, there is little chance of getting it back. If a blank check is lost, no harm is done. _____ Using checks is safer and more convenient than carrying money. _____ Of course, lost money is simply lost money. _____ Next, even if a signed check is lost, the bank can be told not to cash it. _____ In addition, a check can be safely mailed, but money sent through the mail can be stolen. _____ Therefore, if you have a choice, you should certainly carry checks instead of cash.

1. Write a title for this paragraph.

2. Circle the controlling ideas in the topic sentence. What questions are answered in the paragraph that follows?

3. How does the second sentence function in this paragraph?

III

_____

_____ When Indira Gandhi was prime minister of India, she tried to solve this problem by convincing poor people in rural areas to practice birth control. _____ Mrs. Gandhi promised that if a man would agree to have surgery so he could have no more children, he would receive a free transistor radio. Overpopulation is one of India's greatest problems. _____ A radio is a great luxury in some parts of India. _____ Many men agreed, but only after having ten or more children. _____ Mrs. Gandhi then attempted to force poor women to agree to have an operation so that they could have no more children. _____ This caused so much opposition that the problem had to be forgotten, and the problem was never solved.

1. Write a title for the paragraph.

2. Is the topic sentence a statement of opinion, intent, or a combination of both? How do you know?

3. Who is the audience for this paragraph? Describe this audience: age, education, interests, and other background information.

The Point Paragraph Outline

The point paragraph outline is not a pre-writing technique. Instead, it is an organizational strategy that provides a frame for the ideas you want to communicate.

Notice that you must have material—facts, examples, experience, etc.—before you begin to arrange that material for an audience. The point paragraph outline you will study in this chapter is a process that follows (or sometimes occurs at the same time as) the idea-generating, pre-writing processes you studied in the previous chapter.

Journal Assignment

Write for ten minutes. Describe the rules for writing that you learned in elementary and secondary school in your country. What kinds of writing did you do in elementary and secondary school? Be specific.

NOTE: The point paragraph outline that you will learn about and practice in this chapter is, of course, not the only way to organize an academic paragraph. For example, topic sentences do not always occur at the beginning of the paragraph, and sometimes paragraphs do not even have a topic sentence. In addition, the support in an academic paragraph may include a single point or several points and levels of specificity. And, of course, academic paragraphs differ in length depending on their topics, audiences, and purposes. But the overall organization presented in this chapter is a basic, workable format that academic readers will recognize, understand, and expect.

Planning the Point Paragraph Outline

There are two purposes of outlining the material for a paragraph. First, the outline will make the focus and evidence of the paragraph clearer for the writer; it is therefore easier to determine whether or not the support for the opinions and/or information in the paragraph is sufficient. Second, organizing paragraphs by using the point paragraph outline makes the actual paragraph easier for the U.S. academic reader to comprehend; the point paragraph organization is an expected paragraph form. Below is the basic form of the point paragraph outline.

Form: The Point Paragraph Outline

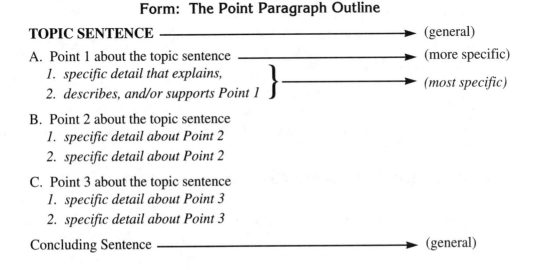

TOPIC SENTENCE ⟶ (general)

A. Point 1 about the topic sentence ⟶ (more specific)
   1. specific detail that explains, ⟶ *(most specific)*
   2. describes, and/or supports Point 1

B. Point 2 about the topic sentence
   1. specific detail about Point 2
   2. specific detail about Point 2

C. Point 3 about the topic sentence
   1. specific detail about Point 3
   2. specific detail about Point 3

Concluding Sentence ⟶ (general)

NOTE: The basic rules for outlining apply to the construction of a point paragraph outline:

1. never an A without a B

2. never a 1 without a 2

The reason for this rule is balance. If you have only an A, for example, you can include that point in the previous line.

The process for planning a point paragraph outline has several steps, but just as pre-writing strategies may differ from writer to writer (and, for some writers, from paragraph to paragraph), planning the detail in a point paragraph outline may occur in different ways. For example, you may begin to construct the paragraph outline in the middle, supplying the details, then identifying the points, and finally forming a topic sentence and a concluding sentence. Or you might begin with a point or two, write a possible topic sentence, work with details, and then modify the topic sentence. Whatever approach you choose (and you should experiment), the general process given below lists some of the steps you might take. Of course, the order you use may be different, and some of the steps may occur simultaneously.

Point Paragraph Outline Guidelines

1. Choose a topic.

2. Use pre-writing techniques to generate ideas about the topic.

3. Construct a possible topic sentence with controlling ideas.

4. Begin constructing the point paragraph outline.
   A. *Think of 2–4 points you want to make about the topic sentence.*
   B. *For each of the points, use two or more specific details (that you have generated) that explain, describe, and/or support that point.*

5. Modify or change the topic sentence (if necessary) to fit the specific detail.

6. Write a concluding sentence that summarizes, offers a solution, comes to a conclusion, makes a recommendation, or makes a prediction, based on the information in the paragraph.

Exercise C

Following is a point paragraph outline. Read it and then answer the questions at the end of the paragraph outline.

TOPIC SENTENCE: **The tourist in Cairo will later remember the smells of the city**.

A. Coffee shops

   1. morning smell of coffee beans being ground   (tell the audience what you're going to tell them)

2. *later, the brewing of the coffee*

B. Spice market
   1. *overwhelming smell of all spices together*
   2. *individual smells: cardamom, cinnamon, ginger*

(<u>show</u> your audience what you're telling them)

C. The Nile River
   1. *mist and fish smells in early morning permeate everything*
   2. *later the smell of fish in riverside restaurants*

<u>Concluding Sentence:</u> For years afterward, the tourist will recall the smells of Cairo whenever he encounters strong coffee, a bakery, or fish in the supermarket.

(tell them what you've told them)

Jim Griswold
(United States)

1. Circle the controlling ideas in the topic sentence.

2. Draw lines from the controlling ideas to the specific details in the outline.

3. What is the purpose of this paragraph? Who is the audience? How do you know?

4. What concluding technique(s) does the author use?

Exercise D

Below are two point paragraph outlines; each is followed by the actual paragraph. Read each outline and paragraph; then answer the questions that follow. Notice that:

1. Only the topic sentence and the concluding sentence are complete sentences in each outline.

2. The other parts of each outline are written in phrases (short, incomplete sentences). Those phrases are written in complete sentences in the actual paragraph.

3. In some cases, specific details that occupy two spaces in the outline are combined into one sentence in the completed paragraph.

I

TOPIC SENTENCE: **This is an old sailor's story about his pipe and women.**

A. Bad men want women like a cigarette
   1. *slender, firm, all in a row*
   2. *selected at will*
   3. *set aflame, discarded*

  B. Fastidious men want women like a cigar
     1. expensive, long-lasting
     2. good appearance
     3. used to the end
  C. Good men want women like a pipe
     1. attached to, knocks gently with love
     2. handles with great care

<u>Concluding Sentence:</u> A man will give you a cigarette, offer you a cigar, but he never shares his pipe.

    This is an old sailor's story about his pipe and women. He told me, "Bad men want their women to be like cigarettes: slender, firm, all in a row, to be selected at will, set aflame, and discarded, only to select another." Then he said, "Fastidious men want their women to be like a cigar: more expensive, longer lasting, with a better appearance, and, if the brand is good, used until the end." After that, the old sailor said to me, "The good man wants his women to be like his pipe: something he becomes attached to, knocks gently with love, and handles with great care always." Finally, he said to me, "Remember: a man will give you a cigarette, offer you a cigar, but he never shares his pipe."

Marcello Villahoz
(Argentina)

1. Write a title for this paragraph.
2. Underline the connectors in this paragraph.
3. What makes this paragraph interesting? Be specific.

II

TOPIC SENTENCE: **Eating in the Student Center is a pleasant experience.**

A. food is excellent
    1. well-prepared and delicious
    2. many different foods (hamburgers, tacos, pizza, and chicken)
    3. self-selection

B. environment is positive
    1. happy young people talking
    2. calm atmosphere for study

C. people are friendly
    1. strangers say "Hi" and share tables
    2. conversation helps my English

Concluding Sentence: It is nice to go to the Student Center cafeteria once in a while to enjoy eating, studying, and talking with new people.

THE STUDENT CENTER

Eating in the Student Center is a pleasant experience. First, the food is excellent. It is well-prepared, it tastes delicious, and there are many different kinds of food like hamburgers, tacos, pizza, and chicken. Moreover, each person serves himself, selecting just what he wants. Second, the environment in the Student Center is positive. Many happy young people are talking and laughing. But the atmosphere is still calm; it's possible to study and do homework. Finally, there are many friendly people at the Student Center. Even the strangers say "Hi!" and offer to share their tables. When that happens, practice in speaking English and friendship often follow. For these reasons, it is nice to go to the Student Center cafeteria once in a while to enjoy eating, studying, and talking with new people.

Sergio Pas
(Honduras)

1. Circle the controlling ideas in the topic sentence of the outline, and draw lines to the details in the outline from each controlling idea.

2. Working with classmates in a small group, suppose that the topic sentence of this paragraph was "Eating in the Student Center cafeteria is an unpleasant experience." What points could you make in the outline? What specific details could you use? As a group, make a single point paragraph outline for that paragraph.

3. Decide, in your group, what concluding technique(s) the author uses in this paragraph.

4. Write a new title for this paragraph.

Writing Assignment 2

Below are four paragraph topics. Choose one. Then choose 2-4 classmates who will be your audience for this paragraph; you will be part of the audience for their paragraphs.

Topics:

1. Describe a room. Remember to use details that will give your audience a clear sense of the room.

2. Write a paragraph about your most relaxing or your most exciting pastime.

3. Write a paragraph explaining why you decided to become a _____ (engineer, teacher, sociologist, etc.).

4. Write a paragraph about a place in your country that you dislike. Explain to your audience why you dislike it.

Peer Feedback: Form a small group with the classmates who will be your audience. Interview your classmates. Discover what they know and what they don't know about your topic, and ask them what they would like to read about your topic. Make notes in your journal about their needs and expectations.

Pre-writing and Drafting:

1. In your journal, write a paragraph about your audience. Describe the classmates for whom you will be writing and what you will write to fulfill those expectations.
2. In your journal, use two pre-writing strategies to generate information about your topic. Write for fifteen minutes.
3. Using the point paragraph planning guidelines given on page 88, plan a paragraph about that topic.
4. Write a rough draft of your paragraph.

Peer Feedback: Meet with the students who are your audience. Read the paragraphs that are not your own. In your journal, write notes about each paragraph: in what ways has each fulfilled your needs and expectations? How should each author modify her/his paragraph to better meet your expectations? When you have finished, discuss your suggestions with your audience; then listen to their suggestions for your paragraph.

Revision: Using the suggestions of your audience and the Revision Guidelines (on the inside back cover of this book), modify your paragraph and write the final draft. Then, in your journal, write a paragraph that describes the changes you made in your paragraph. Tell why you made the changes, and evaluate the ways those changes improved your paragraph.

Journal Assignment

In your elementary and/or secondary school classes, what rules did you learn about writing in your native language? Write a paragraph describing those rules.

Exercise E

Below are three outlines. Read each outline; then, in your journal, write a paragraph using one of the outlines. Be sure to use appropriate connectors so that the paragraph will be unified and complete. Use additional detail when necessary, and give your paragraph a title.

I

TOPIC SENTENCE: **Transportation in Portland is not adequate for people who do not own a car.**

A. Public transportation

    1. very few buses
        a. always crowded
        b. rarely on time
        c. limited schedules

    2. very few taxis
        a. only available from 7 a.m. to 6 p.m.
        b. very expensive
        c. long waits

B. Private transportation

    1. bicycles
        a. inadequate bicycle lanes
        b. danger on the main streets

    2. skateboards or roller blades
        a. difficult to learn
        b. expensive to purchase

    3. on foot
        a. inefficient in a large town
        b. difficult in bad weather

<u>Concluding Sentence:</u> The solution to these problems is simple: if you don't own a car, don't come to Portland!

Abdulaziz Fatoh
(Saudi Arabia)

II

TOPIC SENTENCE: **Palestine is a fascinating country because of its natural beauty, its excellent weather, and its geographical location.**

A. Natural beauty

    1. beaches of the Mediterranean Sea
        (a) yellow sand
        (b) blue water

    2. many beautiful mountains covered with green grass and trees

B. Excellent weather

    1. usually sunshine and moderate temperature

    2. even in cool rainy season, weather is pleasant

C. Geographic location

    1. attractive for tourists
       (a) Egypt on south
       (b) Mediterranean Sea on west

    2. many different cultures
       (a) Lebanon on north
       (b) Jordan on east

<u>Concluding Sentence:</u> All these factors make Palestine appealing for the natives and for visitors.

Mohammed El-Helou
(Palestine)

III

TOPIC SENTENCE: **Soccer is more fun to play than American football.**

A. Less dangerous

    1. no excessive violence permitted

    2. quickness and agility prized more than brute strength

B. Faster

    1. play nearly continuous for each 45-minute time period

    2. players always moving, always playing

C. More integrated tactics

    1. each player both attacks and defends

    2. each team plays both offense and defense

<u>Concluding Sentence:</u> Because soccer is a game of speed and total athletic ability, and because it is exciting to watch as well as play, it is rightly one of the most popular sports in the world.

Nelson Cuervo
(Venezuela)

Modifying the Topic Sentence

The topic sentence of a paragraph should give the reader a clear sense of what the paragraph will contain. However, as you plan your paragraph and organize your material, sometimes the purpose of your paragraph changes. As a result, often the controlling ideas in a topic sentence, or the topic sentence itself, will have to be modified or changed. Usually there are four possible reasons for such a change:

1. You discover, as you generate ideas and plan, that your purpose for writing has changed.

2. You decide, as you plan, that you want to communicate something different to your audience.

3. You find that the information you have presented in the paragraph does not adequately explain or support the topic sentence.

4. The original topic sentence is too general; it needs controlling ideas that focus the paragraph more clearly.

Because one or more of the reasons above may occur in any paragraph you plan, it is necessary to look back and review the purpose and the audience of your paragraph as you write. You may want to:

- restate or reconsider the purpose and/or the audience as you begin to construct the point outline for your paragraph;
- add material to and/or subtract material from the body of the paragraph.

The guidelines below will help you decide whether or not your topic sentence needs modifying or rewriting.

Guidelines for Modifying Topic Sentences

1. Am I still responding to the assignment?

2. Am I fulfilling the needs and expectations of my audience?

3. Does my topic sentence still express the main idea of the paragraph?

4. Do the controlling ideas in the topic sentence adequately introduce the paragraph that follows?

5. Is there any material in the body of my paragraph that is not directly related to the topic sentence?

6. Does the concluding sentence in the paragraph reflect the main idea in the topic sentence?

Exercise F

The writers of the paragraphs below were asked to communicate information about their countries that would be of interest to their international classmates. Each of the paragraphs needs one or more of the modifications listed above so that they will communicate more successfully. Working with a small group of classmates, decide:

- how the title of each paragraph could be modified to help the reader
- how the topic sentence of each might be modified to better communicate the purpose of the paragraph

Then answer the questions that follow each paragraph.

I

The Medellin Climate

My city is Medellin, and it is located in a valley surrounded by big, green mountains with many rivers. Medellin, like many Latin American cities, is in a tropical zone; therefore, it has a warm climate with moderate rains. The temperature in the city never falls below freezing, and, because the city is in the mountains, the days are usually sunny and warm, and the nights are always cool. Because of this, Medellin is called by Colombians "The City of Eternal Spring" and "The City of Flowers." The people of Medellin enjoy the climate and the many fragrant flowers; they spend much of their lives in their gardens, and they prefer casual clothing for their activities.

Gloria Arango
(Colombia)

1. Why did the topic sentence in this paragraph need modification?

2. Circle the controlling ideas in your modified topic sentence. Draw lines from the controlling ideas to the support for those ideas in the paragraph.

3. Write a concluding sentence for this paragraph.

II

Marriage in Iraq

Marriage in Iraq is a complicated system. Plenty of rules must be followed before making the decision to marry. At first, the bridegroom and his mother have to go to the bride's house and talk with her father; the bride's father may agree, or he may need time to make a decision. This depends on various factors. Second, the bridegroom's mother must go to the bride's house to see about the bride's father's agreement. If the two sides agree, the bridegroom must buy two golden rings, hand rings, and a necklace. Then the two families decide on the bridal day.

Subhi Jawad Hamza
(Iraq)

1. Why does the topic sentence in this paragraph need modifying? What is the paragraph really about?

2. Might the second sentence of this paragraph become the first, and the topic, sentence? Why or why not? How might that sentence be modified to better fit the paragraph?

3. What questions could you ask this author to answer in a revision of this paragraph? That is, what additional detail is needed to fulfill the expectations of the audience?

III
QATAR

During the past two decades, my country, Qatar, has witnessed tremendous changes in almost every area except social mores; this aspect remains unchanged, a fact about which we are proud. The transportation system has been modernized significantly; a network that previously consisted of several trails and dusty roads has now been transformed into a system of modern highways and wide streets with lights and green trees on both sides. Communications have also been modernized; in the past, there were no telecommunications systems at all, but now the country has an up-to-date telecommunications system connected to the rest of the world by satellite. In addition, the industrial sector has grown from virtually no factories to industries in cement, petrochemicals, food canning, and fish processing. All these factors make Qatar appealing to both the natives and to visitors.

Hussa Al-Hitmi
(Qatar)

1. How did you modify the topic sentence in this paragraph?

2. What questions could you ask the author to help her add detail to this paragraph? Be specific.

3. Could the author write more than one paragraph about this topic? What might the topic sentences for several paragraphs be?

Exercise G

Below are two point paragraph outlines; each is followed by its paragraph. The outlines are incomplete. Read the paragraphs and complete the outlines. Then answer the questions that follow each paragraph.

I

TOPIC SENTENCE: **There are three ways I would improve the appearance of my apartment.**

A. Insulate it

    1. _____

    2. _____

B. Paint it

    1. _____

    2. _____

C. Change the rugs

    1. _____

    2. _____

<u>Concluding</u> <u>Sentence:</u> If I made these changes, my apartment would be much more comfortable.

Improving My Apartment

There are three ways I would improve the appearance of my apartment. First, I would insulate the walls because now the walls are so thin that I hear all the noises from the other apartments, even when the neighbors take a shower. For this reason, I don't feel I have any privacy; I have to be careful even when I walk on the floors so I don't disturb the neighbors. Secondly, I would paint the inside of my apartment another color. Now it is a dark green, and the color makes the apartment very dark and gloomy. I become depressed by this color and would prefer something lighter. Finally, I would change the rugs in my apartment because they are now badly stained and very dirty. Also, because they are a light color, they are difficult to get clean and even more difficult to keep clean. If I made these changes, my apartment would be much more comfortable.

Beatriz Rodriquez
(Venezuela)

1. Is the topic sentence a statement of opinion, intent, or a combination of the two?

2. Circle the controlling ideas in the topic sentence. Is the word "appearance" supported by the first point? How should the author modify the topic sentence?

3. Underline the repetition of the controlling words in the paragraph. How does the repetition of those words help the paragraph to be more coherent?

II

TOPIC SENTENCE: **Colors are interesting.**

A. blue

    1. sad or cold

    2. "She's feeling blue"

B. yellow

    1. cheerful

    2. decorate kitchens

C. red

    1. anger ("see red")

    2. Christmas

D. Green

   1. calm

   2. "green with envy"

     Colors are interesting. For many Americans, blue is a color that means sadness or coldness; an idiom says, "She's feeling blue" when someone is sad. Most Americans think that yellow is a bright, cheerful color, so yellow is often used to decorate kitchens in houses. Red represents anger for some people; an American idiom states that people "see red" when they are furious. However, red is also the symbolic color of Christmas celebrations. Green is another color that can have two meanings. Some people think it is a calming color, and so many schools and hospitals paint their walls light green. But for other people, green represents jealousy: "She is green with envy" is a common idiom.

Amber Beyer
(United States)

1. Modify the topic sentence to make it clearer and more interesting for the reader.

2. How does the second sentence help the reader focus the paragraph?

3. Write a title and a concluding sentence for this paragraph.

Writing Assignment 3

Choose one of the subjects below (or choose another subject that interests you). Narrow the subject to a topic, and write a paragraph for a small group of your classmates.

Subjects:	Breakfast	Hobbies	Music
	Study Habits	Television	Diets

    Pre-writing and Drafting: In your journal, use a pre-writing strategy that you have not yet used to generate ideas for your paragraph. Use the Paragraph Planning Guidelines (on the inside front cover of this book) to formulate a topic sentence and a second sentence, and construct a point paragraph outline for your paragraph. Remember that the steps you use to develop a paragraph may not be in the same order as the guidelines, and some of the steps may occur simultaneously. Write a rough draft of your paragraph. Then reread your paragraph: Does the topic sentence need to be modified? Follow the guidelines on page 88 to review the purpose and the focus of your paragraph. Then write another draft of the paragraph.

    Peer Feedback: With the small group of classmates who are your audience, read two paragraphs not your own. For each paragraph:

- cover all of the paragraph except for the topic sentence
- in your journal
  write a second sentence for that topic sentence
  write two questions that you expect will be answered in the paragraph
- read the paragraph: does it fulfill your expectations?

After you have read two paragraphs, discuss your paragraph with your peers. Ask for their suggestions to improve your paragraph, and offer suggestions to them.

Revision: Using the advice of your peer audience and the Revision Guidelines (on the inside back cover of this book), revise your paragraph. Then write the final draft.

Exercise H

Following are two paragraphs followed by outline forms. Read the paragraphs and complete the outlines. Then, with a small group of classmates, answer the questions that follow.

I
Three Difficult Words

In English, three words are very troublesome for me. "Chili" is the first word. When I am near Americans, I am afraid to say the word for "chili" in Thai because the word has a bad meaning in English. For example, last week in the supermarket I asked my friend in Thai where the chili was. Two American women looked at me and thought how impolite I was. "Can't" is the second difficult word because I can't distinguish between "can" and "can't" when Americans say this word. Therefore, I often misunderstand what someone is saying, or I miss the point of a story because of this word. The last word is my name, Srirathane. When someone says my name in English, I feel unpleasant because what they say, in Thai, has a bad meaning. My Thai friends always laugh when they hear an American say my name. For these reasons, I avoid the first two words, and I have adopted a nickname, "Kee."

Srirathane Janoenchaiyopeong
(Thailand)

TOPIC SENTENCE: _____

_____

A. _____

1. _____

2. _____

B. _____

    1. _____

    2. _____

C. _____

    1. _____

    2. _____

Concluding Sentence _____

_____

1. Circle the controlling ideas in the topic sentence. Draw lines from those controlling ideas to the supporting detail in the paragraph.

2. Mark with an asterisk (*) in the margins of the paragraph where two or more specific details have been combined into one sentence.

3. What techniques of support have been used in this paragraph? Be specific.

4. How does the second sentence in the paragraph help the reader anticipate what the paragraph will be about?

II
GOOD ADVICE!

    Before I came to the U.S., many people gave me advice about my trip, my studies, and my life in the U.S. My father told me to study, not to waste my time, and to look for some U.S. real estate investments. My mother advised me to learn about other customs and cultures while I studied English. My friend, Maria Pecina, who had studied in the U.S., told me not to speak Spanish with other students from Latin America and to make many American friends. She also warned me about drugs and alcohol in the U.S.; she advised me to be very careful. All of these people gave me advice so that I would succeed, and I have found that they were right.

Noemi Ramirez
(Mexico)

TOPIC SENTENCE: _____

_____

A. _____

    1. _____

    2. _____

B. _____

    1. _____

    2. _____

C. _____

    1. _____

    2. _____

Concluding Sentence _____

_____

1. Who is the audience for this paragraph?
2. In the margin, label the parts of this "hamburger" paragraph: top bun, meat, and bottom bun.
3. What additional questions could you ask the author about this paragraph?
4. Could this paragraph be expanded to several paragraphs? How?

Expanding the Point Paragraph Outline

Not all academic paragraphs follow the point paragraph outline exactly. Although the overall format of the point paragraph outline will remain the same (topic sentence, points about the topic sentence, details supporting the controlling ideas), expanded point paragraphs will have (a) more specific details and/or (b) even more points about the topic sentence than the outlines you have been constructing. The amount of specific material in a paragraph depends on:

- the number of controlling ideas in the topic sentence
- the material you have to communicate
- the audience
- the assignment

NOTE: Expanding a paragraph outline does not mean adding more points without more specific detail. **Each point requires additional supporting evidence.**

Although the point paragraph outline can vary in detail and the number of points, if it is expanded too much, it is hard for the reader to focus on the number of ideas and their support. Therefore, the length of academic paragraphs must be limited. When a paragraph becomes too long, it may need to be reorganized into more than one paragraph. Each of those paragraphs will have its own topic sentence and a point paragraph outline. Writing multiple paragraphs from the ideas in a single paragraph is a skill you will practice in later chapters.

Exercise I

Examine the outlines and paragraph below. Each has a slightly different format from the other point paragraph outlines in this chapter, but all have the overall form of the point paragraph outline. Moreover, each of the paragraphs might be expanded into more than one paragraph. With a small group of classmates, answer the questions that follow each paragraph.

I

TOPIC SENTENCE: **Students whose governments send them to study in foreign countries deserve a better chance to have a high position than locally trained students.**

1. Because they are talented

    A. *strong competition*

    B. *students win with exceptional abilities*

2. Because they overcome many difficulties

    A. *leaving their country and loved ones*

    B. *adjusting to a new country*
       (1) learning to speak the language
       (2) managing finances

3. Because the struggle makes them stronger

    A. *adversity strengthens the character*

    B. *Proverb: "If you wish to be the best man, you must suffer the bitterest of the bitter"*

4. Because their education is superior

    A. *modern knowledge in the field of study*

    B. *intensive study*

    C. *knowledge of another culture and language*

Chii -Pin Chen
(Republic of China)

1. Circle the controlling ideas in the topic sentence. Draw lines to the places in the outline where those controlling ideas will be explained, defined, or illustrated.

2. Who is the audience for this outline: classmates? parents? government administrators? teachers? others (who)? Use specific detail to support your opinion. How might the other audiences listed here respond to the paragraph?

3. What is the purpose of this paragraph outline: to inform? to persuade? to entertain? How do you know?

4. Could this paragraph outline be expanded into multiple paragraphs? What might the topic sentences for each of the multiple paragraphs be? What kinds of supporting detail might you use for each of the paragraphs?

II

TOPIC SENTENCE: **Heart disease is the leading cause of death in the U.S. today because of its wide-reaching effects on the body.**

1. Decrease of blood pumped by the heart causes
   A. *decrease of oxygen to the body tissues*
   B. *decrease of nutrients to the body tissues*

2. Consequence: body tissues deteriorate

3. Decrease of blood pumped by the heart causes
   A. *less efficient transport of carbon dioxide*
   B. *less efficient transport of other products of metabolism*

4. Consequences
   A. *less effective elimination of toxic elements*
   B. *poisoning of the body*

5. Decrease of blood pumped by the heart causes
   A. *decrease of distribution of hormones*
   B. *decrease of distribution of other cell function regulators*

Concluding Sentence: Heart disease, therefore, is not the simple destruction of one part of the body; rather, it can be considered the death of the whole body.

Heart disease, that is, the decrease or disorder of cardiac output, is the leading cause of death in the U.S. today because it has wide-reaching effects on the entire body. For example, when the amount of blood pumped by the heart decreases, the transport of oxygen and nutrients to the body tissues decreases. Consequently, the body tissues deteriorate. Also, the transport of carbon dioxide and other products of metabolism to the lungs and kidneys becomes less efficient and so less effective in eliminating toxic elements from the body. Therefore, the body is slowly poisoned by its own toxic wastes. Finally, the distribution of hormones and other substances that regulate cell function decrease as the blood from the heart decreases; consequently, damage occurs to the cells of the body. Heart disease, therefore, is not the simple destruction of one part of the body; rather, it can be considered the death of the whole body.

Akira Fujimoto
(Japan)

1. Circle the controlling ideas in the topic sentence of the paragraph. Draw lines from those controlling ideas to the support for those ideas in that paragraph.

2. Who is the audience for this paragraph? Use specific vocabulary and sentence structures from the paragraph to support your opinion.

3. If you were the audience for this paragraph, what questions would you ask the author?

4. Could this paragraph be expanded to an essay? What might the topic sentences for the multiple paragraphs be?

Writing Assignment 4

Below are three subjects. Choose two of those subjects (or two other subjects you are interested in) and narrow them to two topics. Then construct two point paragraph outlines about the topics. Your outlines may be the basic point paragraph outline or an expanded form of the point paragraph outline. Clearly identify the audience for your paragraph: the age, educational background, interests, knowledge about your topic, and expectations about your paragraph.

<u>Subjects:</u>   Vacations   Weather   Houses

Pre-writing and Drafting: In your journal, identify and describe in detail the person for whom you are writing this paragraph. During your pre-writing processes, construct a possible topic sentence, an appropriate second sentence, and a point outline. As you draft your outline, reconsider your purpose and audience; modify the topic sentence if necessary, and complete the rough **outlines** of both paragraphs.

Peer Feedback: Exchange outlines with a partner. Describe your chosen audience to your partner and ask that partner to function as your chosen audience. Then read your partner's outlines as if you were your partner's chosen audience. For each outline:

- circle the controlling ideas in the topic sentence
- label in the margins the possible techniques of support used in the outlines
- label in the margins the concluding techniques in the outlines
- at the end of each outline, write one question to help your partner improve the outline

Discuss with your partner which of the two outlines you think will make a better paragraph for your chosen audience.

Revision: Using the suggestions made by your partner, as well as the Paragraph Revision Guidelines (on the inside back cover of this book), select one of the point outlines and make changes that will improve that outline. Then write the rough draft of that paragraph.

Peer Feedback: Exchange paragraph drafts with your partner-audience. Read your partner's paragraph and:

- at the end of the paragraph, write any suggestions that might help your partner write a more successful paragraph
- circle any connectors that were used to combine sentences
- underline any grammatical or mechanical errors you see; check especially for subject-verb agreement, sentence structure, punctuation, and spelling

Discuss your suggestions and your underlined language with your partner.

Revision: Using your partner's suggestions, revise and write the final draft of your paragraph.

Journal Assignment

Write a paragraph about how you wrote the paragraph above. Indicate what changes you made as you revised your outline and your rough draft, and write about your reasons for making those changes.

Sentence Combining Exercise

The jokes below are written with short, choppy sentences, and some information is repeated. Combine the sentences to make the jokes flow more smoothly. Use connectors to help the reader.

I

There was a teacher. There were students. There were two of them. The students were late. They were late to class. The teacher spoke. She asked, "Why are you late?" The first student spoke. He responded, "I had a dream. I dreamed that I lost something. I lost my money. So I began searching." Then the teacher questioned the other student. She asked, "And you?" The student answered. He answered quickly. He said, "I was helping him!"

Nada Abahsain
(Saudi Arabia)

II

I rent an apartment. I live on the second floor. A man lives on the first floor. He is old. One night, it was midnight. I had been dancing. I came back. I came to my apartment. I took off my boots. I threw them. They landed on the floor. I heard a knock. The knock was on the door. I wanted to sleep. I got up.

I answered the door. The old man who lived on the first floor was there. He told me, "Please put your boots lightly on the floor because every night I must wait until your boots hit the floor before I can go to sleep." I apologized. I said, "Sorry about that." I said, "I won't do that again." The next night, I came home. I threw one boot. Suddenly I remembered. I remembered my promise. So I put the other boot down. I put it down lightly. Early the next morning, the old man came. He said, "What about your other boot? I waited. I waited. I waited until now. I waited for the other boot to drop. What happened?"

Jie Li
(People's Republic of China)

5

Explanation Paragraphs

I have a bad attitude toward writing. I think that as an engineer, I don't need to know how to write, so I don't practice enough.

Lars Erik Holte
(Norway)

The U.S. academic audience expects that an academic paragraph will contain information that explains an idea. An explanation paragraph can:

- explain a process (that is, how to do something or how something works)
- define a term
- make a concept clear

In this chapter, you will learn how to generate ideas for explanation paragraphs, and how to plan and organize those paragraphs for a U.S. academic audience. You will study the connectors most often used in these paragraphs, and you will practice analyzing the audiences and purposes for these paragraphs.

Process Paragraphs

The process paragraph describes how to do something: how to get a visa, how to buy a house, how to do a folk dance, etc. Academic process paragraphs are a part of most laboratory reports (how to do an experiment such as dissecting a frog or performing a chemical reaction) in which the supporting technique of physical description is important. Describing a process (how to write a successful paragraph, how to play frisbee golf, how to apply for university admission, etc.) is an essential academic skill.

Process paragraphs are generally organized in chronological order (that is, according to time). *Chrono* means time, and *chronological* means logic in time. When you write a process paragraph, you will:

- choose a topic that is narrow enough to be described in complete detail for your intended audience
- give details of the process in the correct order
- give reasons for the order (if appropriate)
- include negative directions (or warnings) if necessary
- use chronological connectors to help the reader

Chronological Connectors

Sentence Introducers

First, ... Second, ... Then, ... After that, ... Finally, ...

Time Introducers

... before ... after ... when ... while ... until ... during ...

Exercise A

Read the point paragraph outlines and the explanation paragraphs below. Then do the exercise that follows each paragraph.

I

How to Plant a Garden

TOPIC SENTENCE: **After you have prepared the garden soil, you need to follow a procedure for planting the seeds.**

1. Choosing the seeds
   A. flowers or vegetables?
   B. early and late species

2. Planning the planting
   A. what to plant where
   B. why?

3. Follow directions on the seed packets
   A. soak before planting?
   B. depth to plant
   C. watering the planted seeds

Concluding Sentence: If you follow this process, you will surely have a successful garden.

Ani Sala
(Argentina)

1. What is being <u>explained</u> in this paragraph outline? For whom?

2. Modify the title of this outline so that it more accurately describes the paragraph.

3. Write a second sentence for this paragraph.

4. What technique(s) of support could be used in this paragraph?

II

Because I am a curious person, I take every chance I get to travel and learn about different countries and customs. Before I leave on a trip, I prepare myself for the new country by reading about it. I investigate the things I am interested in and, later, I can compare my opinions about the country before and after my visit. When I arrive in the country, I try to find places outside the regular tourist attractions so that I will come in contact with the native people who can often tell me more about the country than the tourist guides. In addition, I try to stay with a native family while I am visiting a country; in this way, I discover more about the inside feelings and the lifestyle of the people. In these ways, I learn more about the country and, usually, more about myself.

Per Nystrom
(Sweden)

1. With a small group of classmates, write a title for this paragraph.

2. What process is this paragraph explaining?

3. With the group, modify the topic sentence of this paragraph so that it more accurately reflects the paragraph.

4. Underline the chronological time connectors in this paragraph.

III

Teaching an American Spanish

TOPIC SENTENCE: **When I teach an American to speak my language, Spanish, I begin by teaching him basic vocabulary.**

    <u>first:</u>

1. Courtesy phrases
    A. greetings   (examples)
    B. compliments   (examples)
      <u>next:</u>

2. Important information questions
    A. about accommodations
        (1) where?
        (2) how much?

B. about interesting places to see
   (1) where?
   (2) how far?
   (3) how to get there?

<u>then:</u>
3. language related to food
   A. names of foods (examples)
   B. how to ask for restaurants (examples)
   C. how to order food in a restaurant (examples)

<u>Concluding Sentence:</u> In a very short time, with practice in vocabulary, this American will at least be able to survive in my country.

Aleida Perez de Chavez
(Venezuela)

1. Circle the controlling ideas in the topic sentence. Does it need to be modified? Why or why not? Modify it if necessary.

2. What is the process described in this outline? Who is the audience for this paragraph? How do you know?

3. Write a second sentence for this paragraph.

4. What concluding technique(s) does the author use?

IV

How to Prepare for Deep Sea Diving

TOPIC SENTENCE: **Deep sea diving can be a safe and exciting sport if you prepare carefully.**

1. Take a class
   A. physical fitness exercises
   B. rules about diving

2. Buy proper equipment

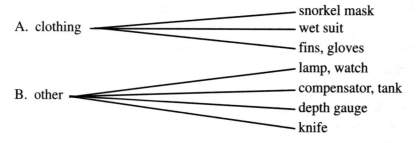

A. clothing — snorkel mask, wet suit, fins, gloves

B. other — lamp, watch, compensator, tank, depth gauge, knife

3. Choose a safe place
   A. quiet water
   B. good weather

Concluding Sentence: When you enter the water for the first time, you will be delighted at the colors, the fish, and the pleasant feel of the water.

Francisco Salas
(Venezuela)

1. With a small group of classmates, decide whether the topic sentence is a statement of intent, opinion, or a combination of the two. How do you know?

2. Is the paragraph outline chronological? How do you know? With your group, discuss what chronological connectors might be used in the paragraph that is written from this outline.

3. With your group, suggest specific details that the author might add to the outline for his audience.

4. Could the outline be expanded into several paragraph outlines? Discuss how with your group.

Writing Assignment 1

Your American friend is going to visit your country. Write a basic paragraph outline (or an expanded paragraph outline) and then a paragraph that shows the first things you would teach an American about your language. Use specific examples to support your ideas.

> **Pre-writing and Drafting:** In your journal, use the pre-writing strategies that are most successful for you in generating ideas about your topic. Also, in a paragraph in your journal, analyze your audience; use the Audience Guidelines (on the inside front cover of this book). As you draft your paragraph, use chronological connectors to help your reader.

> **Peer Feedback:** In a small group of classmates, read paragraph drafts that are not your own. As you read each paragraph, notice how that paragraph follows (or does not follow) the point paragraph outline. At the end of each paragraph, write one suggestion or question for the author of the paragraph that you think will improve that paragraph. Then underline any language or sentence-structure error that you find in the paragraph. After that, discuss your suggestions and questions with your classmates, and listen to your classmates' advice concerning your paragraph.

> **Revision:** In your journal, write a paragraph about what you learned about improving your paragraph from (a) reading your classmates' paragraphs, (b) your classmates' suggestions about your paragraph, and (c) the Revision Guidelines (on the inside back cover of this book). Then, in your journal, write a paragraph describing the changes you intend to make in your paragraph. Explain why you are making those changes. Finally, make the changes to improve your paragraph and write the final draft of that paragraph.

Passive Voice

In many process paragraphs, especially academic paragraphs that are scientific or technological, passive voice verbs are used to give the paragraphs more objectivity. That is, the form of academic scientific and technological writing requires that the researcher(s) remain less important than their work, and passive voice allows the research to be more important. Instead of saying "I did this," the researchers write, "The work was completed ..."

This objectivity is achieved by focusing on the action instead of the actor (the doer). In an active sentence, the subject is the doer. The subject performs the action.

Active Voice Verb: The <u>people</u> elected the President.
　　　　　　　　　　(doer of the action)

In a passive voice sentence, the subject is not the do-er. Instead, the subject is the receiver of the action.

Passive Voice Verb: The <u>President</u> was elected by the people.
　　　　　　　　　　　(receiver of the action)

To change an active to a passive sentence:

* begin the sentence with the object/receiver as the subject

* change the active verb to an auxiliary verb (is, are, was, were, has, have, had) + the past participle

* add "by" before the actor/object of the sentence

Example:

The <u>student</u>	wrote		the <u>paragraph</u>.	(*active voice*)
(doer)	(past tense)		(receiver/object)	
The paragraph	was written	**by**	the student.	(*passive voice*)
(receiver)	(past participle)		(doer)	

<u>NOTE:</u> The test for passive voice: can you say "by X" at the end of the sentence?

Examples:

The phone call <u>was made</u> BY SOMEONE.

The essay <u>is being read</u> BY SOMEONE.

The apple pie <u>could be made</u> BY ANYONE.

When to Use the Passive

1. When the doer is not important.
   Examples:
   Watches <u>are made</u> in Japan. (By whom? It's not important.)
   French <u>is spoken</u> in France. (By whom? It's not important.)

Pets <u>are forbidden</u> in many apartments. (By whom? It's not important.)

2. When the doer is not known.
    Examples:

    John F. Kennedy <u>was murdered</u>. (By whom? We don't know.)

    The politician <u>is being criticized</u>. (By whom? We don't know.)

    The child <u>had been</u> kidnapped. (By whom? We don't know.)

3. When the doer/researcher wishes to remain less important than his research.
    Examples:

    The survey <u>was administered</u> to 120 students. (By the researcher)

    The chemicals <u>were combined</u>. (By the researcher)

    The results <u>were analyzed</u> statistically. (By the researcher)

Exercise B

Below are two process paragraphs about scientific and technical subjects. Underline the passive voice used in each paragraph. Then do the exercises that follow.

I
Making Ethanol in Indonesia

Ethanol can be produced from the fermentation of some crops that contain starch: corn, wheat, sugar cane, and, in Indonesia, sweet potatoes and, especially, cassava. In the process of converting cassava to ethanol, the first step is milling (the reduction of the size of the particles). Next, the milled particles are cooled; the cassava is cooled; the cassava is hydrated, and its starch is gelatinized. Following that step, the starch is converted by enzymic hydrolysis into sugars, and then the ethanol from the sugars, including limited dextrin conversion, is fermented. In the final step, the ethanol is recovered through distillation, and the cassava residues are recovered by evaporation and waste treatment.

Ismail Tontowi
(Indonesia)

1. Why is passive voice used in this paragraph?

2. Change the passive voice verbs to active voice verbs in this paragraph.

3. How do the new verbs change the paragraph?

4. Underline the chronological connectors.

II
The Greenhouse Effect

Trapped heat in the atmosphere of the earth results in the greenhouse effect, but how does it happen? First, the sun warms the earth, and then heat is trapped by certain gases in the atmosphere that act like the glass in a greenhouse. Usually this heat is essential to prevent freezing temperatures on earth, but as the levels of these gases are increased, more heat is created than is necessary. Yet that is exactly what is happening on earth today. The rising level of gases comes from two major man-made sources: chloroflurocarbons (a gas that escapes from refrigerators, air conditioners, plastic foams, and spray cans) and carbon dioxide (a gas that comes from burning fossil fuels like coal and automobile gasoline emissions). The amount of carbon dioxide in the atmosphere has grown more than 25% since the Industrial Revolution, and over 11% since 1958. As a result of the raised level of these two gases, "global warming" is occurring; the earth is getting warmer.

Sosa Abraham
(Malaysia)

1. How does the second sentence in this paragraph help the reader?

2. The purpose of the paragraph is to define and clarify as well as to describe the process. Identify where each of these occurs in the paragraph.

3. Is the topic sentence a statement of intent, opinion, or a combination?

4. Which of the two paragraphs do you find more interesting and valuable? In your journal, write a paragraph describing why.

Exercise C

Following are notes about a process topic (how a telephone is installed). Using this information, write the process paragraph. Use passive voice when necessary, and use chronological connectors. Combine two or more steps into single sentences when it is appropriate.

TOPIC: **how a telephone is installed**

NOTES: consumer places an order with the telephone company
order is processed
line of telephone is connected at the switching office
installer comes to the place the telephone will be installed
total installation may include rewiring and/or installation of outlets
new telephone number is assigned
number is checked for accuracy
number is filed with directory assistance telephone operators
employee at assignment center connects telephone to central office
original order is sent to company's completion department
order is put into a central computer for storage and later updating
entire process takes two to four days
the result is a working telephone

Reducing Passive Voice Use

Because passive voice slows down the sentence, it is sometimes better to reduce or eliminate it from non-scientific process paragraphs. Two ways of reducing passive voice verbs are:

- to use commands (imperative voice) in describing the process
  Example:

  The tree was planted.   (passive voice)

  Plant the tree.   (imperative)

- to use the first person in describing the process
  Example:

  The coffee is made with cardamom.   (passive voice)

  I make the coffee with cardamom.   (first person)

Exercise D

Read the paragraphs below. Notice that the authors avoid passive voice in these non-scientific process paragraphs: The first two use the imperative, and the third uses first person. Then do the exercise that follows each paragraph.

I
How to Make a Stained Glass Panel

Making a stained glass panel is not as easy as it looks. The first thing to do is to choose the pattern and glass colors. Then, draw the model on a piece of thick paper and cut it out. Next, put the pieces of paper over the glass; mark it, and break the glass. [Don't be afraid of hurting yourself if you are using the correct method of breaking the glass.] Following this, place the lead between the glass pieces to hold them together. Then, with the hot iron solder, affix the lead, being sure that all of it is soldered. Finally, attach a nylon thread at the top of the panel to hold it at the window.

Estella Solomon
(Brazil)

1. Is the topic sentence in the paragraph a statement of intent, opinion, or a combination of both? How do you know?

2. What verb tense is used in this paragraph? Why?

3. The bracketed sentence [ ] is a step that is incomplete. What questions could you ask about this step, and what answers could be given in the paragraph?

4. Could this paragraph be expanded to several paragraphs? What might be the topic sentences for those several paragraphs?

II
How to Fail a Big Test

It's easier to fail a big test than to pass it. Simply take it easy, and keep thinking that there's plenty of time to prepare for it. What's the point of going to the first meeting of the class since the teacher is only going to introduce the students to the subject? As the class progresses, remember that sleep is too sweet to ignore, so keep on sleeping. There's always another class next week. The exercises assigned for homework are really stupid and easy; better watch football on TV instead of doing them. The book might be helpful, but by the middle of the course there are no more left in the bookstore. Oh, well, no need to worry; there's plenty of time to study. On the night before the test, stay up late and party with your friends. Then, during the test, do what you can and then take a nap. After the test scores are announced, it's easy to put the blame on the teacher and claim that he gave you an "F" because of personal hatred. Now wasn't that easy?

Pavlos Alexandrou
(Greece)

1. What is the purpose of this paragraph: to inform, to persuade, and/or to amuse? How do you know?

2. Underline the imperative verbs used in this paragraph.

3. How does the second sentence function in this paragraph?

4. Does this paragraph communicate successfully? Why or why not? Use evidence from the paragraph to support your opinion.

III
How to Cope With Stress

My special ways of coping with stress are simple and effective. Sometimes, I feel really low, like when I screwed up an easy Math test, or I go through three hours of boring lectures, or I don't eat lunch because I didn't have time. Then I escape to my dorm room, get my handy walkman set, pick one of my favorite loud, blaring, uninterrupted rock cassettes, put on my comfortable mini-headphones, and let my mind receive a full bombardment of smooth, relaxing, classic rock music. I close my eyes, get comfortable on the couch, and turn the volume up. The outside world seems so far away as I float about in space. My books and homework are forgotten as I snap my fingers and tap my feet with the beat. Suddenly I do not feel moody or stressed out anymore. Finally, I lie quietly, music in my ears, not giving the slightest concern to what's going on around me. Even though I have only undergone a few minutes of this "treatment," I feel better. After an additional few minutes, I am able to get out of my trance and face reality again. This process is, for me, the best possible way to deal with stress.

Leung Lai
(Singapore)

1. Circle the use of the first person pronoun (I) in the paragraph.
2. Underline the controlling ideas in the topic sentence. Draw lines from those controlling ideas to the support in the paragraph.
3. Underline with wavy lines (~~) the use of physical description (that is, sense images).
4. In what ways does the author of this paragraph persuade his readers?

Writing Assignment 2

Write a process paragraph about one of the topics below. Be sure to (a) carefully identify and analyze your audience and purpose, (b) use adequate detail and steps in the process, (c) write a point paragraph outline, and (d) use appropriate chronological connectors.

TOPICS: How to Make … (a food from your country)
How to Find an Apartment in …
How to Apply for University Admission in the U.S.
How to Avoid Injuries in Soccer
How to … (a topic of your choice)

Pre-writing and Drafting: In your journal, use two pre-writing strategies to develop ideas for your paragraph. Use the Audience Guidelines and the Paragraph Planning Guidelines (on the inside front cover of this book). Remember: Your writing processes may not follow the same order as the steps in these guidelines, and some steps may occur simultaneously. Formulate a possible topic sentence, and construct a basic (or an expanded) point paragraph outline. Follow the directions for the assignment (above). Then draft your paragraph.

Peer Feedback: Exchange paragraphs with a partner. As you read your partner's draft:
- underline the topic sentence and circle the controlling ideas
- study the second sentence: does it help the reader focus the paragraph?
- identify the audience: academic? peer? child? other:_____?
- underline the chronological connectors with wavy lines (~~)
- examine the steps in the process: at the end of the paragraph, offer your partner two suggestions (or ask two questions) that will improve or clarify the paragraph
- help your partner by marking any grammatical or sentence structure problems that you find

Discuss the results of your analysis of your partner's paper with your partner.

Revision: Using the advice of your partner and the Revision Guidelines (on the inside back cover of this book), make changes that will improve your paragraph. Then write the final draft of the paragraph. Finally, **in your journal**, write a paragraph describing the changes that you made; evaluate the success of those revisions.

Process Paragraph Problems

The problems that writers of process paragraphs have are:

• inadequate detail OR	• too much detail
• incomplete physical description OR	• too much description
• confusing organization	
• missing steps in the process	

When <u>readers</u> encounter the problems in the first column, they are unable to predict, or in some cases even to understand, the process. In contrast, if they find the problems in the second column, they may become confused or bored and not finish reading the paragraph. To avoid all of these problems, writers must carefully analyze their audiences:

• who are they?	• what do they know?
• what do they need to know?	• what will interest them?
• what will they expect to find in the paragraph?	

Exercise E

With a partner, do one of the following exercises. Later, for homework, in your journal, write a paragraph that describes the process you followed and evaluates the success of that process. If you were to repeat the exercise, how could you improve the results?

1. Sit <u>back</u> to <u>back</u> with a partner. Each of you should have a small (secret) object, a piece of paper, and a pencil/pen. One person describes the (secret) object without using the name or the function of that object. The other person draws that object, using only the descriptive words of the partner. When both partners finish their descriptions, exchange drawings. How successful were you in describing/drawing the object?

2. In a small group of classmates, one person describes an action (examples below), and the other members of the group follow the oral description exactly. When you finish, evaluate the success of the description.

   Examples:

   tying a shoelace

   putting on a coat/sweater

   making a paper airplane

Exercise F

Following are two process paragraphs. With a small group of classmates, read the paragraphs carefully. If you are the audience, are the processes clear? Could you complete the process? Which of the problems listed above are present in each paragraph? Do you have any questions about the processes that are not answered in the paragraphs? What suggestions do you and your group have that will make the processes more complete for the audience?

I
Catching Squid

How do fishermen catch squid in the country of Thailand? The fishermen go to the sea at night. They use only a small boat, two lamps, and the instruments they make by hand. Two or three men usually go in the same boat, and this boat always uses a sail instead of an engine. Their instruments are made from a 2-inch diameter and 6-inch long pipe with a hole at one end and 12-16 hooks around the other end. They tie a rope at the holed end and tie a small fish in the middle of each instrument; then they throw it into the sea. One man usually uses two or three of these instruments. They pull the wire quickly if a squid comes to eat the fish; then they have caught the squid. If they are lucky, they may get more than 100 kilograms of squid in one fishing trip.

Arthorn Boonsaner
(Thailand)

II

How I Cope With Unhappiness

When I am unhappy, I confide in my best friend because she is a good listener. For example, when I was worried about my grades, I confided in her. I told her my study problems, and she listened very carefully. She did not utter a single word until I had finished my talking. Then she gave her opinion and advice to me. She told me to stop worrying and start to work harder. She also told me that worrying would not take me anywhere. I listened to what she was saying, and for the next several hours I thought about everything that she had told me. It was hard for me to accept her opinion and advice even though she was right. Then I persuaded myself to accept them. The best part of confiding in my best friend is that I feel really good after telling her my troubles. I feel as if all the burden I have been carrying has gone.

Hartini Mussa
(Malaysia)

Definition/Clarification Paragraphs

Another kind of explanation paragraph defines words or ideas and/or makes those words or ideas clearer for a reader. In academic writing, definition/clarification paragraphs are frequently required in course writing tasks to explain concepts, synthesize reading, or demonstrate knowledge of the course.

Paragraphs that define or clarify words or ideas differ from process paragraphs because:

- they are not organized chronologically. Although the connectors <u>first</u>, <u>second</u>, etc. can be used, these connectors do not necessarily indicate either time or importance. Often they simply indicate the number of points to be made.

- they do not tell "how to." Instead, definition/clarification paragraphs answer the question "What?"

What does _____ mean?

What does _____ look like?

What is _____ ?

What ways are there to _____ ?

What kinds of _____ are there?

Definition/clarification paragraphs often present points of equal value and interest. Generally, these points are supported by facts, examples, personal experience, and physical description. Often the topic sentences of definition/clarification paragraphs are statements of intent.

Exercise G

Below are paragraphs of definition and/or clarification. Read the paragraphs, and do the exercises that follow them.

I

Routine

Routine is a regular and habitual way of working or doing things. Some people are very much pleased by the routine of their lives. They like it when nothing breaks the even course of their existence, and they feel strangely unprotected when something upsets their routine. These people are usually very faint-hearted, and it's difficult for them to adapt themselves to a new way of life. However, more interesting people find routine a vicious circle. As a rule, these people have very rich imaginations, and when their routine life becomes unbearable, they escape to a different dimension, to the world that they have invented themselves. But not all people who find themselves inside the vicious circle of routine want to live outside it. There is another kind of person who finds routine burdensome, but at the same time, these people know how to carry their burden. As their outward lives are routine, their inner thoughts never stop;

the more they see, the cleverer the thoughts that come into their minds.

Tanya Kurganova
(Russia)

1. How does the author support the definition of routine she gives in the topic sentence? What technique(s) of support does she use?
2. Make a point outline for this paragraph.
3. Write a concluding sentence for this paragraph.
4. Do you agree with this author's ideas? Why or why not?

II

Oh, *Kendo*!

Kendo is a kind of Japanese fencing which I practice and enjoy. It is a form of traditional "budo" sports. Many Japanese high school students learn this sport. They compete in tournaments all over Japan for prizes. The main equipment for *kendo* is a stick made from a special tree called "Take." Participants in *kendo* wear protective gear, including helmets to protect their heads and padded clothing. *Kendo* is a fight between two people; often the participants are injured. But it's not only a game of power; it's also a game of spirit. When I practice *kendo*, I react instinctively. I also feel spiritual power when I win. I am like many people in my country because I enjoy the challenge of *kendo*. It improves both my body and my spirit. I hope this popular Japanese sport will expand to the U.S.

Roy Sato Isao
(Japan)

1. With a small group of classmates, analyze the purpose of this paragraph. How does the author clarify the term *kendo*?

2. With your group, define *kendo* in your own words. What questions might you ask this author to help you complete your definition of *kendo*?

3. Work with your group to try to make a point paragraph outline of this paragraph. What problems did you encounter? What suggestions about the organization of this paragraph might you make for the author?

4. **In your journal**, write a paragraph evaluating these two paragraphs. Which one is more successful for you? Why? Be specific.

III
Origami

Origami, the Japanese art of paper folding which originated in China, is a very inexpensive and rewarding hobby. Traditionally, origami figures are always made by folding, not cutting or pasting. For example, good-luck animals such as cranes, tortoises, and lobsters can be made by simply folding a piece of perfectly squared paper. Origami is very inexpensive; only paper is necessary, and any paper can be used. Moreover, inexpensive gifts, such as earrings, can be made by folding small cranes and attaching pins or loops through the cranes' backs. Origami is also extremely rewarding; using the imagination, one can develop his creativity by turning a plain, simple piece of paper into a fish, a frog, or a house. The greatest reward, however, is that origami can be enjoyed by every member of a household.

Winnie Chan
(Hong Kong)

1. Who is the audience for this paragraph? How does the author present her ideas successfully for her audience?

2. What technique(s) of support are most effectively used in this paragraph? Be specific.

3. What concluding technique(s) does the author of this paragraph use?

4. Which of the paragraphs above is most interesting and valuable for you? **In your journal**, write a paragraph explaining and supporting your choice. Be specific.

Writing Assignment 3

It is said that the Alaskan Inuit Indians have nearly 100 different words that describe snow (words for first snow, snow that falls gently, heavy snow, etc.). Think about two or more words in your language that describe a single concept or phenomenon (for example, sand, politeness, rain). Write an explanation paragraph about those different words. Narrow the subject to a topic, and identify your specific audience. Then focus on the purpose for your communication as you draft your paragraph.

Pre-writing and Drafting: In your journal, use two-prewriting strategies to generate ideas and details for your paragraph. As you pre-write, include an analysis of your audience and purpose. Use the Audience Guidelines and the Paragraph Planning Guidelines (on the inside front cover of this book) to help develop your paragraph draft.

Peer Feedback: With a small group of classmates, read the paragraphs that are not your own. Help the author of each paragraph by (a) making suggestions and/or asking questions that will improve the paragraph and (b) marking any grammar or sentence structure errors you see. Then ask your classmates two specific questions about your own paragraph that will help you revise that paragraph.

Revision: Using the advice of your classmates and the Revision Guidelines (on the inside back cover of this book), make changes in your paragraph and write the final draft. Then, **in your journal**, write a paragraph describing the revisions that you made in your final draft. Explain why you made those changes and how they improved your paragraph.

Explanation Paragraph Connectors

Below are some other words and phrases that you might use in the explanation paragraphs you write in this chapter. These connectors help the reader by signaling the relationships between—and within—sentences. Those relationships are indicated on the left side of the chart below. You will use these connectors not only in process paragraphs but also in all other paragraphs you write for academic assignments.

EXPLANATION PARAGRAPH CONNECTORS

	Short Words	**Long Words**	**Other**
Introductory			First, The first …
Additional Information (Middle Paragraph Connectors)	…, and …	Furthermore, Moreover, In addition,	Also, …also …
Expected Information (Middle Paragraph Connectors)	…, so …		Of course, Naturally, Surely,
Clarifying Information (Middle Paragraph Connectors)			In fact, As a matter of fact, That is, In other words,
Example Signal (Middle Paragraph Connectors)			For example, For instance, To illustrate,
Conclusion Signal		Therefore,	To conclude, In conclusion, In summary, To summarize,

Exercise H

In the following explanation paragraphs, fill in the blanks with appropriate paragraph connectors. Use the list of connectors above, or use other connectors that you know. The relationships between and within the sentences are indicated under each blank: additional information, example, etc. Then do the exercises that follow each paragraph.

I
The Mango Tree

The mango tree is big, beautiful, and useful. Its height is 4-8 meters; its trunk is very fat and strong, _____ and its roots are deep. The leaves

(additional information)

are small and and light green, _____ the tiny flowers are white and

(additional information)

yellow. Mango trees grow in the hot, humid areas of the tropics. _____, they grow near the equator in countries like Colombia,

(example signal)

Venezuela, and Brazil. Usually these trees grow wild (_____,

(definition information)

uncultivated). _____, there are two kinds of mango trees. One is the

(additional information)

mango-manga (_____, the mango-female). The mango-manga

(definition information)

produces fruit twice a year. The mango fruits are delicious; they _____ have high protein and many vitamins. The

(additional information)

other kind of mango tree is the mango-male; it is smaller than the mango-female, _____ it doesn't produce mango fruit. However, it has flowers with

(additional information)

male cells that fertilize the mango-manga. _____, mango trees are

(conclusion signal)

plentiful and beautiful throughout the tropics, _____ their fruit is

(additional information)

eaten by millions of people.

Christian Blanco
(Colombia)

1. What is being defined and clarified in this paragraph?

2. Why is this paragraph written in the present tense?

3. Who is the audience for this paragraph: children? graduate students in horticulture? the general public? How do you know?

4. What other questions could you ask about the topic sentence? That is, what additional information would you like to read about mango trees?

II
Monfort Feedlot

American beef cattle feeding is mechanized and computerized. Cattlemen feed thousands of cattle in a single feedlot; _____, at the Monfort

(clarifying information)

Feedlot in Greeley, Colorado, 14,000 steers are fattened for market at the same time. These cattle are kept in large pens rather than in barns, _____they

(additional information)

are fed by trucks. The forage (_____, the food) consists of corn,

(defining information)

silage, and hay; it is mixed by machine according to a formula made by a computer. _____, the computer is given facts about the cattle to

(expected information)

determine just how much food they need each day. _____, specific

(additional information)

amounts of vitamins and minerals are mixed into the forage to keep the cattle healthy. The amount of nutrients, and even the amount of water, is determined by machines; _____, even the cleaning of waste products from the

(clarifying information)

feedlots is done by machine. _____, after I saw the Monfort

(conclusion signal)

Feedlot, one of the largest feedlots in the world, I believe that American beef cattle feeding practices are very efficient.

Masanori Kiyota
(Japan)

1. What is being defined and clarified (that is, explained) in this paragraph?

2. Underline the passive voice verbs in this paragraph. Why is the passive voice used?

3. Decide on an appropriate connector to begin the second sentence; think about what signal would most help the reader.

4. Who is the audience for this paragraph? What is the purpose?

Writing Assignment 4

The map of the U.S. below indicates the summertime temperatures for several cities on June 15th. Write a letter to a friend in your country. Explain the general weather patterns on this map. Use the cities and their temperatures to explain the differences between the weather in the northeast, the southeast, the northwest, and the southwest. If you live in the U.S., or if you have visited the U.S., include the summertime weather in a city you are familiar with. Use the form of the personal letter you studied in the first chapter.

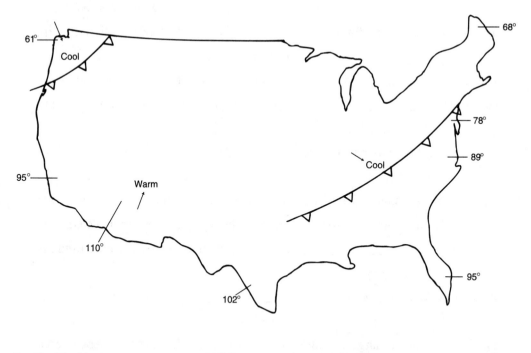

Seattle, Washington	61 ° F	Augusta, Maine	68 ° F
Los Angeles, California	95 ° F	Boston, Massachusetts	78 ° F
Phoenix, Arizona	110 ° F	Raleigh, North Carolina	89 ° F
El Paso, Texas	102 ° F	Miami Beach, Florida	95 ° F

Exercise I

Below are paragraphs of explanation (process, definition, and clarification). Read each paragraph and do the exercise that follows.

I

SEMPOI

   Sempoi is a term used by high school students in northern Malaysia. At my former high school, the word *sempoi* was used when we saw something or someone that was beautiful and smart. It could also mean a compliment when someone had done a good job. We often used this term for our athletic team. For example, when one person on the basketball team successfully tricked his opponent and managed to get a basket, we said that he was *sempoi*. We also used the word when we saw something dazzling. For example, when we saw a beautiful sleek car, we said that the car was *sempoi*. The term *sempoi* has a lot of meanings, depending on the sentence in which it was used, but it always means something wonderful.

Hartini Nor Musa
(Malaysia)

1. With a small group of classmates, examine the purpose of this paragraph: to inform, persuade, and/or amuse? to describe a process, define, or clarify? How do you know?

2. Who is the audience for this paragraph? How do you know?

3. With your group, make a point outline for the paragraph.

4. Are there informal words in your native language (probably used by young people) like *sempoi*? Discuss these words in your group.

II

Ways of Treating Pets in the U.S.A.

   When I first arrived in this country, I found the way pets were treated was surprising. The first week after my arrival, my friend took me to the grocery store to buy food. Inside the store, I saw a pile of sacks. I asked my friend about those sacks, and he said they contained pet food. In all the countries I have been, I haven't seen such big sacks containing food just for pets. Also, in some countries, people don't have enough food for themselves, let alone special food for pets. Two days after that, I went for dinner at one of my roommate's friend's house. There I saw the way this woman was holding and kissing her cat after giving it food. I was shocked because I had never seen a person kissing a cat! Two weeks after that, I went to another friend's house. Suddenly, I saw her feeding her big snake an entire baby chicken, but the snake could not eat because it was sick. My friend was so sad and worried that she took the snake to the veterinary hospital for treatment as though the snake were a human being. One month later, I took a trip to Tucson, Arizona, to my host family's house. Again, I saw the way their daughter treated their dog. She groomed it, fed it, and waited a little while, and then took it out for a walk. This way of treating pets makes me feel that pets are something special in American society.

Casimiro Diaz
(Sao Tomé)

1. Is this paragraph persuasive? Why or why not?
2. How does the second sentence help the reader?
3. Underline the chronological connectors in this paragraph.
4. Have you had similar experiences? Discuss your experiences with your classmates.

III

The western region of the Ivory Coast contains the richest resources in the country. The area, situated 700 km from the country's capital city, is very beautiful and heavily forested. Most of its resources are related to the forest: coffee, cocoa, rice, and lumber. The Ivory Coast is the second largest producer of coffee in the world and the fourth largest producer of rice. The second important resource is tourism. Man, the capital of the region, is located in the cool mountains. Many natives and foreigners go to Man to escape the heat and enjoy the artistic work of the inhabitants: sculpture and weaving. There is also a dude ranch outside the village of Gouessesso where many foreigners spend their holidays. Because of these resources, the western Ivory Coast is important to the economic success of the country.

Diomande N'Vafoumgbe
(Ivory Coast)

1. Circle the controlling ideas in the topic sentence. What is the purpose of this paragraph (process, definition, and/or clarification)? How do you know?

2. Write a title for this paragraph.

3. What technique(s) of support does the author use?

4. Who is the audience for this paragraph?

IV
My Writing Rituals

Before I start to write, I clean the surface of my desk a little bit; I make a space for writing because my desk is always messy. Then I make my favorite tea, green tea or red tea or other kinds of tea. I turn off the music or the television or any kind of sounds because I like a quiet environment for writing. After that, I make a writing plan in my mind. I think about the topic, the topic sentence, and the conclusion. Then I pick examples to support my topic. After I do this thinking, I make a memo about these thoughts, and I start writing. But because of my rough outline, I sometimes change my paragraph; I add a new example or delete a part of my plan. Therefore, though it's necessary for me to make a rough outline, I can change some details in that outline as I write. For me, my outline is fundamental and flexible.

Fumiko Suzuki
(Japan)

1. What is the purpose of this paragraph? Who is the audience?

2. Underline the chronological connectors in this paragraph.

3. Discuss with your group the writing rituals you use when you write a paragraph. Do your rituals differ from theirs? In what specific ways?

4. Which of the paragraphs above is most interesting and valuable for you? **In your journal**, write a paragraph evaluating the reasons why you chose that paragraph. Use specific examples to support your opinion.

Writing Assignment 5

Write a paragraph about one of the topics below (or choose another topic that interests you). Select your audience and purpose as you narrow your topic and generate supporting detail for your paragraph.

TOPICS: describe your processes for writing; include your writing rituals

define a technical term in your major field for a non-technical audience

explain a popular superstition in your country for a U.S. audience

Pre-writing and Drafting: In your journal, narrow your topic so that you can communicate one main idea to your audience in a single paragraph. Use two pre-writing strategies to generate ideas and details for your paragraph. Use the Audience Guidelines (on the inside front cover of this book) to fully analyze your audience.

Peer Feedback: With a small group of classmates, read the paragraphs that are not your own. Help the author of each paragraph by (a) making suggestions and/or asking questions that will improve the paragraph and (b) marking any grammar or sentence structure errors you see. Then ask your classmates two specific questions about <u>your own</u> paragraph that will help you revise that paragraph.

Revision: Using the advice of your classmates and the Revision Guidelines (on the inside back cover of this book), make changes in your paragraph and write the final draft. Then, **in your journal**, write a paragraph describing the revisions that you made in your final draft. Explain why you made those changes and how they improved your paragraph.

Journal Assignment

Write a paragraph describing the paragraphs of your classmates that you read (above). Indicate the audience and purpose, the topic, and the focus for each paragraph. Write one specific detail that you remember from each paragraph.

Finally, write another paragraph describing the paragraph that was most interesting and valuable for you. Use specific details that you remember from the paragraph to support your opinion.

Writing Assignment 6

Look at the following chart. Write a paragraph for an academic audience that explains the chart. Explain to the audience, in a clear and coherent paragraph, the information given in the chart.

How the Use of Fuels to Generate Electricity in the United States has Changed since 1973

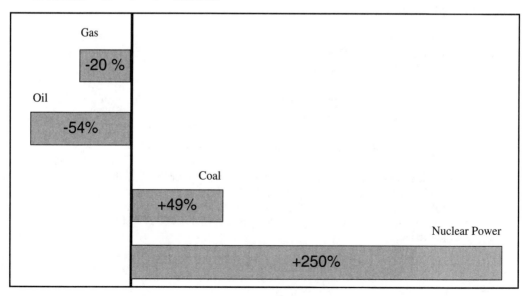

Decrease ⟶ 0 ⟵ Increase

Gas	-20 %
Oil	-54%
Coal	+49%
Nuclear Power	+250%

Pre-writing and Drafting: In your journal, use a pre-writing strategy to develop and organize your paragraph. As you pre-write, identify and analyze your audience and your purpose for this paragraph (use the Audience Guidelines on the inside front cover of this book). Construct a topic sentence of intent that states the purpose of the paragraph. Then write a rough draft of the paragraph.

Peer Feedback: Exchange paragraphs with a partner. As you read your partner's paragraph, help your partner by underlining any grammar or sentence structure errors that you find. Then discuss the paragraph with your partner, offering suggestions or asking questions that will help your partner improve the paragraph.

Revision: Using your partner's advice and the Revision Guidelines (on the inside back cover of this book), make necessary changes to your paragraph. Then write the final draft of the paragraph.

Sentence Combining Exercise

The jokes below are written in short, choppy sentences, and some information is repeated. Combine the sentences so that the jokes flow more smoothly. Use connectors to signal the reader about the relationships between (and within) the combined sentences. Then underline those connectors.

I

Kon Ton is a child. He is very smart. He is five years old. He is famous in his hometown. One day, there is a party. Everyone admires Kon's genius. Suddenly a person says: "A smart child doesn't mean he will also be smart when he grows old." Kon replied. He replies immediately. "I think you must have been pretty smart when you were a child, right?"

Cheng-hsiung Hung
(Republic of China)

II

There were soldiers. There were ten of them. They were from different nationalities. There were on an airplane. There was a captain. Suddenly, the captain spoke. He announced that the airplane was losing altitude. He said that the airplane would crash. It would crash because of the weight in the plane. It was too heavy. He added that the plane could continue to fly. It could continue if weight was released. He said that a certain amount should be released. The amount of weight was 170 to 200 pounds. Unfortunately, there was not even one parachute. One soldier had to die. He had to jump. He had to do this in order to save the others. The Russian soldier volunteered. He jumped. As he jumped, he yelled "Viva Russia!" Two minutes passed. Then the captain made another announcement. He said exactly the same thing. This time, the French soldier jumped. He yelled, "Viva France!" This situation went on. It went on until two soldiers were left. One soldier was Italian. The other soldier was Turkish. Then the captain made the announcement again. The Turkish soldier responded. He pushed the Italian soldier. He pushed him out of the plane. As he pushed, the Turkish soldier spoke. He yelled "Viva Turkey!"

Mukemmel Sarimsakci
(Turkey)

Comparison/Contrast Paragraphs

I like to write, but in a foreign language it is difficult for me because I have to express my feelings in a different system of language. It's like I have to think twice to write in a foreign language.

Rochmah Agustrina
(Indonesia)

Writers make many decisions about their writing. Choosing a method of development for a paragraph is one of those decisions. In the last chapter, you learned ways to develop explanation paragraphs through the methods of process, definition, and clarification. Another way to develop a paragraph is to use comparison or contrast (or both).

COMPARISON: identifies and analyzes <u>similarities</u> between two persons, places, things, or ideas

CONTRAST: identifies and analyzes <u>differences</u> between two persons, places, things, or ideas

Choosing to use comparison/contrast as a method of development means deciding on a reason for using that method. In U.S. academic writing, comparison and contrast paragraphs are sometimes used to <u>explain</u> (that is, in an explanation paragraph) a topic. More often, they are used to support the evaluation of two persons, places, things, or ideas. For example, X is better, more beautiful, easier, more helpful, etc. than Y, and so X is preferable to Y. Writers whose purpose is to compare (or contrast) in order to <u>evaluate</u> and select one of the persons, places, events, or ideas develop **criteria** (factors by which they can judge their topic) to make the comparison (or contrast). These criteria* are the points in the point paragraph outline that are supported by the facts, examples, physical description, and/or personal experience generated by the writer.

A comparison paragraph usually contains both the differences and the similarities of the two people, places, events, or ideas of the topic; similarly, a paragraph of contrast contains similarities as well as differences of the two "sub-topics." However, the emphasis and most of the detail in each paragraph is usually on either comparison or contrast.

NOTE: Some academic writing tasks will ask students to "compare" when the professor actually means "compare and/or contrast."

Writing Assignment 1

You have been traveling around the U.S. during your vacation, and your friend in your native country has written you a letter asking you to describe two of the cities you visited. Below is a table with basic information about two cities. Look at the criteria carefully. Select three of the criteria (below) for evaluation, and select which city you would prefer. Then write a personal letter to your friend. In the letter, evaluate the cities and describe the city you prefer. Follow the personal letter form you studied in the first chapter.

Criteria	City X	City Y
population	15,000	225,000
location	northwest U.S.	southeast U.S.
average daytime temperature	winter: 43°F summer: 78°F	winter: 62°F summer: 91°F
major industries and businesses	John Deere Farm Implements, pickle factory	Monsanto Chemical Company, IBM Computers, Chevrolet industrial plant, Kodak
colleges and universities	vocational-technical school, community college	state university, two private colleges, three vocational schools
intensive language programs	small program at the community college: 50 students	large program at the university; 300 students
entertainment	two movie theaters, community college-athletic	26 movie theaters, city opera and ballet, two theater companies

* *criterion* is the singular of *criteria*.

Organization of Comparison/Contrast Paragraphs

In most comparison/contrast paragraphs, parallel points about the topic must be made. There are two ways to organize a comparison/contrast paragraph: (a) application of one criterion to both of the **"sub-topics"** within the topic at the same time, and (b) discussion of each sub-topic separately, using all criteria with each sub-topic. Each form of organization can be equally successful. The decision of which organizational format to use depends on the assignment (or purpose), the audience, and the available material.

Discussion of Both Sub-Topics

The basic point paragraph outline (or the expanded point paragraph outline) that you studied in the previous chapter can be used for this comparison/contrast organizational form. For example, the writer of a paragraph that contrasts the advantages of traveling by plane (labeled X in the outline below) or by ship (labeled Y) will first select criteria by which s/he will evaluate the two types of travel. Then s/he should make the same points about both sub-topics (X and Y). The organization of this paragraph will be orderly and <u>parallel</u>. Notice that X always comes first in both of these outlines , and Y always comes second. Being careful to make these points parallel helps the reader.

Basic Comparison/Contrast Point Paragraph Outline

TOPIC SENTENCE (**X is preferable to Y**)

1. X and Y   (Criterion 1)
   A. Supporting Detail
   B. Supporting Detail

2. X and Y   (Criterion 2)
   A. Supporting Detail
   B. Supporting Detail

3. X and Y   (Criterion 3)
   A. Supporting Detail
   B. Supporting Detail

<u>Concluding Sentence</u>

Below is a basic point paragraph outline on the topic of ship versus plane travel. Notice that ship travel is discussed first after each criterion is stated so that the reader will not be confused.

TOPIC SENTENCE: **I prefer traveling by ship to traveling by plane.**

1. The longer time on the ship is more restful than an airplane trip.
   A. ship: a change of pace from my daily life
   B. plane: hurried just like my daily life

2. Ship travel is a more interesting time than air travel.

   A. ship: swimming, playing games

   B. plane: sitting, reading

3. The variety of people on a ship is entertaining.

   A. ship: meet many different people

   B. plane: meet only one seatmate, perhaps

Concluding Sentence: For all these reasons, if I had a choice, I would travel by ship.

Nejah Al-Kazemi
(Kuwait)

Discussion of Each Sub-Topic Separately

The alternative form of the point paragraph outline organizes the two people, places, things, or ideas that will be compared and/or contrasted separately. The first sub-topic (X) is discussed and completed, using each of the criteria (see A and B in the outline below). Then the second sub-topic (Y) is discussed, using the same criteria in the same order. Being careful about the order of the criteria helps the reader.

NOTE: the alternative point paragraph outline can also be "expanded" in the same way the basic point outline can be expanded.

The Alternative Comparison/Contrast Point Paragraph Outline

TOPIC SENTENCE **(X is preferable to Y)**

1. X

   A. Criterion 1

      (1) Supporting Detail

      (2) Supporting Detail

   B. Criterion 2

      (1) Supporting Detail

      (2) Supporting Detail

2. Y

   A. Criterion 1

      (1) Supporting Detail

      (2) Supporting Detail

   B. Criterion 2

      (1) Supporting Detail

      (2) Supporting Detail

Concluding Sentence

Below is an alternative point paragraph outline on the topic of studying English with a private tutor versus studying English in an English class. Notice that private tutoring

(X) is discussed first, and studying in an English class (Y) is discussed second. Notice also that the criteria A, B, and C (rate of learning, participation, and meeting goals) are discussed in the same order for English class (Y) as they are for private tutoring (X). In that way, the reader will not be confused.

TOPIC SENTENCE: **Studying English with a private tutor is more helpful than studying in an English class.**

1. Studying with a private tutor (X)
   A. student has the opportunity to assimilate information at his/her own pace (rate of learning)
   B. student participates orally during the last half of each class (participation)
   C. student can make and achieve individual goals (meeting goals)

2. Studying in an English class (Y)
   A. student must progress at the rate of the class (rate of learning)
   B. student may be able to participate during only a small percentage of the class (participation)
   C. student must accept class goals (meeting goals)

Concluding Sentence: After investigating the advantages above, I have decided to stop taking English classes and hire a private tutor.

Iara Wrege
(Brazil)

Exercise A

Below are two paragraphs. Both are about the same topic; both contain the same information. However, the organization of the paragraphs differs. Read both paragraphs. Then answer the questions that follow.

I

Colorado snow conditions are much better than Japanese snow conditions for downhill skiers like me. First, Colorado mountain snow is drier than Japanese snow. For example, in ski areas like Vail and Aspen, I can't make a complete snowball because the snow isn't sticky enough, but in Japanese ski areas, making snowballs is easy. The drier snow in Colorado has two advantages: my clothes stay dry even when I fall, and my skis move through the "powder" snow quickly because they do not stick. In addition to the quality of the Colorado snow, the weather conditions make the ski season both more pleasant and longer in the U.S. Most Japanese ski areas open in the middle of December and close in mid-March, but Colorado skiers can begin skiing in November, and sometimes the ski areas are open until the end of April. Moreover, ski areas in Japan are known for their cloudy, damp weather, but in

Colorado, the bright sun and dry weather make it possible to ski comfortably, sometimes even in shorts and a shirt! For these reasons, many Japanese skiers dream of coming to the U.S. to ski.

II

Colorado snow conditions are much better than Japanese ski conditions for downhill skiers like me. Most Japanese ski resorts have wet, sticky snow; I can easily make snowballs with it, but it is not easy to ski on wet snow. Moreover, the ski season in Japan is short and not always pleasant; most areas are open in mid-December and close by mid-March, and the weather at these resorts is generally cloudy, damp, and consequently very cold. In Colorado, however, conditions are far better. First, Colorado snow is dry; for example, in ski areas like Vail and Aspen, I can't make a complete snowball because the snow isn't sticky enough. This dry snow has two advantages: my clothes stay dry even when I fall, and my skis move through the "powder" snow more quickly because they do not stick. In addition to the quality of Colorado snow, the ski resorts open early in November and sometimes stay open until the end of April, giving skiers a long season. Finally, the bright sun and dry weather in Colorado make it possible to ski comfortably, sometimes even in shorts and a shirt! For these reasons, many Japanese skiers dream of coming to the U.S. to ski.

Hiro Yabuki
(Japan)

1. With a small group of classmates, decide which of the two paragraphs is organized according to the basic point outline. Which is organized according to the alternative point outline?

2. With your group, decide which is more effective. Use specific detail to support your opinion.

3. **In your journal**, write a point paragraph outline for <u>one</u> of the two paragraphs.

4. In what ways does the paragraph evaluate its topic? List the criteria.

Exercise B

With a partner, use one of the topics below to complete both the basic outline and alternative outline below. Decide on appropriate criteria for an audience of your classmates. Your purpose is to <u>evaluate</u> the sub-topics for that audience.

TOPICS: two new cars (X versus Y)
          two kinds of pizza (X versus Y)
          two stereo systems (X versus Y)

I. Basic Point Outline

TOPIC SENTENCE: _____

_____

1. _____

    X. _____

        1) _____

        2) _____

    Y. _____

        1) _____

        2) _____

2. _____

    X. _____

        1) _____

        2) _____

    Y. _____

        1) _____

        2) _____

3. _____

    X. _____

    Y. _____

Concluding Sentence: _____

_____

II. Alternative Point Outline

TOPIC SENTENCE: _____

_____

X. _____

   A. _____

      1) _____

      2) _____

   B. _____

      1) _____

      2) _____

   C. _____

      1) _____

      2) _____

Y. _____

   A. _____

      1) _____

      2) _____

   B. _____

      1) _____

      2) _____

   C. _____

      1) _____

      2) _____

Concluding Sentence: _____

_____

Writing Assignment 2

With your partner from the exercise above, write one paragraph about the topic you chose from one of the outlines you constructed.

Pre-writing and Drafting: With your partner, discuss the necessary detail that will support your topic sentence, and generate that detail together. Use the Paragraph Planning Guidelines (on the inside front cover of this book) to help you plan your paragraph. Write a draft of the paragraph.

Peer Feedback: Meet in a group with another pair of partners. Exchange paragraphs. With your partner, read the paragraph draft that is not your own. Then, with your partner:
- underline the topic sentence and circle the controlling ideas
- draw lines from the controlling ideas to details in the paragraph draft that support those ideas
- underline with wavy lines (~~) the connectors in the paragraph draft
- mark any grammar or sentence structure error you find

At the end of the draft
- indicate which paragraph outline form was used: basic or alternative
- identify the purpose and the audience for the paragraph
- ask two questions that will help the authors improve their paragraph

Finally, discuss the paragraph with the authors.

Revision: Using the written and oral advice of your classmates and the Revision Guidelines (on the inside back cover of this book), revise your paragraph with your partner. Write the final draft of the paragraph. Then, **in your journal**, write a paragraph (by yourself) that compares and/or contrasts writing a paragraph alone with writing a paragraph with a collaborator (your partner). Discuss which of these two you prefer, and support your preference with specific detail.

<u>NOTE</u>: Each of the comparison/contrast organizational forms has some disadvantages. Writers using the **basic outline**, for example, must be careful to use appropriate connectors (see below) so that the reader is adequately directed through the paragraph. In contrast, writers of the **alternative outline** must focus on presenting their criteria without repeating details, and they must carefully join the two parts of the paragraph.

Comparison/Contrast Connectors

Clear connectors are necessary for successful comparison/contrast paragraphs. Below is a chart with some common comparison and contrast connectors. Notice that there are more contrast connectors, perhaps because comparison/contrast paragraphs more often focus on differences than they do on similarities. Notice also the use of punctuation (commas and periods) in the sentences using the connectors.

Figure 6:1 Comparison/Contrast Connectors
Common Comparison Connectors

Long Words

Likewise, ~~Также, подобно~~

Similarly,

In like manner,

In the same way,

Other Words

… also …

… , too.

… the same …

… the same as …

Common Contrast Connectors

Short Words	Long Words	Subordinating Words	Other Words
, but	However, *однако*	Although	Unlike
, yet	In contrast,	Even though	Whereas
		On the other hand,	
		Nevertheless,	

[handwritten annotations: как бы ни / какой бн ни, / хотя бн, даром что / тогда как, / поскольку, / принимая / то внимания / тем не менее / несмотря на / therefore]

Exercise C

Read the paragraphs below. Use appropriate comparison or contrast connectors to complete the paragraphs. Then answer the questions that follow each.

I

I am _____ my brother in many ways. First, his face is _____ to mine. He has brown skin with wide eyes, and he wears glasses. I _____ have brown skin and need glasses. He and I are _____ height: 1.85 meters. His hair is brown; _____, I have brown hair. When he is walking his steps are long _____ mine, as my relatives tell me all the time. For these reasons, many people, even my close friends, often think that my brother is me when they see him.

Kamil Al Maksossi
(Iraq)

1. Is this a comparison or a contrast paragraph? How do you know? Does it evaluate or explain? Use details in the paragraph to support your opinion.

2. Is the paragraph organized according to the basic outline or the alternative outline?

3. Who is the audience for this paragraph? How do you know?

4. Circle the controlling ideas in the topic sentence. Then draw lines from those controlling ideas to the details that support them in the paragraph.

II

_____

There are many differences between my grandmother and me. I think the first and greatest difference is our age. She is 70 years old, _____ I am only 25. Second, my grandmother has blue eyes; my eyes, _____, are brown. In addition, my grandmother is very fat. In fact, she weighs about 200 pounds. _____, I weigh only 120 pounds. We also have different personalities. _____ my grandmother is always happy, I am often angry. She smiles all the time, even at people on the street. _____ her, I smile only when I feel very happy. Finally, my grandmother talks so much that her sons say, "Don't talk all the time because it is very boring," and she answers, "It's good for your to hear me." _____, I don't like to talk much. I prefer to think. _____ my grandmother and I are very different, I am fortunate because we are good friends.

Esmeralda Salomon
(Venezuela)

1. Is this paragraph organized according to the basic outline or the alternative outline?

2. What is the purpose of the paragraph? Does it evaluate and/or describe? Use detail from the paragraph to support your opinion. Who is the audience? How do you know?

3. How did you make the decisions about which connectors to use? Use specific details from the paragraph to support your answer.

4. Write a title for this paragraph.

Writing Assignment 3

Choose one of the following topics, or choose another topic that interests you. Write an <u>evaluative</u> comparison/contrast paragraph for classmates who are not from your country. Use either the basic point outline or the alternative point outline, and use appropriate comparison/contrast connectors.

TOPICS:
- two ways of meeting Americans (Which is better? Why?)
- two ways of dealing with homesickness (which is more successful? Why?)
- two holidays (Which is your favorite? Why?)
- two restaurants you have eaten at (Which was more enjoyable? Why?)

Pre-writing and Drafting: In your journal, use pre-writing techniques to generate ideas and specific details about the topic. As you pre-write, consider the needs and expectations of your audience, and select the criteria that will interest your readers. Use the Audience Guidelines and the Paragraph Planning Guidelines (on the inside front cover of this book) to help you. Choose a comparison/contrast outline form, and construct an outline for your paragraph. Make your paragraph consistent and parallel so that your readers will not become confused. Write a rough draft of your paragraph.

Peer Feedback: With a small group of classmates, read several paragraphs that are not your own. As you read, help your classmates by making suggestions (or asking questions) that might improve the paragraph, and underline any grammar or sentence structure errors that you find. Discuss your suggestions and underlining with your group. Then, **in your journal**, write a paragraph describing the most interesting and valuable paragraph draft that you read. Describe why you found the paragraph interesting, and describe the suggestions you made for improvement. Below is a journal entry by another student to show you how to write your journal entry:

I liked Sahil's paragraph about high school students in the U.S. who take drugs. It was informative, and it had a lot of good points. He has four main points about health problems that come from taking drugs. The most interesting point was that some students get liver damage from taking drugs. The suggestion I made was that he should only discuss three points (so he must modify his topic sentence) because he doesn't have any detail for the fourth point in his paragraph.

Sverre Nyquist
(Norway)

Revision: Using your classmates' advice (and what you learned from reading your classmates' paragraphs), make changes in your draft to improve your paragraph. Then write the final draft of your paragraph.

Exercise D

Read the following comparison/contrast paragraphs. Decide which outline form each follows (and use specific detail from each paragraph to support your decision). Then answer the questions that follow.

I

Life in the bush is preferable to life in the city. The bush is calm and clean; there are no problems of overpopulation, noise, or air pollution. Your life is quiet, independent, and happy as you walk from house to house, talk with friends, and enjoy the smell of freshness. Your neighbors work together and live like brothers. However, the city is a chaotic and filthy place. Unlike life in the bush, the noise of the traffic, the crowded streets, and the terrible pollution from factories make life unpleasant. Life in the city is fast paced, regulated by others, and isolated. You cannot walk alone for fear of being harmed by strangers, and even your neighbors regard you with distrust. For these reasons, I prefer to live in the bush.

Halimatou Tiemogo
(Niger)

1. With a small group of classmates, outline this paragraph.

2. Discuss how the second sentence helps to direct the reader.

3. The paragraph is evaluative. Does this paragraph persuade the audience? Which criteria in the paragraph need more support? What questions might you ask the author to help him improve the paragraph?

4. Underline the comparison/contrast connectors.

II

Americans are more frugal than I had thought. Before I came to the U.S., I thought that Americans used everything and ate as much of everything as they wanted. However, my experiences have shown me that Americans conserve many things. For example, when I first arrived in the U.S., I stayed with an American family. One day, after I had taken a shower, one of the household members told me that I was using too much water; however, I had thought that my shower had been very conservative! Soon after that, I began my studies at the university, and I discovered that American students are especially careful about their money. For example, many of these students have cars; however, they choose to ride bicycles to school in order to save gas money and to conserve energy. In the same way, most university students eat salad or doughnuts and a drink for lunch because they aren't expensive. In fact, some students even bring their lunches in paper bags to save more money. For me, the most surprising discovery was how American students entertain. Although in my country parties have plentiful and beautiful food, in the U.S. students enjoy themselves at parties with only some wine and some cheese. From all these examples, I now realize that a neighbor's grass isn't always greener!

Etsuzo Tomita
(Japan)

1. What is the purpose of this paragraph? How do you know? What is evaluated? Use detail from the paragraph to support your opinion.

2. After reading the information in the topic sentence, what questions did you expect would be answered in the paragraph? Were your questions answered? How might the author modify his topic sentence?

3. What techniques of support are used in this paragraph? Use specific details from the paragraph to support your answer.

4. Underline (a) the comparison/contrast connectors and (b) the middle paragraph connectors in this paragraph.

III

In my country, Nepal, we prefer dogs rather than cats. One reason for this preference is that cats are not easily available in Nepal. They have to be bought, and they are very expensive. However, dogs are easily available, so we don't have to pay for dogs. In fact, they are often given as gifts by neighbors. Superstition plays a part in our distaste toward cats, too. Cats are said to be a sign of a bad omen; they bring bad luck. For example, if a person sees a cat at the time he is leaving the house, he will stay home. But the case is very different for dogs. We train dogs for various purposes: to watch our property, to hunt, and to guard people. Finally, we believe that cats are not friendly; therefore, they will not make good pets. Dogs, however, are loyal and friendly; consequently, they make excellent pets.

M. Wagley
(Nepal)

1. Is the purpose of this paragraph primarily evaluative or explanatory? Support your opinion with specific details from the paragraph.

2. How does the second sentence help to focus the paragraph for the reader?

3. Underline the comparison, contrast, and middle paragraph connectors.

4. Write a title for the paragraph.

IV

Drying Clothes

Since living in the United States, I dry my clothes with a machine, whereas in Malaysia I do it quite differently. In the U.S., I wash my clothes in the dormitory laundry room, and after that I put the newly washed clothes carefully in the dryer. Then I simply put two quarters in a slot on the top of the dryer, select a temperature (cool, warm, hot), and push the start button. Then I can spend forty-five minutes working or just relaxing. When I open the dryer, I can feel the warm air on my face. I do not have to worry about the weather, whether it is raining or hot. In contrast, in Malaysia, the weather conditions were really important. After the clothes were washed, I had to spend time hanging each piece of clothing in the hot sun. Every half hour, I had to go out and check the clothes so that they would get dry, but not too hot. If it was raining, the clothes would end up hanging in the kitchen; they would be in the way for many hours as they dried. While using the dryers in the U.S. costs money, I prefer it to drying clothes at home because it is quick and easy.

Hartini Musa
(Malaysia)

1. Circle the controlling ideas in the topic sentence, and draw lines from those ideas to the details in the paragraph that support them.

2. Underline the connectors in this paragraph.

3. Mark the details in the paragraph that are evaluative. Mark the details that are explanatory.

4. Ask two questions that would help the author improve her paragraph.

Writing Assignment 4

Write either a basic outline or an alternative outline for a comparison OR contrast paragraph about the responsibilities of the mother and the father for raising children in your country. Unlike the previous paragraphs you have written in this chapter, the purpose of this paragraph is to inform your readers; that is, you will describe and explain the topic rather than evaluate it. Your audience is a classmate who does not know about child raising in your country.

> **Peer Feedback:** With a small group of classmates, discuss the responsibilities of parents in your country. Ask your classmates questions about child raising in their countries, and answer their questions about child raising in your country. **In your journal,** take notes about the details about your topic that interest your classmates.
>
> **Pre-writing and Drafting: In your journal,** use pre-writing strategies to develop your topic. Select an appropriate outline for your material, and begin drafting your paragraph. Use the Audience Guidelines and the Paragraph Planning Guidelines (on the inside front cover of this book) as you develop your draft. Use appropriate connectors in your draft, and write a title for your paragraph.
>
> **Peer Feedback:** In a small group of peers, read the paragraph drafts that are not your own. Help the authors of those paragraphs by:
> - making suggestions about narrowing the topic of each paragraph so that the authors can write interesting, valuable final drafts
> - asking the authors questions that will help them add detail to their paragraphs
> - marking any grammar or sentence structure error you find (and discussing

those possible errors with the author)

Revision: Using the advice of your classmates and the Revision Guidelines (on the inside back cover of this book), revise your paragraph and write the final draft. Then, **in your journal**, write a paragraph describing how you might expand that draft into several paragraphs about the same topic. What might possible topic sentences for multiple paragraphs be?

Overall Organization of Comparison/Contrast Paragraphs

While the process paragraphs you studied in the last chapter were organized chronologically (that is, according to time) and used chronological connectors (first, second, next, etc.), many comparison/contrast paragraphs arrange their explanatory points or their criteria from most to least important, or from least to most important.

NOTE: Some paragraphs have points of equal importance. In that case, the writer must decide which criterion or point would be most persuasive or clear if it were used first (or second, or third, or last).

Writers must therefore decide on the relative importance of their explanatory points or their evaluative criteria. Then they must arrange them in an order that the audience will understand and accept. Of course, sometimes the judgment of what is more or less important depends on the assignment, the available material, and, especially, the audience. Consequently, the writer must analyze the audience and purpose of the paragraph carefully. The paragraphs below are examples of each form of organization.

Exercise E

Read the paragraphs below. Notice how each is organized, and discuss that organization with your classmates. Write an appropriate title for each paragraph. Then answer the questions that follow.

(From Most to Least Important)

Chinese differs from English in several ways, and these differences make learning English difficult. First, the most complex difference is the word order. For example, in English, a greeting is "How are you?" but in Chinese, the same greeting is "You are how?" Next, in Chinese, our verbs don't have past tense; instead, we know the time from the adverb. In English, however, time is designated by tense. Besides these important basic problems, Chinese and English have many small differences. Chinese, for instance, does not distinguish between "he" and "she," nor is there a difference between "a" and "an" as there is in English.

Cheng-Hwa Hu
(China)

1. With a partner, modify the topic sentence of this paragraph so that it more accurately reflects the paragraph that follows.
2. Underline the words that demonstrate the most-to-least important overall organization of this paragraph.
3. Discuss how the second sentence of this paragraph helps direct the reader.
4. With your partner, write a concluding sentence for this paragraph.

(From Least to Most Important)

In industry, especially on assembly lines, robots are better workers than human beings. Unlike men, robots work in boring or dirty or unpleasant jobs without complaint or absence. They will drill holes or make sheet metal parts for weeks and years at a time. In addition, robots on the assembly line are more cost-effective than men. They can work 24 hours a day, and their "up time" (that is, the time they are operable) is nearly 95%, as opposed to 75% for the average human worker. More importantly, robots also work in jobs too dangerous over a long period of time for men, jobs that cause disease, or jobs in which frequent accidents occur with fumes or radiation. Most important, robots are accurate. Human error is responsible for a 10% rejection rate, but the robots' rejection rate is zero. For all these reasons, industries are moving from human to robot employees.

Abdalla Saadawi
(Libya)

1. Is this an explanatory and/or an evaluative paragraph? How do you know?
2. Which outline form is used by the author of this paragraph: basic or alternative?
3. What technique(s) of support are used? Label each in the margins of the paragraph.
4. What questions might you ask this author to help him improve this paragraph?

(Points of Equal Importance)

There are three main differences between advertisements on television in Hong Kong and advertisements on television in the U.S. First, there are only a few kinds of advertisements in Hong Kong. For example, almost all the ads on television in Hong Kong are about food and cigarettes. In the U.S., however, there are different kinds of ads: in addition to food and cigarettes, there are also ads for cars and cosmetics, household utensils and clothes, and many other items. Second, the TV ads in Hong Kong waste a lot of time. There is a five-minute break every ten minutes for advertisements. In contrast, the frequency of TV ads in the U.S. is low, and the time for the breaks is short. For example, the longest ad I have seen lasted only for three minutes. Therefore, the watcher will not be disturbed and forget the situation of a good program. Third, advertisements in Hong Kong are very boring, and they all have the same style: for instance, all the cigarette ads have the same scene of a beautiful beach. On the other hand, the ads in the U.S. have different styles, and they are interesting too. For example, the special effects in one car ad amazed me, and the creativity in the ads for jeans is very stimulating. In conclusion, I love to watch TV ads in the U.S., but in Hong Kong, I turn off the TV when the ads come on.

Yik Lee
(Hong Kong)

1. Circle the controlling ideas in the topic sentence. Based on the controlling ideas, what questions do you expect will be answered in the paragraph that follows?

2. Underline 3 evaluative details and 3 explanatory details in the paragraph.

3. Underline the connectors in the paragraph with wavy lines (∼∼).

4. The author of this paragraph had equally important points to present to his readers. What might have made him decide to organize the points in the way he did?

Writing Assignment 5

Write a paragraph that discusses some differences (or similarities) between your native language and English. You will choose either to explain *the differences (or similarities) or to* evaluate *them. Your audience is a native speaker of English who wants to know more about your language.*

Pre-writing and Drafting: With a small group of classmates (who are not from your native country), discuss similarities and differences between English and your native languages. Take notes **in your journal** as you talk. Tell your classmates which information about their languages you find most interesting. Write ideas from your classmates about your language in your journal, too. Then begin to draft your paragraph. Use the Audience Guidelines and the Paragraph Planning Guidelines (on the inside front cover of this book) to help your develop your paragraph. Remember: Your writing processes may not follow the steps in the Guidelines in the same order, and some steps may occur simultaneously. Make decisions about the narrowed topic, specific detail, outline form, overall organization, and connectors. Think about your audience and purpose as you write your rough draft, and make revisions in your paragraph as you write.

Peer Feedback: With the same small group of classmates, read paragraph drafts that are not your own. Help each author by:

• putting an asterisk (*) in the margin where you find interesting detail

• making suggestions that will help each author improve her/his paragraph

• marking any grammar or sentence structure error that you see

Revision: Using the written and oral advice of your classmates as well as the Revision Guidelines (on the inside back cover of this book), make changes in your draft that will improve your paragraph. Then write the final draft of the paragraph. Finally, **in your journal**, write a paragraph about the best paragraph draft you read in your group. Use specific details that you remember from that paragraph to show why it was the best.

Using Parallel Sentence Structures in Comparison/Contrast Paragraphs

Comparison/Contrast paragraphs often contain parallel grammatical structures. Grammatical parallelism means that parts of a sentence have similar forms. The rule for parallelism: Elements in a sentence that are similar in <u>ideas</u> should be similar in <u>structure</u>.

Examples:

1. Ali wanted *to go* to the U.S., *to study* at a university, and *to return* to Libya. (parallel infinitive verbs)

2. The doctor recommended *aspirin*, *bed rest*, and a *liquid diet*. (parallel noun objects)

3. Successful jokes are *clear*, *fast*, and *short*. (parallel adverbs)

Sometimes separate sentences are "reduced"; that is, they are combined with parallel grammatical structures.

Examples:

Mehdi enjoys traveling. His brother, Ali, enjoys traveling, too.

<u>Both</u> Mehdi and his brother, Ali, enjoy traveling.

OR

<u>Like</u> his brother Ali, Mehdi enjoys traveling.

Exercise F

The paragraph below has many short, choppy sentences. Combine some of the sentences so that the paragraph flows more smoothly. Eliminate some of the words, and make some of the grammatical structures <u>parallel</u>. Add comparison connectors when necessary.

Seattle and San Francisco are very much alike. Seattle is a seaport city. San Francisco is a seaport city. Seattle is on the northwest coast of the U.S. San Francisco is on the northern California coast at the edge of the western U.S. Their climates are similar. Seattle has mild winters with very little snow. San Francisco has very little snow and mild winters, too. The summer in Seattle is often cool and rainy. San Francisco has cool, rainy summers. Mark Twain, the famous writer, once said, "The coldest winter I ever spent was summer in San Francisco." Both cities have wonderful shopping and restaurants. San Francisco is famous for Fisherman's Wharf, where dozens of excellent restaurants serve fresh seafood. Seattle is also famous for its seaside restaurants and open air fish markets.

Writing Assignment 6

Write a paragraph of personal experience that contrasts your <u>expectations</u> of a situation with the <u>reality</u> of that situation. Choose one of the topics below (or another topic that interests you). Notice that this paragraph will be chronological (that is, *"before" and "after") and that it may be either evaluative or explanatory. Your audience for this paragraph is a classmate who does not know you well.*

> **TOPICS:** a visit to another city in your country (before and after you visited)
> a job you have had (before and after you began that job)
> an aspect of the U.S. (before and after you arrived)
> a visit to the dentist (or doctor) (before and after you visited)
>
> **Pre-writing and Drafting:** In your journal, use the Paragraph Planning Guidelines (on the inside front cover of this book) to (a) select and narrow your topic, (b) generate details that will interest your reader, and (c) select a purpose (and an overall organization) for your audience. Then construct a basic or an alternative point outline and a possible topic sentence for your paragraph. Draft your paragraph. Then reread the paragraph, and, using the Audience Guidelines (on the inside front cover of this book), consider your audience. If necessary (a) modify the topic sentence, (b) add detail, or (c) revise the second sentence of the paragraph. Then write <u>another</u> draft of your paragraph.
>
> **Peer Feedback:** In a small group of classmates, read several paragraphs that are not your own. In your journal, take notes about each paragraph. Note:
> - whether the paragraph is explanatory or evaluative or both
> - whether the paragraph comes from a basic or an alternative outline
> - the purpose of the paragraph
> - how the second sentence helps the reader (or doesn't help the reader)
>
> In the margins of each paragraph:
>
> - put <u>one</u> asterisk (*) where you find the best detail
> - write the type of one successful technique of support that you identify
>
> At the end of each paragraph, write one suggestion to help the author improve the paragraph. Then discuss your findings with your classmates. Use your journal notes to help you remember.
>
> **Revision:** Using the oral and written advice of your classmates, as well as the Revision Guidelines (on the inside back cover of this book), make improvements in your paragraph draft. Then write the final draft. Finally, **in your journal**, write a paragraph comparing and contrasting the rough draft of your paragraph with the final draft. Use specific details to support your ideas.

Sentence Combining Exercise

The jokes below are written with short, choppy sentences, and some of the information is repeated. Combine some of the sentences so that the jokes flow more smoothly. You will eliminate some of the words in order to combine the sentences effectively. Use appropriate connectors when necessary.

I

A group of jokers were sitting. They were sitting together. They were exchanging jokes. They were familiar with the jokes. Therefore, they simply numbered the jokes. Then they mentioned each number. A number had been given to each joke. The others would respond to the number. They would respond by laughing. They laughed because they knew the number. One day, one of the jokers spoke. He said, "Joke number 43." All of the others laughed. They laughed for a while. Then they stopped. But one person kept laughing. He continued laughing for a long time. The others asked him why. He answered, "This is the first time I have heard that joke."

Kamalian Shaat
(Palestine)

II

I had an uncle. He had no friends. Instead, he had a dog. The dog went with him. The dog went everywhere with my uncle. One day my uncle went to the movies. It was a typical cinema. It was a small-town cinema. Of course, the dog went with him. At the end of the film, the cinema owner came over. He came to my uncle. He decided to play a joke. The joke was on my uncle. The cinema owner said, "Did your dog like the movie?" My uncle replied, "No." The cinema owner was surprised. It had been a good movie. So he asked a question. He asked my uncle, "Why not?" My uncle replied, "Because he already read the book."

Rodolfo Siles
(Honduras)

III

China is a country. China might have an earthquake. It is very likely that China will. After all, it is a populated country. In fact, it is the most populated country in the world. A billion people live there. Therefore, they might cause an earthquake. If they all did something. If they did it simultaneously. If they jumped. Then the world would certainly quake.

Hung-chi Kuo
(Republic of China)

7

Cause-Effect Paragraphs

I like writing. But writing in English is a tough job for me.

Jinlai Shyu
(Republic of China)

Cause(s) and effect(s), like comparison and contrast, can occur either in the same paragraph or separately; that is, there can be <u>cause</u> paragraphs, <u>effect</u> paragraphs, or <u>cause-effect</u> paragraphs. **Cause paragraphs** discuss the causes (or reasons) for effects (or consequences). **Effect paragraphs** discuss the effects (or consequences) of an action, result, or occurrence.

NOTE: Sometimes a writing assignment labeled "cause-effect" means either cause or effect; sometimes it means both. You will need to clarify the assignment with your professor.

A **cause paragraph** usually answers the question **"Why?"** As writers investigate an answer to a question, they may ask, for example:

Why does a volcano erupt?

Why do headaches occur?

Why do some apples turn red?

Writers of cause paragraphs, then, usually begin with the effect (the volcano erupting, the headache occurring) and then explain the causes for these effects. In cause paragraphs, time is important. That is, the causes for an effect are explained in their chronological order: First this happened, and then that happened, and after that…

An **effect paragraph** often answers the question **"What?"** Writers investigating the effects of an occurrence, an event, or a result, might ask, for example,

What are the effects of an earthquake?

What are the effects of a high fat diet?

What are the effects of failing a test?

Writers of effect paragraphs usually begin with a topic sentence that describes the event, the occurrence, or the result. The paragraph that follows describes the effect(s) of that event, occurrence, or result. Often, the effects can be subdivided (and the paragraph topic and topic sentence narrowed): the effects of an earthquake on people, cities, or the earth's surface; the effects of a high fat diet on the human heart, on body weight, or on life span; the effects of failing a test on a personal level or on a professional level.

Sometimes paragraphs include both causes and effects. This happens particularly when, for instance, in a series of effects, an effect becomes a cause for another effect. A writer describing a laboratory experiment, for example, might describe the steps in the experiment, or the writer might analyze a complex series of events, such as the causes and/or the effects of secondary school students holding part-time jobs. In the outlines below, effects (E) become causes (C) which in turn lead to new effects.

TOPIC SENTENCE: **High school students who are also employed gain experiences that help them live a better life.**
(C) Student has a job
    (E) learns skills: responsibility, time management, independence ⟶ (C)
       (E) applies those skills in school and improves grades ⟶ (C)
         (E) is therefore able to go to a better university ⟶ (C)
           (E) consequently, s/he has a more successful career

TOPIC SENTENCE: **High school students who hold part-time jobs help the U.S. economy.**
(C) Student has a part-time job
    (E) earns money ⟶ (C)
       (E) spends money (cars, clothes, entertainment, fast food) ⟶ (C)
         (E) as a result, the U.S. economy expands to fill the needs
           (more production, more U.S. jobs) ⟶ (C)
         (E) therefore, more U.S. taxes are collected ⟶ (C)
           (E) so the federal deficit decreases

Organization of Cause-Effect Paragraphs

Generally, cause-effect paragraphs are organized in the same way as most explanatory paragraphs: with **the basic point paragraph outline** (or the expanded point paragraph outline). Many cause or effect paragraphs are organized from most-to-least important, or from least-to-most important causes or effects. Other cause-effect paragraphs are organized with points of equal importance. Some cause or effect paragraphs (and most paragraphs that contain both causes and effects) are organized chronologically—that is, according to time.

Exercise A

Read the following basic outlines and paragraphs. With a small group of classmates, decide whether each paragraph is a cause or an effect paragraph. Then, with your group, answer the questions that follow.

I

TOPIC SENTENCE: **I play soccer for three reasons.**

1. It's easy fun.
   A. known the rules for a long time
   B. not dangerous; a challenge

2. It relaxes me.
   A. enjoy playing with friends
   B. a good break from studying

3. It allows me to meet new people
   A. competition with strangers
   B. travel to new places for games

Concluding Sentence: For these reasons, my favorite pastime is playing soccer.

Zamil Al-Anazi
(Kuwait)

1. What is the purpose of this paragraph? Is it explanatory or evaluative? How do you know?

2. Are the points in this outline organized from most important to least important point? Or are the points equally important? How do you know?

3. Under point 1A, the specific details are not directly related to the stated point. Modify either the point or the specific details so that the details support the point.

4. What would you add or change to make the details in this outline more interesting for your group?

II

COOKING

Cooking is my hobby; when I cook, good things happen to me. If I am lonely or homesick, cooking lifts my spirits. When I make a delicious dessert, and ask someone to share it with me, my depression disappears. When I am bored or very tired, cooking makes me feel alive, especially if I know I am cooking dinner for some friends. Cooking also reminds me of home. Before I left my country, my sisters and I would cook together every Sunday, and everyone in my family would eat and laugh together. [Now I enjoy cooking something savory for my roommates because their joy in eating makes me remember the happy times with my family.] For me, cooking is an excellent escape, and without it I wouldn't be able to be so happy.

Ma Mu-der
(Republic of China)

1. What is the action/occurrence/result in this paragraph? What are the effects?

2. Circle the controlling ideas in the topic sentence. Could the sentence be modified to make it clearer for the reader?

3. How does the second sentence help to direct the reader?

4. Sometimes an effect becomes a cause and vice-versa. In the bracketed sentence [ ], which is the cause and which is the effect?

III

When I think about returning to Buenos Aires, I get very apprehensive because I will face many problems there. First, politically, Buenos Aires, like the entire country of Argentina, is very unstable, and frequent changes of government often result in unemployment and general insecurity of the population. Another problem is the highly inflationary economy in Buenos Aires, which reached 170% last year. Such inflation means that saving is useless, and the buying power of the people is very limited. Many people cannot even afford to pay the huge rents on their apartments. Finally, Buenos Aires has all the problems of most large cities: crowding, noise, pollution, and traffic jams. For all of these reasons, I am dreading my return to Argentina.

Ani Sala
(Argentina)

1. Label the technique(s) of support used in this paragraph in the margins.

2. Underline all the connectors in the paragraph.

3. This paragraph be expanded into an entire essay. Which sentences could be used as topic sentences for multiple paragraphs?

4. What questions might you ask about those topic sentences that the author could answer in the multiple paragraphs?

Writing Assignment 1

Write a cause paragraph about your most *relaxing, enjoyable, difficult,* or *exciting* pastime. Show **why** that hobby is relaxing or enjoyable or difficult or exciting by using facts, examples, description, or experience. Your audience for this paragraph is your teacher.

> **Pre-Writing and Drafting:** In your journal, use two pre-writing strategies to develop detail for your paragraph. Consult the Paragraph Planning Guidelines (on the inside front cover of this book) as you begin to draft your paragraph. Remember: Your writing processes may not follow the order of the steps in the Guidelines, and several of the steps may occur simultaneously. Using the Audience Guidelines (on the inside front cover of this book), analyze your teacher's needs and expectations concerning your topic. As you draft this paragraph, consider the arrangement of causes (from most-to-least important, or vice versa).

> **Peer Feedback:** Exchange paragraph drafts with a partner. Then, using the audience analysis of your audience from your journal, pretend you are the teacher. Read your partner's paragraph draft, and:
> - underline the topic sentence and circle the controlling ideas
> - underline with wavy lines (~~) all the connectors
> - label one technique of support in the margin
> - put an asterisk (*) in the margin where you find successful detail
> - mark any grammar or sentence structure error you find

> At the end of the paragraph draft:

> - identify the organization of the paragraph
> - write two questions (or two suggestions) to help your partner improve the paragraph

> **Revision:** Using your partner's advice, make changes that improve your paragraph. Use the Revision Guidelines (on the inside back cover of this book) to help with the revision. Write the final draft of the paragraph. Then, **in your journal,** write a paragraph discussing the reasons you made specific changes in your paragraph draft. Support your reasons with specific detail.

Cause-Effect Connectors

Because cause or effect paragraphs are often explanation paragraphs, some of the connectors your have already learned will also be used in these paragraphs: middle paragraph connectors like *for example* and *in addition*, and concluding connectors such as *in conclusion*. In addition, some cause or effect paragraphs use comparison-contrast connectors (*but, however, although, even though*, etc.) to help the reader understand what is and what is not an effect or a cause.

However, some connectors are used specifically with cause or effect paragraphs. These connectors help the reader to distinguish between causes and effects. To write successful cause-effect paragraphs, then, you must be able to use cause-effect connectors correctly and appropriately. Some cause-effect connectors are listed below. Notice the placement and the relationship between causes (**C**) and effects (**E**), and note the punctuation used with these connectors.

Cause-Effect Connectors

C = Cause   E = Effect

Short Words	Long Words	Subordinating Words	Other Words
E..., so...C	Therefore, ...E	E...because...C	First, ...C or E
	Consequently, E	E...because of C[*]	Second, C or E[**]
	As a result, ...E	E...due to...C[*]	
	For this reason, ...E	E...since...C	

Exercise B

Read each pair of sentences. Determine which is the cause and which is the effect. Label them C (cause) and E (effect). Then write a combined sentence from each pair of sentences; use some of the connectors from the chart above.

1. Ayed got up late.
   He missed the bus.

2. He was hungry.
   He stopped at McDonald's for breakfast.

3. He'll get fat.
   He always eats junk food.

---

[*] The addition of the preposition requires the effect to be a noun phrase rather than a clause.
[**] Sometimes chronological connectors (first, second, etc.) are used in cause-effect paragraphs to indicate time. Morte frequently, however, these same chronological connectors (first, second, etc.) are used in cause-effect paragraphs to innumerate causes or reasons and/or effects. That is, these connectors are used to list the numbers of the causes and/or effects.

4. It's easy for him to gain weight.
   He likes to eat.

5. There are always new foods to try.
   Eating has become an enjoyable hobby for him.

6. The fast-food chains like McDonald's and Pizza Hut are doing a booming business.
   Many people eat several meals a week there.

7. We often grab any food in easy reach.
   We are always in a hurry.

8. The fast food restaurants prepare so much food so quickly.
   Sometimes there are problems with the cleanliness of the food.

9. There are many food preparation regulations.
   A lot of sloppy processing slips by.

10. One consumer was astonished.
    He found a dead mouse in his bottle of soda.

Exercise C

Using the following four sentences as causes, make up meaningful effects to go with each sentence. Use appropriate cause or effect connectors from the chart above. Try to use a different connector in each sentence.

1. Miami is a magnificent place.

   Effect: _____

2. Most of America's wine is produced within 100 miles of San Francisco.

   Effect: _____

3. Santa Fe, New Mexico, is famous for its artisans.

   Effect: _____

4. Dubuque, Iowa is built on seven hills.

   Effect: _____

Exercise D

Use the following four sentences as effects. Make up a meaningful cause to go with each sentence. Use appropriate connectors from the chart above. Experiment with different connectors.

1. It was terribly cold last Friday night.

   Cause: _____

2. I slipped and fell on the street.

   Cause: _____

3. I was late getting home.

   Cause: _____

4. A friend needed help pushing his car.

   Cause: _____

Exercise E

Add a cause or an effect sentence to each of the sentences below, and indicate which you are adding by <u>circling</u> the C (cause) or the E (effect) at the beginning of each sentence. Use an appropriate cause-effect, comparison-contrast, or middle paragraph connector in each sentence. Try to experiment with as many different connectors as possible.

1. I am a (hard OR lazy) worker.

   C   E _____

2. Emma wants to go to (New York OR Dallas) for her vacation.

   C   E _____

3. He wants to take a (history course OR biology course) next semester.

   C   E _____

4. I (always OR never) get my homework finished.

   C   E _____

5. People (always OR never) have to wait for me.

   C   E _____

6. Men (ought to OR don't need to) prepare their own meals.

   C   E _____

7. Finding a part-time job would be (easy OR difficult) for me.

   C   E _____

8. Nadia likes (hot OR cold) weather.

   C   E _____

Exercise F

Read the following sentences. Then construct both a cause (C) and an effect (E) for each of the sentences. Use appropriate cause-effect, comparison-contrast, and/or middle paragraph connectors.

1. The skiing is excellent at Aspen this year.

   C _____

   E _____

2. The Russians lost to the U.S. in ice hockey.

   C _____

   E _____

3. Bobsledding is a very fast sport.

   C _____

   E _____

4. Jackie skates so gracefully.

   C _____

   E _____

Exercise G

In the paragraph below, write the appropriate cause-effect connectors in the blanks. Choose the connectors on page 162.

Some students fail in college _____ their academic background is weak. For example, one student might not have had an adequate mathematics course, _____ he fails his university math class. Another student may not attend classes regularly _____ he has never learned the importance of attendance. _____ he may not be able to pass the tests in class _____ he does not know the answers. _____ financial problems, other students may fail university classes. For example, students who have to take jobs don't have as much time to study. _____, they may fail their classes. Others may worry _____ they have too little money, and _____ they may not be able to concentrate on their studies. Finally, there are students who fail _____ their energies are not directed toward their classes. Some of these students are not interested in college, _____ they spend their days doing other things. _____ other students are distracted by other activities—parties, movies, etc.—they do not study enough. _____ they fail. _____ of all these problems, numerous students fail in college every year.

Shams Othman
(Saudi Arabia)

Writing Assignment 2

In your journal, write five sentences about one of the topics below. Each sentence must have a <u>cause</u> and an <u>effect</u>. Underline the cause in each sentence. Circle the effect. Use appropriate cause-effect connectors.

TOPICS: Why I like my best friend
Why teachers in the U.S. are different from teachers in my country
Why I like (or dislike) the weather in my hometown

Exercise H

With a small group of classmates, read the following paragraphs. Underline the connectors in each paragraph, and identify them as cause-effect, comparison-contrast, chronological, or middle paragraph connectors. Then answer the questions that follow each paragraph.

I

I never drink cola because it is really bad for your health. I discovered this when I worked with some biologists last summer. We did two simple experiments. In the first, we measured the pH (that is, the grade of acidity) of the cola. We found that the cola has a pH of 3.2. That is extremely acidic, and so it is bad for your body. In the second experiment, we decided to examine the effects of high acidity in cola. We put a shark's tooth in a glass of cola. In just seven days, the tooth had completely disappeared: the cola had dissolved it! If cola can do that to a tooth, what can it do to human teeth or to a human stomach or intestine? For these reasons, I never drink cola, and I advise my friends not to drink it either.

Ruben Perez
(Mexico)

1. Is this paragraph about causes or effects or both? Use specific detail from the paragraph to support your opinion.

2. Is the topic sentence a statement of opinion, intent, or a combination of the two? How do you know?

3. Modify the topic sentence so that it more accurately reflects the rest of the paragraph.

4. Is the paragraph persuasive? What questions do you think the cola company might ask this writer about his experiments?

II

Solar Cell Energy

There are three reasons why solar cell energy generation has not developed more rapidly. First, the cost per watt of solar cell generation is more expensive than that of steam power or nuclear power generation. Therefore, researchers are still looking for ways to make solar cells cheaper. Second, nature plays a large part in solar cell generation. For example, some days are cloudy and rainy; because there is not always fine weather, solar energy can't be generated every day. Also, no solar energy is generated at night. Consequently, solar cells must have the capacity to store energy for use during these times, and these storage cells are very expensive. As a result, only in low latitude areas can enough solar energy be generated effectively at this time. Finally, building plants for solar cell generation is extremely expensive. A very large space is needed, and the need for maintenance is constant. To illustrate, the surface of the solar cell plant has to be cleaned daily. For all these reasons, it is very difficult to develop solar cell plants and make solar cell energy available to the general public for a competitive price. Despite all these problems, I believe the day will come when we use solar energy cells because they are a form of clean energy with no pollution.

Kiho Kato
(Japan)

1. Does this paragraph explain causes or effects? Of what?

2. Make a basic point paragraph outline for the paragraph.

3. Who is the audience for this paragraph? How do you know? How does the vocabulary and sentence structure differ from the previous paragraph? Why?

4. The last sentence of this paragraph introduces a new idea into the paragraph. Cross it out. Could that sentence be used as the topic sentence for another paragraph? What questions could you ask the author about the controlling ideas in that sentence that could be answered in another paragraph?

III

American football is a good sport for commercial television. First, because it is such a popular game in the U.S., football has a huge audience that watches both college and professional games on television. The result is a large audience for advertisers. Second, the way the game is played (that is, with many short plays with breaks between each play) allows frequent insertions of commercials, so a lot of money can be made by the television companies. For example, a 30-second commercial during a regular football game costs about $100,000, and that same commercial during a championship football games could cost nearly three times as much. The most valuable time for television stations is the long break between the halves of each football game; advertisers and others who want publicity have nearly twenty minutes. The Super Bowl, the last game of the season and the game that determines the national championship, is the best example of the financial success of American football on television. Although the game only lasts about two hours, the television program lasts nearly four. While the teams are not playing, the commercial sponsors have a very long time to advertise their products. [Other forms of publicity also take place. The television stations advertise their other programs, and once, during half-time at the Super Bowl, even the President of the U.S. took advantage of the opportunity for publicity. He called the television broadcasters to talk with them (and to be heard by the 40% of the American public who were watching the Super Bowl!) about football… and politics.]

Onofre Gabaldo
(Spain)

1. Is this paragraph about causes or effects? Of what? Use specific detail from the paragraph to support your opinion.

2. How does the second sentence help to direct the reader?

3. What technique(s) of support do you find in the paragraph? Identify them in the margins.

4. The last bracketed [ ] sentences of the paragraph may be ideas that are outside the paragraph. Write another concluding sentence for the paragraph, and suggest ways that the other final sentences might be used in another paragraph about this topic.

IV

Walking Tours

In my opinion, the most enjoyable means of travel is the walking tour. First of all, walking allows the traveler to enjoy the tour by seeing everything on the way instead of hurrying and missing the surroundings. In addition, walking tours are useful for health. At the end of the journey, one feels a delicious physical weariness in spite of feeling a little exhausted. One also has the possibility of meeting people who live in the tour area, to learn about their traditions and ways of living. The members of a tour group also become friendly, and they share many memories, both of the troubles (and sometimes the dangers) they encounter and of the pleasures of the trip. Moreover, walking tours are inexpensive; there are no high fares for transportation, and the walker doesn't have to rely on the schedules of trains, planes, or other people. Finally, people on walking tours are repaid for their hardships by getting to know wild, uninhabited places as they interact with nature.

Natasha Helnyk
(Ukraine)

1. With a small group of classmates, decide on the overall organization of this paragraph (most-to-least important, least-to-most important, or equal points). How do you know?

2. With your group, discuss the ways in which the audience for this paragraph differs from the audience of the previous paragraph. Be specific.

3. This paragraph could be expanded to several paragraphs. With your group, underline the possible topic sentences for at least three different paragraphs. Then discuss the specific details you and your group might use to support each of the topic sentences.

4. Which of the paragraphs in this exercise was the most interesting and valuable for you? Why?

Writing Assignment 3

Choose one of the topics you wrote cause and effect sentences for in your journal (Writing Assignment 2 above) and write a paragraph for your classmates about that topic.

> **Pre-Writing and Drafting:** In your journal, use the Paragraph Planning Guidelines (on the inside front cover of this book) to generate ideas for your paragraph, to construct a basic (or expanded) point outline and topic sentence, and to write and revise the paragraph draft.

> **Peer Feedback:** Exchange paragraph drafts with a partner. Immediately cover the paragraph except for the topic sentence. Then read the topic sentence and, **in your journal**, write for two minutes about what you think the paragraph will be about. Include the questions you expect will be answered in the paragraph. Then discuss your expectations with your partner, and read your partner's paragraph. Were your expectations fulfilled? What changes might your partner make to improve the paragraph? Make suggestions about focus, detail, and grammar.

> **Revision: In your journal**, write a paragraph about what you learned from your partner about improving your paragraph. Describe the plans you have for revising your paragraph. Then, using the advice of your partner, and the

Revision Guidelines (on the inside back cover of this book), make necessary changes in your paragraph. Write the final draft.

Developing Academic Cause-Effect Paragraphs

When you complete academic writing tasks, you will often have to develop detail for your paragraphs from information that is not from your personal experience. There are at least three ways to find information. One way is to use secondary sources in the academic library. The next chapter focuses on the necessary skills for library use. Two other sources of information give primary (or first-person) evidence; they are:

1. interview an authority about the topic

2. construct and administer a survey to a group of people

Information from interviews and surveys can be used not only in cause-effect paragraphs but also in any academic paragraph: explanation, comparison-contrast, or any other method of paragraph development.

Interviews

If an academic writing assignment requires you to gather information about a topic, you may want to **consult an expert**. This authority may be a professor (an expert in, for example, cellular cofferdams), a person outside the university (for example, the director of a city office or the president of the city council about a problem in the city), or even a classmate (who might be an authority about a topic such as rodeos, quarterbacking a football team, or the use of snow fences). Guidelines for conducting a successful interview include:

1. make an appointment to meet with the expert

2. write the interview questions carefully; make sure that they are

   A. clear; simple, easy to understand, and relevant to the topic

   B. sequenced; each question follows logically from the previous one

3. listen carefully, and take notes during the interview

4. after the interview, review your notes and add details you remember

Using interviews to develop evidence for academic paragraphs is not limited to cause-effect paragraphs. Interviewing authorities is an excellent strategy for any academic assignment. Below are the questions developed by three students for interviews that answered the question "Why?" Notice that the fourth set of interview questions answers the question "What?" Interview information can also be used for explanation (and other) paragraphs.

I
TOPIC: Why do flowers smell sweet?

Expert: **Dr. Greg Brown, Professor of Botany**

<u>Questions</u>:

1. Why do flowers smell good?

2. What causes the odor?

3. Why do some flowers smell different from others?

4. Who benefits from this smell?

5. Why do humans think flowers smell good?

Chris Fogstad
(Norway)

II
TOPIC: Why is Mexican food served at the dormitory cafeteria every day?

Expert: **Washakie Center Manager Lorene Helweg**

<u>Questions</u>:

1. How often do you serve Mexican food?

2. Why do you serve it every day?

3. Do you think that this food is acceptable to the students? Why (or why not)?

4. Do the non-Mexican students request it? Is it a popular kind of food?

5. Do you have to consider nutritional requirements?

6. Is Mexican food considered nutritious?

Mayda Martinez
(Puerto Rico)

III
TOPIC: Why did you choose this university?

<u>Questions</u>:

1. What is your native country?

2. When did you arrive in the U.S.?

3. Tell me about your life in your native country.

4. Why did you leave to come to the U.S.?

5. What was your principal reason for choosing X University?

6. Had you heard about the university before you came here? How?

7. Have your expectations about this university been fulfilled?

Xi Zhen Peng
(People's Republic of China)

IV
TOPIC: What are the attitudes of students toward homework?

Experts: **Students in an intensive English language program**
<u>Questions:</u>

1. Is homework helpful to you?

2. Do you get good grades on homework?

3. Do you think the IELI teachers give too much homework?

4. How would you change the amount of homework?

Shelley Reid's ESL writing students
Intensive English Language Institute
State University of New York/Buffalo

Reporting the Results of an Interview

Reporting the results of an interview requires the identification of the person interviewed and information concerning her/his authority, and the appropriate use of connectors. Readers need signals that indicate that the information they are reading are the result of an interview with an expert. Some structures for introductions of authority and introductory connectors are below. Notice the use of commas.

- **According to X, Chair of the Physics Department of Harvard University, ...**

- **As X, who is the Mayor of Washington, D.C., states, ...**

- **X, two-time national rodeo champion, states (indicates, reports, suggests), ...**

- **As X stated, (indicated, reported, suggested, pointed out), ...**

- **X also indicated (stated, suggested, advised, pointed out) that ...**

Exercise I

Read the paragraphs below. Each paragraph uses an interview to develop the paragraph. Notice the method(s) of development used in each paragraph (narration, process, definition, comparison-contrast, cause-effect). Underline the connectors in each paragraph. Then answer the questions that follow each paragraph.

I

According to Dr. William Brown, Professor of Botany at Colorado State University, there are two important ways to improve olive production: replanting and regeneration. Of the two, regeneration is better because it is quicker and easier. As Dr. Brown stated, "Replanting consists of prolonged and difficult preparations of the soil, and this preparation must be done by hand because plows cannot get between the trees." As Dr. Brown went on to explain, the next step in replanting is digging a hole that is one meter square and one meter deep, and the ovule is placed there and covered with soil. The ovule is the protuberance on the old olive tree; ovules exist on many parts of the trunk, often just below the ground's surface. From the ovule comes the new olive tree. On the other hand, regeneration involves cutting back the old, diseased olive trees. Dr. Brown described the process: "The ovules beneath the ground remain, and the parent tree above ground is removed. The ovules root easily, form their own root systems, and they absorb water and nutrients from the parent root." Thus, with one simple operation, the olive tree is regenerated. The results are the same for both methods: younger, healthier, more fruitful trees.

Abdessatar Omezine
(Tunisia)

1. With a small group of classmates, decide the method(s) of paragraph development used in this paragraph: explanatory (process, definition, answering questions), comparison and/or contrast, and cause and/or effect. Use details from the paragraph to support your opinion.

2. With your group, identify the techniques of support used in this paragraph: facts, examples, description, and/or personal experience.

3. Discuss with your group the punctuation used in the direct quotations in this paragraph.

4. Write a title for this paragraph.

II
Why Do Flowers Smell Good?

Usually the smell of a flower can range from sweet (like vanilla) to fresh, like the smell of spring. According to Dr. Greg Brown, Professor of Botany at the University of Wyoming, flowers do not smell good in order to please humans, but rather to attract "a specific pollinator," that is, an insect or bird that will carry pollen from one flower to another for reproduction. Dr. Brown stated that "pollination is biology;" different flowers smell different because of differences in the chemistry of the plant. The actual odor is produced by volatile oils on the hairy stems in the middle of the flower that are called "osmophores."

Flowers smell different, Dr. Brown indicated, because the insect pollinators expect different smells. For example, bats like fruity or musty odors, but some butterflies prefer sweeter "vectors" (fragrances). Some insects even prefer flowers that smell like rotten meat or burnt rubber! Dr. Brown also pointed out that, in this respect, people are similar to insect or bird pollinators. That is, humans' sense of smell as well as their preferences for different fragrances are individual; we all smell flowers slightly differently.

Chris Fogstad
(Norway)

1. Who is the audience for this paragraph? How do you know? How does the audience for this paragraph differ from the audience of the previous paragraph? Contrast the vocabulary of the two paragraphs to support your opinion.

2. Underline the signals to the reader that this paragraph is the result of an interview. How does the use of the expert's knowledge help the success of the paragraph?

3. What techniques of support are used in this paragraph? Be specific.

4. Write a concluding sentence for this paragraph.

Writing Assignment 4

Choose one of the topics below (or choose another topic of interest to you). Interview an authority about this subject. Then write a paragraph that reports some of the results of your interview. Use appropriate introductory information about the person you interviewed, and use appropriate connectors. Your audience for this paragraph is your teacher (or another university professor).

TOPICS: McDonald's' restaurants are very popular
Children should/should not be given everything they want
A law in my country that should be changed

Pre-Writing and Drafting: In your journal, write a paragraph about why you chose your topic and who, exactly, you will interview to gather information for your paragraph. Then construct the questions for your interview (use the guidelines on page 170).

Interview the authority. Study your notes, and begin to draft your paragraph. Remember that some of the information you have gathered will not fit into your paragraph. Construct a basic (or expanded) point paragraph outline and a possible topic sentence. Use the Audience Guidelines and Paragraph Planning Guidelines (on the inside front cover of this book) to help develop your paragraph. Revise your draft to make it more effective for your reader.

Peer Feedback: With two other classmates, share the rough draft of your paragraph. Cover the draft of each of your classmates' paragraphs before you read them. Read just the topic sentence of each. Then, at the end of the paragraph, write the questions that you think will be answered in the paragraph. Then read each paragraph. Were your questions answered? Help your classmates as you read their rough drafts by:

- suggesting modification of the topic sentence
- suggesting additional detail in the paragraph (be specific!)
- marking any grammar or sentence structure errors you find

Discuss the results of your reading with your classmates.

Revision: Using the advice of your classmates and the Revision Guidelines (on the inside back cover of this book), write a paragraph **in your journal** that describes the changes you will make in your paragraph draft. Explain <u>why</u> you will make each change. Then make those changes, and write the final draft of your paragraph.

Surveys

Sometimes the opinions, preferences, or views of a number of people are necessary as evidence. Like interviews, surveys (also called questionnaires) are a way of gathering evidence about a topic. While you could write a paragraph about just your opinion, an audience might be interested in a variety of viewpoints, or your academic writing task may ask you to include the opinions of others.

The results of a survey can be used to support ideas in any kind of paragraph: explanation, comparison-contrast, cause-effect, or another method of development. Moreover, results from a single survey can be used in several (multiple) paragraphs. For example, you may want to write about whether students on your campus prefer to live in dormitories or in apartments (comparison-contrast); in another paragraph, you might report on the results of a survey question about why the students chose either dormitory life or apartment life (cause-effect). Evidence for both of these paragraphs could come from the same survey.

Constructing a simple questionnaire (survey) is not difficult if you follow these guidelines.

1. At the beginning of the survey, write one or two sentences that describe the purpose of your survey for the people who will complete it.

2. Collect information about the people who will respond to your survey (called "respondents"). For example, at the beginning of your survey, ask for information concerning age (or year in school), gender (male or female), native country, amount of time in the U.S., or any other piece of information that might be relevant to the results of your survey. Do not ask for the name of the respondent.

3. Limit your survey questions so that those people completing the survey (the respondents) can answer the questions quickly. For example, ask questions that can be answered "yes" or "no" or <u>give</u> the possible answers such as

    A. always, usually, sometimes, or never

    B. one week, two weeks, three weeks, or more than three weeks

    C. agree, disagree, don't know

    D. excellent, very good, good, fair, poor

4. Keep your questions objective. Do not make judgments. For example, write:

Do you prefer ice cream or yogurt?   NOT

Do you prefer <u>wonderful</u> ice cream or <u>terrible</u> yogurt?

5. Ask classmates or friends to read and complete the rough draft of your survey, and to make suggestions for improvement.

6. Include a copy of the survey with the final draft of the writing assignment.

Exercise J

Below are three surveys written by students to gather information for several paragraphs. The first survey was designed to answer the question "Why?" The results will describe several <u>reasons</u> why people like or do not like the theater. The second was designed to gather information to answer the questions about homework given in an intensive English language program. The third gathers information about a drinking law. The resulting paragraphs will answer such explanatory questions as "How much?" "What?" and "How do you feel about homework?"

With a small group of classmates, analyze the survey questions. Do they fulfill the guidelines for surveys above? How could each survey be improved?

I
TOPIC: Why do/don't you like to go to the theater?

    This is a survey I am doing so that I can write a paper for my freshman composition class. Please answer questions below and return the survey to me. In questions 2-7, please mark one **X** for each statement under **SA** (strongly agree), **A** (agree), **U** (undecided), **D** (disagree), or **SD** (strongly disagree). Then please write your opinion in response to question 8.

    Thank you for your help.

1. Demographic Data

Name _____   Age _____

Country _____

	SA	A	U	D	SD
2. I like to go to the theater.	—	—	—	—	—
3. I go to the theater often.	—	—	—	—	—
4. Going to the theater is a pleasant event.	—	—	—	—	—
5. Going to the theater is an unpleasant event.	—	—	—	—	—
6. The theater is an unreal world that is not important.	—	—	—	—	—
7. The theater reflects our life and makes it better.	—	—	—	—	—
8. Why do you like (do not like) to go to the theater?	_____

Evelyn Kim
(Russia)

II
TOPIC: Homework in the IELI

Please complete the following survey by circling the answer that best describes your attitudes and schedules about homework. All students in the IELI will have an opportunity to complete this survey. Your name will not be used in the results. I will post a copy of the results of this survey outside of classroom 604. Thank you for your help.

Age _____   Gender: (male, female)   English Level:_____

1. When do you do homework? (Morning; Lunch; Afternoon; Night)

2. Where do you do homework? (Dorm room; Cafeteria; Other: _____)

3. Do you like homework? (Yes; No; Maybe/Sometimes)

4. Is the homework difficult for you? (Yes, always; Yes, some of it; No, not usually)

5. How long does it take to do homework? (1–2 hours; 3–4 hours; 5–6 hours; 7+ hours)

6. Do you always finish your homework? (Yes; No; Maybe/Sometimes)

7. Which subject has the most homework? (Reading–Writing; Grammar; Speaking; Listening)

8. Does someone help you with your homework? (Yes; No; Sometimes)

9. Do you get good grades on your homework? (Yes; No; Maybe/Sometimes)

10. Do you have homework every day? (Yes; No)

Shelley Reid's ESL writing students
Intensive English Language Institute
State University of New York/Buffalo

III
TOPIC: State Drinking Laws

This survey is about the state drinking law which went into effect on January 1, 1990. This law prohibits drinking alcohol for anyone under the age of 21.

This survey is just for a class project. I would appreciate it if you would give an honest answer. Thank you for your help.

1. Your sex: male _____   female _____

2. Your age: _____

3. Have you heard about the state drinking law which prohibits anyone under 21 years from drinking alcohol?   yes _____   no _____

4. Do you drink alcohol?   yes _____   no _____

   A. If <u>yes</u>, when was the last time you drank alcohol?

      date: _____

   B. If <u>no</u>, is it because you honor the state drinking law?

      yes _____   no _____

5. Do you know any student at the university who is under 21 years old and drinks alcohol?   yes _____   no _____

6. Do you think the state drinking law should remain at 21 years?

   yes _____   no _____

   A. If no, what do you think the age should be? _____

7. Why or why not do you think this drinking law is justified?

   Comment: _____

Olé Peter Skuusrud
(Norway)

Writing Assignment 5

With a small group of classmates, use Survey II above (about homework in an intensive English language program). Each student in your group will ask four friends to complete the survey. With your group, tabulate the results of the survey; that is, count how many people answered each of the questions in what ways. Make a chart that reports the survey results.

Then, with your group, write a single paragraph reporting the results of the survey. Use appropriate connectors. Your audience is a group of students not in your class.

> **Pre-Writing and Drafting:** In your journal, use information from the survey and the survey results to construct a basic (or expanded) point paragraph outline and a possible topic sentence.

> **Collaborative Writing:** With your group, decide on the most appropriate topic sentence for your paragraph. With one person in the group serving as the "writer," decide what sentences, and what details, should be in the paragraph. Write a rough draft of that paragraph.
>
> Make copies of that paragraph for each person in the group. As you read your copy of the paragraph, use the Revision Guidelines (on the inside back cover of this book) to improve the paragraph. Then discuss your revisions with other members of your group.

> **Revision:** Revise the rough draft of the paragraph, using the advice of the group and the Revision Guidelines (on the inside back cover of this book). Write the final draft of the paragraph.

Writing Assignment 6

With a small group of classmates, select one of the topics below (or another topic that interests your group) to construct a 5-8 question (or statement) survey. The survey results may be used in an explanation, comparison-contrast, or cause-effect paragraph. Ask about 20 people to complete the survey (that is, each group member will survey 4-6 people).

As a group, tabulate the survey results. Each group; member will then write about some of the results of the survey in a well organized paragraph. Your audience is your teacher (or another academic professor).

- Smoking
- Music
- Diets

- Secondary school students holding part-time jobs
- Teachers giving grades in university classes
- Children learning foreign languages

> **DAY 1: Collaborative Pre-Writing and Drafting:** With your group, use the Paragraph Planning Guidelines (on the inside front cover of this book) to choose a subject and decide on a purpose for the group survey. Then narrow your subject to a topic. Construct the draft of 5-8 questions (or statements). In addition, construct the top part of the survey that describes the survey for your

respondents and asks for information about the respondents. Follow the guidelines for survey construction on pp. 175–176. Make 3-5 copies of your survey draft.

DAY 2: Peer Feedback: Assign a number to each person in your group (1, 2, 3, 4, 5). Then, the Number 1 people from each group should form a new group, and the Number 2 people another group, and so forth. Read and complete each of the surveys in the group. As you complete your classmates' surveys, help your classmates by:

• writing suggestions on the survey about the vocabulary, sentence structure, or content that will result in a clearer survey

      A. do you understand each question/statement?

      B. is each question/statement easy to answer?

      C. are there any judgmental words in the statements?

• discussing what you think the purpose of each survey is

• marking any errors in sentence structure or grammar

DAY 3: Collaborative Revision: With your <u>original</u> group, revise your survey. Use the advice of your other classmates to make the survey clear, objective, and easy. Then write a final draft of the survey.

DAY 4: Administer the survey.

DAY 5: Peer Feedback: With your original group, tabulate the results of the survey. Then discuss the results.

1. Were any of the results expected? Which? Why did you expect them?

2. Were any of the results a surprise? Which? Why?

3. What were the most interesting results? Why?

With your group, decide who should write paragraphs about which of the data. Choose from the possibilities below, or make your own choices.

1. introduction: why the group chose the topic (the purpose of the survey)

2. paragraph of summary about the first half of the survey results

3. paragraph of summary about the second half of the survey results

4. paragraph discussing the most interesting results

5. paragraph discussing the most surprising results

6. paragraph discussing the ways in which the results were expected

7. paragraph comparing (and/or contrasting) the expectations of the group with the reality of the results

DAY 6: Peer Feedback: With your <u>numbered</u> group of classmates (1, 2, 3, 4, 5), read the paragraph drafts that are not your own. At the end of each paragraph:

- write two questions (or suggestions) that will help the author
- write what you think is the most interesting detail in the paragraph

Then discuss the survey results and the paragraphs in your group.

DAY 7: Collaborative Revision: Using the advice of your classmates, revise your paragraph draft. Then write the final draft of your paragraph.

Sentence Combining Exercise

The jokes below are written in short, choppy sentences, and words are often repeated. Combine some of the sentences so that the jokes flow more smoothly. Eliminate some of the repeated words, and use appropriate connectors.

I

A scientist did an experiment. He tested a fly. He tested its hearing. He cut off something. It was one of the fly's legs. Then he spoke to the fly. He told it to move. The fly moved. It moved very slowly. The scientist cut off all the legs. They were the fly's legs. Then he spoke again to the fly. He told it to move. The fly didn't move. The scientist wrote. He wrote his results. This was the result: If you cut off all the fly's legs, he can't hear.

Mohamed Azrak
(Syria)

II

In ancient China, there was a temple. It was on the mountain. It was on top. The mountain was high. It was so high. The monk had to go downhill. He went downhill every day. He went to fetch water. The water was for drinking. He used a bar. He use two buckets. The buckets hung on the bar. Each bucket hung at the end of the bar. The buckets hung on opposite ends of the bar. One day, another monk came. He helped the first monk. They fetched water together. Each man held the bar. Each held one end of the bar. They put one bucket in the middle. The next day, a third monk joined them. They became lazy. All three monks carried the bar. One monk was at each end of the bar. One monk was in the middle of the bar. But there was no bucket. So they had no water to drink.

Now, in a university in China, a student wrote this story in English: "One monkey had water to drink, two monkeys had water to drink., but three monkeys didn't have water to drink."

Yuming Deng
(People's Republic of China)

III

There was a man. He was rich. He was sitting. He was on a park bench. He was looking at the birds. Suddenly a man got close. The man was poor. He was a tramp. He said, "I haven't tasted food. I haven't tasted it for five days." The rich man didn't want to be bothered. He spoke. He said to the poor man, "Don't worry. It still tastes the same."

Sergio Paz
(Honduras)

8

Multiple Paragraphs

I have trouble with writing because I always want to say too much and begin to construct sentences that are too complicated. I know exactly what and how I want to write, but suddenly I don't know any words anymore. I try to translate the sentence from German to English but that never really works out.

Nanna Meyer
(Switzerland)

U.S. academic prose often requires more than one paragraph. Furthermore, because academic prose requires **evidence**, often a single point paragraph outline is not sufficient for the amount of essential specific detail to support ideas or opinions. Therefore, it is often necessary to construct **multiple paragraphs**. Each paragraph of an essay, a technical report, a critique, or a research paper will have the same general form: a general **topic sentence** with **controlling ideas** followed by facts, examples, physical descriptions, and/or personal experiences that explain, define, clarify, and/or illustrate those controlling ideas.

Developing Multiple Paragraphs

Many of the paragraphs in this book could be expanded to two or three or more paragraphs of 125–225 words. The expansion of these single paragraph ideas to multiple paragraphs involves:

- a topic sentence with controlling ideas for each of the paragraphs
- the addition (sometimes) of one or more points that further explain the controlling ideas in the topic sentence
- the addition of more specific detail to the points in the paragraph

Almost any paragraph can be expanded into two or more paragraphs. For example, a single paragraph could be written about the assignment "Write about the problems you had during your first weeks in the U.S." The writer could write a single paragraph about a single problem s/he had, or the writer could write several paragraphs about several problems, as the paragraphs below demonstrate. Notice the "overall topic sentence" that acts like an umbrella over all the paragraphs. Each underlined topic sentence in the paragraphs that follow relates to the overall topic sentence.

OVERALL TOPIC SENTENCE: I had several problems during my first week in the U.S.

The first problem was about my dress. I am accustomed to dressing in long clothes and covering my head because my Islamic religion requires this. Therefore, I decided not to change my style of dress when I came to the U.S. When I first arrived at the airport in New York, I observed many people looking at me because my clothes were very strange for them. Two strangers asked me why I was dressed in those clothes. My husband answered their questions, and the people admired his answers. But most of the people didn't ask me; they just stared at me a long time, and some of them laughed. At this time I felt angry and thought that Americans were very impolite.

Another problem made me cry. When I first arrived, I didn't speak English very well, and that caused a serious problem. When my husband went to the airport to meet his friend, I stayed in our new apartment to cook dinner and wash our clothes. But when I went to the laundry room, I closed the door to the apartment, and I forgot the key inside. After that, I was afraid because I didn't know what to do. I saw other women in the laundry room, and I tried to tell them my problem, but they didn't understand me. Finally, they knew what I needed, and they helped me. They found the apartment manager, and he unlocked my apartment. But when I was alone in my apartment, I cried because I had been so afraid.

The problem that made me the most sad when I first came to the U.S. was loneliness. I came here with my husband because he was going to attend graduate school. But when he went to the university, I was alone. Always before in my country, I had my family and many friends. When my husband went to work, I had a busy and happy life. But my first days alone in the U.S. were very difficult. I missed my family, especially my mother, and I missed my other relatives, too. After I cleaned my house each morning, I had nothing to do and no one to talk with. I wrote many long letters to my family, but still I remained very lonely. Fortunately, this problem has become less difficult as I have made new friends, but the first weeks were terrible.

Suha Al-Shuwai
(Kuwait)

Other multiple paragraphs are written when the author is telling a story that has several parts. Below is an example of a **narrative** (that is, a story). Notice the chronological organization of the story, which the author indicates for the reader by using chronological connectors. Each paragraph describes a single "scene" in the story.

NOTE: Stories do not usually follow the forms of academic writing (that is, topic sentences and use of evidence).

A Fable

It happened <u>one day</u> that, as usual, King Lion the 4th fell asleep after a full dinner. He hadn't slept twenty minutes when he was awakened by a little green fly. She was so importunate and buzzed so noisily that the lion couldn't help waking up. The fly displayed utter disrespect for the lion by interrupting his dreams.

The lion felt extremely frustrated. <u>First</u> of all, he thought that it was a criminal conspiracy of his enemies or that somebody wished to overthrow him. But <u>then</u>, on reflection, the lion put these thoughts away. There were no enemies in nature for him. Still, he was in a foul humor. <u>Meanwhile</u>, the culprit was making rounds over the lion's head at full throttle. She didn't care a straw that the lion felt pummeled and bruised because she was convinced that he was occupying her territory. So the lion was at his wit's end.

<u>Then</u>, suddenly he remembered about the retired sparrow who had been forced into retirement like a broken chair. The sparrow's temper was very short, and that accounted for his forced retirement. The lion thought that it would be a pretty good idea to bring the sparrow back. <u>When</u> the sparrow stood in front him, the lion set his task: to kill the fly. That was an easy job for the sparrow; in a flash, not a trace of the fly remained.

But this action played into the sparrow's hands. The lion was very grateful to the sparrow and suggested that the sparrow come out of retirement to serve him, but the sparrow thought, "If I got the sack once, I could get the sack again." He didn't say that to the lion, though. <u>In the end</u>, he just flew away without making any comment.

Igor Ivanov
(Siberia)

Writing Assignment 1

Write three paragraphs about one of the topics below (or a topic of your own choice). Choose your audience for this series of paragraphs. For each paragraph, use the Audience Analysis and Paragraph Planning Guidelines (on the inside front cover of this book).

Topics: Vacation places in your country

Superstitions in your culture

Differences between teachers in your country and in the U.S.

The reasons you are majoring in _____.

Peer Feedback: With two classmates, discuss your chosen topic. Offer your classmates suggestions (and ask appropriate questions) to help them write interesting paragraphs. Ask your classmates to evaluate your ideas and details for your paragraphs. Take notes in your journal. Then, in your journal, write a paragraph evaluating the help you gave and the help you received in your group.

Pre-Writing and Drafting: In your journal, use two pre-writing techniques to collect information for your paragraphs. As you organize your information, consider your audience. Make a point paragraph outline for each paragraph. Then write a rough draft of each paragraph.

Peer Feedback: With the two classmates from your original group, read the six paragraphs that are not your own. As you read the first set of three paragraphs:

- underline the topic sentence and circle the controlling ideas for each paragraph
- write 2-3 questions that you expect will be answered in the paragraph
- put an asterisk in the margin where you find especially good detail

As you read the second set of paragraphs:

- mark any error in grammar or sentence structure that you see
- write one question or suggestion at the end of each paragraph to help the author

Discuss the marks and suggestions that you made with your classmates.

Revision: Using the advice of your classmates, and the Revision Guidelines (on the inside back cover of this book), make changes that will improve each of your paragraphs. Write the final drafts of your paragraphs. Finally, **in your journal,** write a paragraph about:

- what was easy about writing your paragraphs (and why)
- what was difficult (and why)
- what you learned from revising your paragraphs

Peer Feedback: Read the final drafts of paragraphs written by classmates in your original group. **In your journal,** write about the set of paragraphs that you most enjoyed. Why did you find those paragraphs most interesting and valuable? Use specific detail from that set of paragraphs (that you remember) to support your opinion.

Expanding a Rough Draft

Another way to write multiple paragraphs is to expand a single paragraph that you have already written. Often you will be able to divide the original topic sentence and the existing paragraph into two parts (or more), and then add more detail to each paragraph. For example, the comparison/contrast point paragraph outline below can easily be divided and expanded with the use of additional detail (facts, examples, physical description, and/or personal experience). The original paragraph is on page 38 of this book.

Topic Sentence: **There are many differences between the way American parents raise their children and the way parents raise children in Saudi Arabia.**

1. In the U.S., fathers and mothers are equally responsible for raising their children.
    A. both parents teach, play with, and discipline the children
    B. both parents treat their children like adults
        (1) expect them to be responsible and independent
        (2) expect them to earn money

2. In Saudi Arabia, parents have separate roles in raising their children.
    A. father's responsibilities
        (1) earns money to support the family completely
        (2) father makes all family decisions
    B. mother responsibilities
        (1) everyday care and love
        (2) guidance and basic schooling

Concluding Sentence: The result of these differences is that American children, who become adults in childhood, often behave like children when they are adults, but Saudi Arabian children, who have passed through all the stages of childhood, are ready to behave like adults when they reach maturity.

Ahmed Al-Himaidi
(Saudi Arabia)

The author of this paragraph has tried to do too much in one paragraph. There is not sufficient detail to support the controlling ideas and persuade the audience. Below are two point paragraph outlines that divide the outline above. Notice that, following each of the points, the techniques of support that must be used to support that point (facts, examples, physical experience, and/or personal experience) are indicated. The additional evidence for each paragraph will make the paragraphs more substantial and thus more persuasive.

OVERALL TOPIC SENTENCE: There are many differences between the way American parents raise their children and the way parents raise children in Saudi Arabia.

Topic Sentence: **In the U.S., children are raised to be responsible for themselves and to be independent from their parents, and the parents have equal responsibilities.**

1. Both parents raise the children.
    A. teach them   +   (examples)
    B. play with them   +   (examples)
    C. discipline them   +   (examples)

2. Both parents want their children to be responsible for themselves.
   A. parents work outside the home   +   (description, facts)
   B. leave the children with a baby sitter   +   (description, facts)
   C. consequences result in children being responsible
      (1) distance develops between children
          and parents   +   (examples)
      (2) children learn to care
          for themselves   +   (examples)

3. Both parents encourage their children to earn money outside the home
   A. even very young children have jobs   +   (facts, examples)
   B. most teenage children become
      financially independent   +   (examples)
   C. consequences result in children becoming independent
      (1) make their own decisions   +   (examples)
      (2) spend their own money   +   (facts, examples)
      (3) leave home at a very young age   +   (examples)

Topic Sentence: **In contrast, in my country, Saudi Arabia, parents treat their children as dependents, and each parent has separate responsibilities.**

1. father's responsibilities
   A. complete financial support of the family +   (examples)
   B. Authority to make major decisions
      for the children   +   (examples)
      (1) clothes to wear   +   (personal experience, facts)
      (2) friends to make   +   (personal experience, examples)
      (3) schools to attend   +   (facts, examples)
      (4) who to marry   +   (facts, examples)
   C. duty to communicate his experiences
      to his sons to prepare them for life   +   (examples)

2. mother's responsibilities
   A. cares for everyday needs   +   (descriptions, examples)
   B. provides love and guidance   +   (personal experience, description)
   C. teaches the daughters about their
      roles in life   +   (examples)

3. consequences
   A. children are dependent
      on their parents   +   (examples)
      (1) for money   +   (examples)
      (2) for advice   +   (examples)
   B. children behave as children   +   (personal experience, examples)

The Essay

When multiple paragraphs are about one topic (for example, problems you had when you first arrived in the U.S.) and when those paragraphs are related to one another, they form the **body** of an essay. Academic essays begin with a paragraph of introduction. The introduction usually ends with an overall topic sentence (called a **thesis statement**). The thesis statement is the most general, most important sentence in the essay, and it has controlling ideas that will be supported in the paragraphs of the essay. Following the introductory paragraph are the multiple paragraphs, called the body of the essay, that explain, define, and/or illustrate the overall topic sentence (thesis statement). Finally, at the end of the essay, there is a short a concluding paragraph.

Each of the multiple body paragraphs has a topic sentence, each is organized chronologically, most-to-least important (or vice-versa), or by equal points. The points in each paragraph are supported by facts, examples, physical description, and/or personal experience. And the focus of each multiple paragraph can be explanatory (process, definition, or clarification), evaluative, and/or persuasive. In other words, multiple paragraphs, the kinds of paragraphs you have been writing in this class, can become the body paragraphs of an essay.

Exercise A

Below are examples of multiple paragraphs and multiple paragraph outlines that have been developed by students from their pre-writing. Read the paragraphs and outlines. As you read, analyze the organization of each paragraph: process, definition, clarification (that is, making a concept clear), comparison-contrast, or cause-effect. Then answer the questions that follow each.

I

Rough Draft (Brainstorming)

A major problem in Damascus is the cost of housing; many things have caused the price of houses to increase. First, the population of Damascus ten years ago was 700,000; however, now the population is more than two million. As a result, the number of available houses has decreased, and housing prices have escalated. Second, construction materials like iron, cement, and wood have become very costly. World economics, some shortages of supplies, and production expenses have caused the prices of these materials to nearly double in the last decade. Third, the price of land is 15 times higher than it was ten years ago; therefore, ordinary people can't even afford to buy land, much less to build a house. The effects of these prices touch most young people who live in Damascus. For example, many of them cannot marry because traditionally, young couples must be able to buy a house before marriage. In some cases, these young people may marry, but then they will have to spend as much as 50% of their income on renting a small apartment. Consequently, most of the young people leave Damascus, go to other countries, and earn higher salaries for several years before they return to Damascus and settle down. If the government could solve the problem of expensive housing in Damascus, many of the social problems in that city would be eliminated.

Expansion: Multiple Paragraph Outline

OVERALL TOPIC SENTENCE: A major problem in Damascus is the cost of housing; many things have caused the price of houses to increase.

Topic Sentence: **Many things have caused the prices of houses in Damascus to increase.**

1. The population explosion
   A. ten years ago: 700,000
   B. today: two million

2. Construction materials have increased in price because of
   A. world economics   +   (facts, examples)
   B. shortages of supplies   +   (facts, examples)
   C. production expenses   +   (facts, examples)

3. The price of land has increased
   A. 15 times higher
   B. beyond the reach of most people   +   (personal experience)

4. Housing prices have escalated because
   A. fewer houses available   +   (facts)
   B. less money available   +   (facts)

Topic Sentence: **The effects of these prices touch most young people who live in Damascus.**

1. They cannot marry
   A. tradition expects married couple to buy
        their own house   +   (personal experience)
   B. if they cannot, they cannot marry   +   (personal experience)
2. Those who do marry live badly
   A. in small apartments   +   (examples, description)
   B. spend 50% of their salary on rent   +   (facts, examples)
3. Therefore, many young people leave Damascus
   A. to work in other countries
        for better wages   +   (facts, examples)
   B. to save money to return to Damascus
        to buy a house   +   (facts, examples)

Concluding Sentence: If the government could solve the problem of expensive housing in Damascus, many of the social problems in that city would be eliminated.

Mohamed Azrak
(Syria)

1. These paragraphs focus on causes and effects. With a small group of classmates, determine which are causes, and which are effects. Do any causes become effects (and vice-versa)?

2. With this small group of classmates, analyze the audience for these paragraphs. How do you know? What supporting details would be persuasive for this audience?

3. With your group, generate specific supporting details (examples, experience, facts, and description) that the author might use for these paragraphs. Remember: you will have to "create" the detail.

4. With your group, write a draft of the completed paragraphs.

II

Sociologic Baseline Study

OVERALL TOPIC SENTENCE: A socioeconomic baseline study is a scientific method of studying social phenomena that influences the economic conditions of a society.

This method of study is performed collaboratively by a group of scientists consisting of sociologists, economists, and anthropologists. The method is most effective when used to study societies that we know little or nothing about. For example, these scientists try to understand patterns in a little-known society by using multiple forms of investigation that include surveys and interviews (that is, participative investigation), laboratory experiments, and field work. After they have gathered their data, the scientists analyze those data, using statistical methods. Finally, the results of the analysis are interpreted and summarized, and the final report is written.

One such study was conducted by the University of Wyoming in the Bay Region of Somalia, East Africa. [This study was financed partly by the World Bank and by USAID (United States Agency for International Development).] A group of experts, consisting of a sociologist, an anthropologist, and an economist, studied the social conditions of a small Somali tribe called Rahanweyn. This tribe was known to be agropasturalist; that is, they both farm and keep livestock. They play an important role in the Somali economy; consequently, the Somali government was interested in further development of this region. However, very little was known about both how this tribe lived and how it farmed. When the group of experts arrived, they visited randomly selected villages; they gave out surveys and interviewed individuals. Finally, after they had analyzed the data they had collected, they delivered their report to the Somali government, which used their report as a master plan for carrying out policies of development programs.

Ahmed Mohamed Ali
(Somalia)

1. Circle the controlling ideas in the (underlined) topic sentences. Draw lines that connect words in each topic sentence with the overall topic sentence. What questions do you expect will be answered in each of the following paragraphs?

2. Were your questions answered? What advice might you offer the author to improve and/or expand his paragraphs?

3. The paragraphs above are focused on extended definition. What techniques of support does the author use to explain the topic? Use details from the paragraphs to support your answer.

4. The second sentence of the second paragraph, which is bracketed [ ], does not help the reader. How could that problem be solved?

III

(Rough Draft)

The process of developing a dam for hydraulic power (that is, water power) consists of many complex steps and involves many specialists. First, the need for the project must be determined; both the demand capacity and the installed capacity must be considered. Second, the size of the urban area, the kind of area (that is, residential or industrial), and the potential for population growth must be studied. Finally, hydrology research must be conducted: data must be collected concerning precipitation, soil constituents, and river parameters. Only then can the structural designs for both the foundation and the structure itself be made. After all these complex steps, the dam is ready to be constructed.

Christian Blanco
(Colombia)

Plan for a Multiple Paragraph Outline

OVERALL TOPIC SENTENCE: The process of developing a dam for hydraulic power (that is, water power) consists of many complex steps and involves many specialists.

Topic Sentence: **First, the need for the project must be determined; both the demand capacity and the installed capacity must be considered.**

1. Who considers the need?   +   (facts, examples)

2. How is the need determined?   +   (facts)

A. demand capacity	+	(definition)
B. installed capacity	+	(definition)

3. What data result in the decision
   to complete the project?   +   (facts, description)

Topic Sentence: **Second, the size of the urban area, the kind of area (that is, residential or industrial), and the potential for population growth must be studied.**

1. Who considers these problems?   +   (facts, examples)

2. How are the data collected?   +   (examples, physical description)

3. What data result in the decision
   to complete the project?   +   (facts, examples)

Topic Sentence: **Finally, hydrology research must be conducted: data must be collected concerning precipitation, soil constituents, and river parameters.**

1. How is the research conducted?   +   (facts, physical description)

2. What specific data are collected?   +   (facts, examples)

3. What data result in the decision
   to complete the project?   +   (facts, examples)

Topic Sentence: **Only then can the structural designs for both the foundation and the structure itself be made.**

1. Who does the structural designs?   +   (facts, examples)

2. What is involved in the design
   of the foundation?   +   (facts, description)

3. What is involved in the design
   of the actual structure?   +   (facts)

Concluding Sentence: After all these complex steps, the dam is ready to be constructed.

1. Who is the audience for this topic? How do you know? For what audience might the original paragraph be appropriate?

2. What other questions might you ask the author?

3. Underline the passive voice used in the paragraph and the outline. Why is passive voice used?

4. Write the second sentence for one of the outlined paragraphs above. Use appropriate connectors.

Writing Assignment 2

Choose a comparison-contrast paragraph or a cause-effect paragraph you wrote previously in this class. Expand this paragraph to two (or three) paragraphs by dividing the material and adding more specific detail.

> **Pre-writing and Drafting:** Read the original paragraph carefully. Then, **in your journal**, write about how your intend to expand this paragraph. As you write, begin generating specific detail to support the additional paragraphs. Use the Audience Analysis and the Paragraph Planning Guidelines (on the inside front cover of this book) to plan the multiple paragraphs. Make a point paragraph outline for each planned paragraph. Then write a rough draft of each paragraph.
>
> **Peer Feedback:** With a small group of classmates, discuss the reason(s) you chose the paragraph you expanded, and how you expanded your original paragraph. Then read paragraphs that are not your own. Mark with an asterisk (*) any successful detail you find. As you read, take notes about the paragraphs **in your journal**.
> Note:
> - the topic for each set of paragraphs
> - what you learned as you read each set of paragraphs
> - suggestions (or questions) you have for the author

Finally, discuss the paragraphs you liked best with your group. Be specific. Then offer any suggestions (or questions) you have to each author.

> **Revision:** Using the advice from your classmates, and what you learned from reading your classmates' paragraphs, make changes that will improve your paragraphs. Write the final draft of your paragraphs. Then look again at the planning paragraph you wrote earlier **in your journal.** What additional changes did you make? Write a paragraph in your journal that describes the actual changes you have made in your revision. Explain why you made the changes.
>
> **Peer Feedback:** Read the final draft of the sets of paragraphs your original group members have written. **In your journal,** write about the changes made by one of the authors in her/his paragraphs. Were the changes successful? Why or why not?

Exercise B

Read the rough drafts of the paragraphs below. In each case, the paragraphs must be expanded with specific detail so that the audience will be more interested in the topic and the paragraphs will be more persuasive. With a small group of classmates, examine each draft, and answer the questions that follow.

I

Thailand—A Wonderful Resort Area

OVERALL TOPIC SENTENCE: **If I had a two-week vacation, I would go to Thailand because it is an excellent resort area.**

First, the weather is always fine, with 250 days of sunshine each year. <u>In Pattaya, there are beautiful beaches with coconut trees and white sand that last for miles and miles.</u> At the beach, I can smell the fresh breeze from the sea, and the sand is so fine as I try to touch it with my fingers. I cannot help lying on it, enjoying a sun bath. When the sun is too hot, I can jump into the blue water which is so clear that I may see some tropical fish swimming around. <u>If I want to see some of the Thai culture, there are many temples in Bangkok, which are all charming and sparkling under the sun since their windows and doors are usually made of colorful glass, crystal, and gold.</u> I can go inside and worship the Buddha, wishing him to bring me good fortune. <u>Besides the culture, every tourist likes to shop, and Thailand is a great place for shopping.</u> There are a lot of traditional handicrafts and ornaments made of shells. They charmingly sparkle in the golden sunlight. However, I find the most entertaining part of shopping in Thailand is bargaining. <u>After a day's touring, I am so hungry that I would like to enjoy a great Thai dinner in a restaurant built of coconut trees, where I can taste traditional Thai food, so tasty and different.</u>

<u>Concluding Sentence:</u> When I am in Thailand, all my troubles will fly away.

Chui Ho
(Thailand)

1. Examine the focus of this paragraph: process, definition, clarification (that is, making a concept clear), comparison-contrast, cause-effect? Use detail from the paragraph to support your opinion.

2. The author of this paragraph should be writing four paragraphs about this topic. With your small group of classmates, begin planning the paragraphs. Each person in the group should choose one of the (<u>underlined</u>) topic sentences and plan a point paragraph outline.

3. Generate specific supporting detail for the topic sentence you chose. Discuss that supporting detail with your classmates. Ask their advice about your detail, and offer them advice about the details they are generating.

4. Write a rough draft of the paragraph you have planned. Share that rough draft with your group.

II

Expectations and Surprises

INTRODUCTION: **Before I came to the U.S., I really expected two kinds of differences: One was the equality of the sexes, and the other was saying "yes" or "no" clearly.**

OVERALL TOPIC SENTENCE: **My expectations were fulfilled, but I was surprised by some other characteristics of the U.S.**

First of all, I expected to find equality of the sexes. In my country, we draw a distinction between sexes on jobs and opportunity; for example, most people think that it's not good for girls to study abroad by themselves, but it's all right for boys. In addition, it's hard for women to get a job after they are married. Even if they're not married, it's much harder to get a job than it is for men. *** As I expected, I have seen equality of the sexes in the U.S. No one distinguishes any jobs or majors between men and women. *** People don't think of men above women. I love that men and women have the same opportunities.

Secondly, I expected to learn to say "yes" and "no" as frankly as I wish. When I was in Korea, I couldn't say "yes" or "no" definitely. I hesitated to say "no," for instance, when someone asked me to do something for him, even though I didn't want to do it. I said "yes" because I didn't want to make him feel bad; I couldn't express myself as I meant, even when it was not good for me. But as I expected, Americans say directly what they really want. I need to say "yes" or "no" definitely. *** Instead of worrying that I can't express myself well, now I worry that I may express myself "too well" when I go back to Korea!

Although my two expectations were met, I was still surprised by what I didn't expect. [First, I was surprised that American parents educate their children to be so independent.] They try to make their children think and act for themselves, and they really respect the opinion of their children, even if they are young. [Second, I was surprised by the freedom.] Americans live and wear what they like. Some people even wear tattered clothes, but no one cares. Though they act as they want, they never harm others. Furthermore, they hug and kiss just about anywhere. [Third, I was surprised by the fairly conservative laws about alcohol and night clubs.] In my country, after graduating from high school, we can drink and go to the discotheque, but in the U.S., only people over 21 years old with an I.D. can. I thought American would be a more open society.

Heuiseong Lim
(Korea)

1. Notice that this essay begins with an introductory sentence. The Overall Topic Sentence is usually written at the end of the introductory sentence in academic English.

2. The first two paragraphs lack specific detail that will interest the reader. With a small group of classmates, suggest facts, examples, personal experience, and/or physical description that would support the sentences that come just <u>before</u> the three asterisks (***).

3. The final paragraph needs expansion. Possible topic sentences for separate paragraphs are bracketed [ ]. With your group, choose one of the sentences and write a point paragraph outline for that sentence. Discuss specific detail to support the topic sentence.

4. With your group, write a rough draft of that paragraph. Then, assign a number to each person in your group (1, 2, 3, 4). All students with 1 should gather in a new group; all students with 2 should gather in another group, etc. In these "fragmented" groups, share your group's paragraph with other class members.

III

Gossip (Rough Draft)

INTRODUCTION: **Gossip, at first glance, is often an innocent thing, and it is indispensable, even for a business talk. One can hardly imagine a conversation without at least a little piece of gossip; it makes a conversation colorful and light.**

OVERALL TOPIC SENTENCE: But gossip can be a dangerous and hurtful hobby.

<u>Gossip wouldn't do any harm if it weren't for gossip-mongers, people who are in charge of spreading reports about others.</u> They don't simply tittle-tattle; instead, they take great interest and find special pleasure in discussing and spreading gossip. *** In their interpretation, a piece of information acquires lots of disgusting details which are not true, or the information can be totally transformed into a lie, preserving only an external form. ***

<u>In this way, gossip can be a very convenient vehicle for deliberate distortion of facts.</u> And if it doesn't ruin a person's career or affect his family life, which is extreme and rather rare, it can leave a big black (or gray) stain on his reputation.***

<u>Gossip is especially dangerous for people who are going to get a new job, or who want to be elected somewhere, or who are going to marry.</u> *** Then, although the gossip may be "nothing but talk," the listener will subconsciously associate a person with the gossip. *** The effects of such gossip can be tragic.

Renata Tairbekova
(Russia)

1. Circle the controlling ideas in each of the (underlined) topic sentences. With a line, join the words in each topic sentence with the controlling ideas in the overall topic sentence (the **thesis statement**).

2. With a partner, underline the causes and the effects in the paragraphs above. Label the causes (C) and the effects (E).

3. The author of these paragraphs has not used adequate detail to support her points. With your partner, add 2-3 sentences of detail (facts, examples, description, or experience) at each of the five places you see asterisks (***).

4. Form a small group with another set of partners. Share your supporting detail. Select the best supporting detail and write a rough draft (one draft for the group) of the paragraphs.

Exercise C

Many of the paragraphs in previous chapters could be expanded to multiple paragraphs. Work with a small group of classmates. Choose two of the paragraphs listed below. Read the original paragraphs. Then discuss how to expand those paragraphs.

Chapter	Topic	Author	Page
2.	Women's Hair and Clothing	Maria Agaltsova	43
3.	Acapulco for Vacations	Alejandro Maiz	76
4.	Good Advice	Noemi Ramirez	101
5.	The Greenhouse Effect	Sosa Abraham	116
6.	Life in the Bush	Halimatou Tiemogo	147
7.	Returning to Buenos Aires	Ani Sala	160

After your discussion, generate the paragraph point outlines and necessary specific detail for the expansion.

Writing Assignment 3

Choose a topic that interests you. Choose the audience for your multiple paragraphs. Then write three paragraphs about that topic.

Peer Feedback: With a small group of classmates, discuss your chosen topic. Describe your audience, and ask your classmates to become that audience. Then ask those classmates to help you by asking questions about your topic that your audience might be interested in your answering. In your journal, take notes about your group's discussion.

Pre-Writing and Drafting: In your journal, use two pre-writing techniques that you have found successful to gather information about your topic. Analyze your audience **in your journal,** using the Audience Analysis Guidelines (on the inside front cover of this book). Then, using the Paragraph Planning Guidelines (on the inside front cover of this book), begin constructing an appropriate point paragraph outline for each of your paragraphs (a basic outline, an expanded outline, or an alternative outline). Write the rough draft of your paragraphs.

Peer Feedback: With the same group of classmates, read the sets of multiple paragraphs that are not your own. If you are the <u>first</u> reader:

- underline the topic sentences and circle the controlling ideas in each paragraph
- put an asterisk in the margin where you find successful detail
- at the end of the set of paragraphs, write 2 questions to help the author improve the paragraphs

If you are the <u>second</u> reader:

- underline the connectors in each paragraph of the set
- label the technique(s) of support in the margin of each paragraph
- at the end of the set of paragraphs, write two suggestions to help the a u t h o r improve the paragraphs

If you are the third reader:

- at the end of each paragraph, write the overall organization: chronological, most-to-least important (or vice-versa), or equal points
- at the end of each paragraph, write whether the paragraph was explanatory and/or evaluative
- at the end of the set of paragraphs, write an **overall topic sentence** (a thesis statement) for the set

Then, answer questions from your classmates about the comments and marks you made, and ask your classmates questions about their marks and comments on your rough draft.

Revision: Using the advice from your classmates and the Paragraph Revision Guidelines (on the inside back cover of this book), make improvements in your paragraphs. Then write the final draft of your paragraphs. **In your journal,** write a paragraph describing the changes you make; tell why you made those changes, and discuss why you think the changes improved your paragraphs. What did you learn about writing from this multiple paragraph assignment?

Peer Feedback: With your original group of classmates, read the final drafts of the sets of paragraphs. Take notes **in your journal** about the changes you find in those final drafts. Discuss with your classmates the changes they made. Finally, **in your journal,** write about the set of paragraphs that you found most interesting and valuable. Be specific about the changes your classmate made and how these changes improved her/his paragraph.

Sentence Combining Exercise

The jokes below are written with short, choppy sentences, and some of the information is repeated. Combine some of the sentences so that the jokes flow more smoothly. You will eliminate some of the words in order to combine the sentences effectively. Use appropriate connectors when necessary.

I

There was a man. There was another man. They were friends. They were in an asylum. It was an asylum for the insane. The first man spoke. He asked his friend, "Would you climb this tree? Would you catch the bird? The bird that is in the tree? The bird that is green?" The friend agreed. He climbed. What he climbed was the tree. He came back down. He didn't have the bird. The first man asked, "Where is the bird?" His friend replied, "I'm sorry. The bird hasn't ripened yet. It's still green!"

Omar Al-Mofadda
(Libya)

II

There were three people. They came back to their apartment They had been on a journey. It had been long. It had been tiresome. Their apartment was located on the 40th floor. But there was a problem. The electricity was off. The elevator did not work. They had to use the stairway. They climbed. There were slow. One of them made a suggestion. The suggestion was that each of them should tell a story. The story should be interesting. Then the time would pass. It would pass quickly. They all agreed. So the first person talked. He told a story. Then the second one talked. He told a story. By then, they were on the 35th floor. When the third person's turn came, he talked. He said, "I'd like to tell you a miserable and most interesting story. I left the key to our apartment in our car!"

Jiangshan Wang
(People's Republic of China)

III

Two men got angry. They were angry with each other. "I will kill you," A said. "I will kill you," B responded. Then they agreed. They agreed to fight. They agreed to duel. B said,"Where should we go?" A said, "Let's go to a quiet place, so nobody will see us."

The next day, they met. They were together. They took the train. But A bought a round-trip ticket. B bought only a one-way ticket. A said, "So you do not intend to return, eh?" B replied, "I always use my opponent's return ticket."

Xingwu Yang
(Mongolia)

9

Using Secondary Sources

When I began my research, I learned that the controversy I chose was a lot bigger than I thought.
I was very surprised to find as much evidence and examples for my viewpoint.

Anita Gundersen
(Norway)

Academic writing tasks often require (a) multiple paragraphs and (b) research. In the same way that the length of an academic writing assignment is determined by the professor, the type and amount of research depends on the assignment.

There are three basic types of research. Some academic assignments ask students to use their own experience or observation as evidence; a scientific laboratory report is a good example of <u>observational</u> and <u>experiential evidence</u>. Other research assignments will require gathering information from **primary sources** (<u>interviewing an expert</u> or <u>surveying a population</u>); studying a problem at the university (inadequate parking space, dormitory noise, a required computer science course) and writing about solutions to that problem might involve such primary source evidence. Another type of research requires the use of <u>secondary sources</u>: books, magazines, newspapers, and other materials available in the **university library**.

<u>NOTE:</u> many academic assignments require the use of two or all three of these types of research.

Academic Writing Tasks

Academic writing tasks should specify both the type(s) of research and the length of the assignment. For example, the directions below (taken from actual academic assignments) give students information about the assigned tasks. In those assignments that specify types of research, those types are identified in italics.

1. <u>Wood Science</u>: Provide the class with a 250-word *summary*, and a *bibliography* of at least 6 references (no books and no material from non-refereed sources). (library resources)

2. <u>Biochemical Engineering</u>: The maximum length for the paper is *10 single-spaced typewritten pages*, not including tables and figures.

3. <u>Genetics Laboratory Report</u>: Using the data collection sheet, *select* any two traits and *collect* an independent sample from about 35 persons other than members of the class. (survey)

4. <u>Marketing</u>: *Gather evidence* from news or magazine articles, copies of print ads, copies of press releases, *interviews* with company executives, photos of displays or outdoor advertising, samples of sales promotion material, direct mail pieces, *audio* or *videotapes* of ads or public service announcements. (observation, interviews, library resources)

5. The text of the paper should be *1–3 pages, typed, double-spaced*, 1-inch margins, 10- or 12-point type. You may turn the paper in on a *computer disk* in WordPerfect or Wordstar.

6. Environmental Issues: Keep this paper *under 4 pages*, not including the *bibliography* of 6–10 references. (library resources)

Academic Libraries

In previous chapters you studied the strategies of observing, interviewing, and surveying. This chapter will describe academic libraries. You may find that the U.S. academic library differs from libraries in your country in its materials, organization, and policies. For example, students in the U.S. usually have to locate library materials by themselves, although librarians are often available to answer students' questions.

The academic library is the heart and the brain of the U.S. college or university campus. The work you do in this chapter will help you become familiar with the materials available in the academic library for use as secondary sources in your academic writing. Throughout this chapter, specialized library vocabulary is boldfaced. Learning to use this vocabulary will make your library use easier and more successful.

Exercise A

1. Go to an academic library.

2. At the **information desk**, ask about a **library card**.

   A. If you have a student identification card, will it also serve as your library card?

   B. If not, what is the procedure for getting a library card?

3. Ask at the information desk about **library tours**: when are they? If possible, arrange to go on such a tour to learn about the different parts of the library.

Exercise B

*Read the paragraphs below, written by students after they had been to their college or university library. Define the **boldfaced** words of library vocabulary. Then do the exercise that follows.*

I

My college friends and I liked many things about our college library. First, the **magazine** and **newspaper sections** were located just inside the entrance to the library, so when we had a meeting, for example, we could wait for one another and read something interesting; there were newspapers from many countries, even mine! Another aspect of the library that we liked was the classification of materials because it was simple and complete. In fact, we usually didn't have to ask for help because we didn't have many problems **locating** books and other materials. However, if we did have questions, a librarian at the **reference desk** in the library would answer them. The best quality of the library was its private and group places to study. For example, several times we had to do a group project, and we continuously had to consult several different books, so we could meet in the library's **group study area**, speak together, even in loud voices, and not bother anyone. For these reasons, my friends and I spent much time in the library.

Albert Hemosillo
(Mexico)

II

What I Need to Learn About the Library

There are a lot of useful things I should learn about the library. First, I need to find out how to find books that I want to read. I need to find how to locate them and then how **to check books out** so I can take them home to study. Then I need to be able to find specific information on different subjects. For this, the library has many materials available to me: **journals, dictionaries,**

encyclopedias, microfilms, and **audio** and **videotapes.** In order to use these materials, I have to learn how to use machines like the **photocopy machine,** the **microfilm readers,** and the tape recorders that the library has. If I can learn about these things, I will be able to use the library effectively.

Rima Khodadian
(Iran)

III

The library is very useful and necessary for all students. If you have to investigate something in your major field, you can find information about that in the library. There are many special books about your interest. Also, there are many **periodicals,** papers, and **technical reports** in which you can find other ideas about your investigation. If you don't want to investigate something, you can use the library for fun. You can read many books about literature, or about your hobbies, like cooking, gardening, or fixing your car. Finally, if you wish to learn about other countries, you can read many articles about them in books or magazines, and you can study many maps from places all over the world. You can even learn the language of another country from books or from videotapes that you find in the library. For those reasons, to know how to use the library is very important for all students.

Christian Blanco
(Colombia)

1. Underline the topic sentence in each paragraph and circle the controlling ideas. What questions do you expect will be answered in the paragraph that follows each sentence? Were those questions answered?

2. In what ways are the purposes and audiences of each paragraph similar? Different? How does the second sentence in each paragraph help the reader?

3. What techniques of support does each author use? Label those techniques in the margins. What overall organization is used in each paragraph (process, definition, explanation, comparison, contrast, cause-effect)? How do you know?

4. Make a point paragraph outline for one of the paragraphs.

Journal Assignment

Describe the process of locating a book in a library in your country. Use specific examples and appropriate details. Then share your paragraph with a small group of classmates from different countries. Discuss the similarities and differences of using a library in those different countries.

Organization of U.S. Academic Libraries

Suppose that you have been assigned a topic or have chosen a topic to investigate. In order to complete the writing task, you will have to do some research. You may want to interview an expert, but first you need to know more basic information about the topic. Therefore, you need to go to the library. Although U.S. academic libraries are very well organized, and they contain enormous amounts of information, sometimes students have problems locating information because they do not understand the basic organizational principles of the library.

NOTE: All academic libraries index their materials in the same way. Consequently, if you learn to use one U.S. academic library, you will know how to use most academic libraries in the U.S.

Finding materials in the library will be easier if you think about your topic before you go to the library, especially if you try to "think like a librarian." First, think about words that <u>describe your topic</u> or are closely related to your topic. For example, if you are going to write about gasoline prices, you may think of words like the following that *describe* or *relate to* the topic:

oil	fuel	oil production	gasoline
OPEC	fuel prices	oil prices	gasoline prices

These **descriptors** may help you to discover the categories under which librarians have **indexed** (that is, organized) materials about your topic. When you go to the library and begin to search for information, remember your descriptors. If you cannot find materials using one of the words, use one of the other words.

The Card Catalog

Every book and magazine (and every newspaper, videotape, map, encyclopedia, etc.) in the academic library has an identification number. In order to locate a book, you will need that number, the **call number.** In many U.S. academic libraries, you will find that number in the **card catalog,** an alphabetically arranged listing of all the library's materials. There is a card for each book (and all materials) in the library. Usually, the cards are filed in drawers, alphabetically, and students use this card catalog to find the call numbers of the materials they need.

There are three sections in the card catalog:

1. **The title section:** Books are listed alphabetically by the first word of the title. Use this section if you know the title of the book.
   Note: the words *a, an,* and *the* are ignored in the card catalog. If the title begins with one of these words, look up the <u>second</u> word in the title.

2. **The author section:** Books are listed alphabetically by the <u>last name</u> (that is, the family name) of the author. In English, the family name usually comes last: Arden <u>Boyer</u>. However, if the last name is used first, it is followed by a comma, and then the first name: <u>Boyer</u>, Arden. Use the author section if you know the last name of the author.

3. **The subject section:** This is the largest section of the card catalog because it lists books <u>alphabetically by subject</u>. Use this section of the card catalog if you need information (and probably several books) about a topic. The subject section of the card catalog usually has three different sizes of cards. The tallest cards have the names of general categories: for example, <u>Physics, Nutrition, Medicine</u>. The middle-sized cards have the general topics followed by sub-topics: for example Physics, <u>nuclear</u>; Nutrition, <u>animal</u>; Medicine, <u>neurosurgery</u>. Behind the smallest cards are the actual cards with call numbers; each card represents one book (or other kind of material) that the library has on that subject.

Because the card catalog has three sections, most materials are listed at least three times: by title, by author, and by subject. This procedure is called **cross-referencing**; it provides you with three ways to find a book. Below is an example of a card from the subject section of the card catalog.

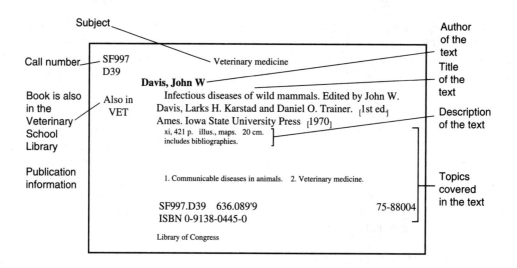

Exercise C

On the next page are two process paragraphs written by students about the card catalog. Read the paragraphs, and define the boldfaced library vocabulary. Then, with a small group of classmates, answer the questions that follow.

I

Using the Card Catalog

Do you know how to use the card catalog in order to find the book you want? There are three ways. First, if you now the author's name, look in that part of the card catalog. If the author's last name is Shiu, for example, look under "S." Then you will find the card with the author's name, the title, and the call number. If you don't remember the author's last name, look up the name of the book in the **title section**. For instance, if the book's title is *The Construction of Cellular Cofferdams*, look under "C" (because you must not consider *a, an,* and *the*). There you will find the card if the library has the book. Finally, if you want information about a subject, instead of just one book, look in the **subject section** of the card catalog. For example, if you want information about microbiology, you will look under "M." Then you will look at many cards until you find several books that look interesting. No matter what you are looking for in the card catalog, always remember to copy the call number, the title, and the author's name completely and correctly. Otherwise, you will not be able to locate the book in the library.

Jun Wang
(People's Republic of China)

II

How to Use the Card Catalog

Every university student in the United States should know how to use the card catalog. The first thing you must do is go to the card catalog; it contains the information that will guide you to the books about your topic. You can look in the subject section, the **author section** (if you know the author's last name), or the title section (if you know the complete title of the book). When you find the card of a book you want, write down the information from the card. Be sure to copy the **call number**, for without it you will not be able to find the book on the shelves of the library. For example, if the book you want is titled *Physical Education and Training*, and the call number is GV342 / A75 / 1989, copy that number carefully. If you do not know how to locate the book by using the number, ask a librarian at the **reference desk** to help you. The librarian will give you a piece of paper that is called the locator. The **library locator** tells you where different call numbers are located in the library. Then you should go to that place, find your book, and **check it out** at the **circulation desk** in the library.

Omar Mussa El-Maghari
(Libya)

1. Identify the techniques of support used in each paragraph. Label those techniques in the margin.

2. Are there steps in each process paragraph that need more explanation? What questions could you ask each author in order to obtain additional information about the card catalog?

3. Underline the connectors in each paragraph. How do the connectors help the reader?

4. Make a point paragraph outline for one of the paragraphs.

Exercise D

Below is a card from the author section of the card catalog. Examine the card, and fill in the information in the blanks that follow.

```
DD43
D5
        Dickinson, Robert Eric, 1905-
            Germany; a general and regional geography, by Robert E.
        Dickinson. [2d ed.] London, Methuen [1964]
            xxiii, 716 p.   illus., maps,  24cm.
            Bibliography: p. 682-702.



        1. Germany—Descr. & trav.—1945-      2. Physical geography—
        Germany.
                DD43D5  1964                                    67-59646


        Library of Congress              [2]
```

1. call number _____

2. author's name _____

3. title _____

4. place of publication _____

5. date of publication _____

6. If you wanted to look for more books on this subject, what part of the card catalog would you look in? _____

The Computerized Card Catalog

Many U.S. academic libraries now have **computerized** their **card catalogs**. That is, the information from all the cards in the card catalog has been put on a **computer database**. Instead of searching through the drawers of cards, students go to a computer terminal to find library materials. Generally, the computer screen will have instructions about how to use the database system, and you will follow those instructions. If the instructions are not clear, the **reference librarian** will answer questions and assist you.

Each system will have slightly different procedures and different commands, but the general process will be similar. You will type the appropriate command (for example, "T" for title or "A" for author) or you will highlight the appropriate line on the computer screen with the computer cursor (for example, <u>name</u> or <u>word</u> or <u>browse</u>). Then you will push the <u>Return </u>key. After that, you will have an opportunity to type an entire word (for example, an author's name, a title, or a subject descriptor) and push the Return key. When the information about the materials arrives on the screen, the call number will be included.

The **computerized card catalog** is more efficient than the card system because the machine is faster than the human hand. Moreover, if you search the subject section, the computer screen will show <u>all</u> the books about your topic, and the reference will contain more information about the book. Below is an example of a typical computer screen for a student who typed the word "Kachina" (an American Indian doll) in her search for information about that subject. Note that the books are listed from the newest to the oldest (from 1991 to 1985). Definitions of the abbreviations have been added at the right of the page (and are <u>underlined</u>). Call numbers are **boldfaced**.

Teiwes, Helga   1991
Kachina Dolls: The Art of Hopi Carvers   photos by author
Tucson, AZ: University of Arizona Press
160 p. illus (some colored), map, refs, index   <u>illus (illustrations)</u>
    E99.H7   <u>refs (references)</u>
    T38

Adams, E. Charles   1991
The Origin and Development of the Pueblo Katsina
Tucson, AZ: University of Arizona Press   <u>p. (pages)</u>
235 p.   illus, maps, refs, index   <u>index: alphabetized</u>
    E99.P9   <u>list at the end of the</u>
    A24   <u>book, with page</u>
                                      <u>numbers where each</u>
                                      <u>topic is discussed</u>

Bromberg, Erik   1986
The Hopi Approach to the Art of the Kachina Doll
West Chester, PA: Schiffer Pub.   Pub. (Publications)
95 p   ill (some colored), indexes, biblio   biblio (bibliography)
    E99.H7
    B85

Dockstader, Frederick   1985
The Kachina and the White Man's Influences on the Hopie Kachina Culture
        Rev. and Enlarged Ed.   rev. (revised)
Albuquerque: University of New Mexico Press   ed. (edition)
134 p., illus (some colored), index, biblio
    Q11.C95
    D35

Of course, once you find the information and the call numbers of the materials that you want, you still must find those sources in the library. U.S. academic libraries are organized in "**open-stacks;**" that is, users (not librarians) locate the materials on the shelves. The opposite is the "closed-stacks" library, in which users give librarians the call numbers of materials they want, and the librarians collect the materials for them.

Writing Assignment 1

Choose a topic that you would like to know more about. Your topic may be one that you have written about earlier in this class (which you will expand to multiple paragraphs), or one of the topics below, or a new topic that interests you. Because you will investigate this topic, try to state that topic in the form of a question (see topics below).

The purpose of this investigation is to explain and/or to evaluate. Your audience for the multiple paragraphs you will write about this topic is a small group of classmates. These classmates will also serve as the peer reviewers for your rough drafts.

Possible Topics: How does El Niño affect the weather?
                 What are Type A and Type B personalities?
                 Can the Leaning Tower of Pisa be fixed?
                 Why do birds sing?
                 How can the TOEFL be improved?
                 What is a "black hole"?
                 Do men and women communicate differently?
                 Should all university students be required to become computer literate?
                 How do water towers "work"?
                 What is "carrying capacity"?

Pre-writing: In your journal, write about why you chose your topic. What do you know about that topic? What don't you know? What do you want to communicate to your audience?

Peer Feedback: With a small group of classmates, share your ideas about your chosen topic. This group of classmates is the audience for your multiple paragraphs. Ask them what they know and don't know about your topic, and ask them what they would <u>like</u> to know. Also, discuss with your classmates appropriate **descriptors** for your topic (that is, other words that describe or relate to your topic). **In your journal**, take notes about your audience and about their expectations.

Pre-writing: In your journal, write about what you learned from your audience/group. What information do you need to generate about your topic? What resources will you use? Write about the plan you have for gathering information.

The General Reference Section

Most academic libraries have a general reference section. In this area you will find materials such as encyclopedias, dictionaries, and maps. Usually, these materials cannot be checked out of the library.

There are many different **encyclopedias**. Some are quite general (for example, the *Encyclopedia Americana* and the *Encyclopedia Britannica*). These general encyclopedias have many volumes. They are alphabetically arranged by subject, and they give basic information about many, many topics. Other encyclopedias are more specialized: *The International Encyclopedia of the Social Sciences, The McGraw-Hill Encyclopedia of Science and Technology, The Encyclopedia of Education*, and many others. These specialized encyclopedias have many volumes, and they also give basic information about a variety of topics. However, the topics are limited to their specializations.

NOTE: Often, beginning library researchers look for general information about a topic in an encyclopedia. While this information can be valuable as a beginning, you should also plan to use other library resources, particularly books and magazine articles.

The Library of Congress (LC) System

Books and other materials in academic libraries are identified and shelved according to a system called the **Library of Congress (LC) system**. Most academic libraries in the U.S. follow the LC system. If you understand how to use the system, you will be able to find materials in any academic library more easily.

Following is a list of the major classifications within the Library of Congress system. Within each category, there are sub-headings (for example, see the Science heading):

Library of Congress Subject Classifications

A	General Works		
B	Philosophy, psychology, and religion		
C	General History		
D	Old World History		
E	U.S. History		
F	U.S. Local History		
G	Geography, Anthropology		
H	Social Sciences		
J	Political Science		
K	Law		
L	Education	QB	Astronomy
N	Fine Arts	QC	Physics
P	Language and Literature	QD	Chemistry
Q	Science	QE	Geology
R	Medicine	QH	Natural History
S	Agriculture and Forestry	QK	Botany
T	Technology	QL	Zoology
U	Military Science	QM	Human Anatomy
V	Naval Science	QP	Physiology
Z	Bibliography	QR	Bacteriology

<u>Sample Call Number:</u>   **QB**156
R20

"QB" is Astronomy
"R" is the first initial of the last name of the author of the book)

Exercise E

Look at the following call numbers. Using the Library of Congress (LC) table above, indicate the major field that each call number classifies.

Call Number	Major Field	Call Number	Major Field
ND573 P42	_____	N42 T5	_____
PN73 C81 **Folio**	_____	NC452 B239 **Sci Ref**	_____
GB4372 H7	_____	PR542 A97	_____
HQ426 D22 **Ref**	_____	VB213 S56 **Doc**	_____
A273 F2 **Special**	_____	BF8879 G49 **Video**	_____

NOTE: The third line of some of the call numbers above (in **boldface**) gives additional information about the cataloged materials:

Folio: the book is taller (larger) than normal; it may be shelved in a different place in the library.

NOTE: A few academic libraries, and many public libraries in the U.S. (city libraries, for example) follow another organizational system called the Dewey Decimal System. Instead of letters and numbers, this system uses only numbers. Following are the major categories in the Dewey Decimal System; of course, each category (such as The Arts) has many subdivisions.

000	General Works	500	Pure Science	
100	Philosophy	600	Technology	701
200	Religion	700	The Arts	702
300	Social Sciences	800	Literature	703
400	Language	900	Geography and History	

Sci Ref: the book is in the **Science Reference** area; probably you will not be able to check out this book. Instead, you will have to use it in the library.

Ref: the book is in the **General Reference** area; probably you will not be able to check out this book. Instead, you will have to use it in the library.

Special: the book is shelved in a **Special Collection**. Ask the reference librarian to help locate the book.

Doc: the material is a **Government Document**. Government documents are difficult to find. Ask the reference librarian for assistance.

Video: this material is available on videotape and will probably be shelved in a special place in the library.

Locating LC Materials in the Library

Library materials are shelved sequentially, according to their call numbers. In order to find a book (or other material):

1. At the reference desk, ask about a **library locator** (a piece of paper or a sign that tells you where different call numbers are located generally in the library).

2. Look at the call number of the book you need to locate. The first letter of the call number (which also indicates the LC subject classification) will tell you the general area. For example:

> Q   1st floor, north wing,   <u>or</u>
> R   basement.

Go to that general area.

3. Remember: everything in the library is in alphabetical and numerical sequence. If, for example, the call number is:

> **PN72**
>
> **R81**

the first letter of the first line indicates that you will be looking for a book about "Language and Literature" (see the LC list earlier in this chapter). First, then, you must find the "Ps." Then you will see the PAs, the PBs, and so on until you find the PNs. After that, you will see PN1, PN2, ...PN26, PN27, ...PN71, and then **PN72**.

In addition to the sequenced Ps, you will also notice the second lines of the call numbers: Each second line begins with a letter and is followed by a number. The first letter is the first initial of the last name of the author of the book. In the case of the call number above, the author's last name begins with the letter R. To follow the second sequence, you should first locate PN72. The first PN72 books will probably be PN72 / A, then PN72 / B, and so on. Continue looking until you find:

PN72	PN72	PN72	PN72
R1	R10	R65	R81

When you have located the entire call number, you have found the book! You may take it from the shelf, look at it, and, if you choose, "**borrow**" it from the library (that is, **check it out**).

NOTE: If you take the book off the library shelf and decide that you do not want to use it, do NOT try to replace it on the shelf. Books are easily misplaced on library shelves, and if the book is out of order, no one will be able to find it. Instead, put the book on a nearby table, or give it to the people at the circulation desk. Then trained workers will reshelve the books.

Journal Assignment

In your academic library, find three books in the card catalog or in the computerized card catalog about your chosen topic. Write the <u>call number</u> and the <u>title</u> of the book **in your journal**. Then, using the <u>library locator</u>, find <u>one</u> of these books in the stacks. <u>Check the book out</u> at the <u>circulation desk</u>. Use the <u>index</u> (at the back of the book) or the <u>table of contents</u> (at the front of the book) to locate information about your topic. **In your journal**, take notes from the book that will help you write about your topic.

Writing Assignment 2

Write a paragraph explaining your process of finding the books in the library. Your audience is a student who has had no experience with this process. Be specific; use examples from your own experience, and use appropriate connectors. Use the Paragraph Planning Guidelines (on the inside front cover of this book) to help draft your paragraph.

Then share your experience, your paragraph, and your notes from your journal assignment with a small group of classmates. Discuss your library experiences with your group.

Finding and Using Magazine Articles

To find books and other materials in the library, you will use the card catalog or the computerized card catalog. However, finding magazine **articles** (called **periodicals** by librarians because they arrive periodically) takes a different sequence of skills. Instead of the card catalog, magazines are cataloged in **indexing journals**. An indexing journal is a list of magazine articles, alphabetically arranged by subject (and sometimes by author as well). The information about articles is gathered and organized for a period of time (for example, every two weeks, or three months, or one year).

Using Periodical Indexing Journals

There are dozens of indexing journals in the academic library (*Business Periodicals Index, Applied Science and Technology Index, Engineering Index*, etc.). But the most popular (and most general) indexing journal in the library is **T*he Reader's Guide to Periodical Literature***. *The Reader's Guide* indexes all the articles in more than 100 popular (not academic) magazines. Once you know how to use it, you will know how to use many other indexing journals that are used in academic fields such as art, medicine, food science, etc.

Each **volume** of The *Reader's Guide* covers a period of time: two years for the thick cloth-bound (**hardback**) volumes, three months for the large paper-bound (**paperback**) volumes, and two weeks for the thin, paper-bound booklets. To use this indexing journal, you will look up your topic (for example, <u>dolphins</u>) in the most recent volume available because <u>the greatest value of magazine articles is their newness</u>. If you cannot find your topic, you will choose one of your other **descriptors** (for example, <u>porpoises</u>) and look for that word. After you have found the word(s) under which you will find information about your topic, you will work backwards in time, looking at the most recent index, then the next recent, and so forth, of *The Reader's Guide* until you have found enough information about your topic.

Magazine articles about your topic are listed **alphabetically under the subject.** Sub-headings and cross-references in the indexing journal will help you find other descriptors and related topics. For example, look at this entry from *The Reader's Guide*:

> MARTIN, Paul
>
> > Marva Collins—a teacher who cares. il pors Good H 187:60+ S ''91

This entry means that there is an article by Paul Martin entitled "Marva Collins—A Teacher Who Cares." The article has **illustrations** and a **por**trait of Ms. Collins. It was published in the magazine *Good Housekeeping*, **volume** 187, page 60 (the + means that there is also a little on page 61). The date of the **issue** of the magazine is September, 1991.

Exercise F

With a partner, read the multiple paragraphs below. Then answer the questions that follow.

How to Use The Reader's Guide

The Reader's Guide to Periodical Literature is a subject and author list of many (but not all) magazine articles published in the U.S. This list, called an index, is sent to U.S. libraries every two weeks so that interested people can find out quickly what current information is available. For university or college students who must frequently do research, this list of subjects written about in magazines of general interest can be valuable. Learning to use The *Reader's Guide* is therefore important to all university students in the U.S.

The content of *The Reader's Guide* consists of subject and author entries to periodical articles (that is, magazines that are published regularly). This information is listed alphabetically. After the subject or the author's name, information is given that tells the student where to find the magazine article. For example, if you want to look up the subject "Education," you should find the most recent volume of *The Reader's Guide* , then look up the letter "E," and then find the word "Education." If you want to look up an author whose last name is "Rodriquez," you should look up the letter "R" and then find the word "Rodriquez." Under the subject or the author listing, you will find articles listed, in alphabetical order, about that subject or by that author. Each article is listed by the first word in the title of the article (except for the words *a*, *an*, and *the*;

these initial words are not considered in the alphabetizing of articles).

    The Reader's Guide also has two kinds of cross-references (that is, information about other places to look in *The Reader's Guide* for more articles about a subject). After a heading, you might find the word **SEE** which is followed by other subject headings also found in that volume of the indexing journal. For example, "Higher Education" isn't a subject heading in *The Reader's Guide.* If you look up "Higher Education," you will find: "SEE Universities and Colleges." Then you will look under "U" for Universities. The other kind of cross-reference is *see also.* For instance, if you look for "Education," *The Reader's Guide* will list articles about education, but it will also say: "*see also:* Adult Education, Elementary Education, Special Education." If you are interested in any of those headings, you can look them up in *The Reader's Guide.*

Noemi Ramirez
(Mexico)

1. What techniques of support does this author use in her paragraphs? Label those techniques in the margin.
2. Underline the connectors in these paragraphs. How do the connectors help the reader?
3. Make a point paragraph outline for the last paragraph.
4. What questions could you ask this author to answer (or answer more completely) in the paragraph?

NOTE: Some of the information in *The Reader's Guide* is abbreviated. A page at the beginning of each volume lists the abbreviations used in the individual entries. Examine the sample below, taken from a recent **Reader's Guide.**

Some Abbreviations Used in The Reader's Guide

abr	abridged	Mr	March
Ag	August	My	May
Assn	Association	N	November
Ave	Avenue	por	portrait
bibl	bibliography	pseud	pseudonym
bi-m	bi-monthly	q	quarterly
bldg	building	rev	revised
Co	Company	S	September
cont	continued	sec	section
Corp	*Corporation*	Spr	*Spring*
D	*December*	St	*Street*
Dept	*Department*	supp	*supplement*
il	*illustrated*	tr	*translated*
Ja	*January*	v	*volume*
Je	*June*	w	*weekly*
Jl	*July*	Wint	*Winter*
m	*monthly*	y	*year*

<u>Remember:</u> not all magazines are indexed in *The Reader's Guide.* For example, many academic magazines (often called **journals**) are not listed. A list at the beginning of each volume of *The Reader's Guide* indicates the periodicals that have been indexed. For instance, if a professor has suggested that you check for articles that appeared in the journal *Newsweek*, you would find articles from that journal in *The Reader's Guide* (see the list below). However, if the professor suggested that you check for articles in *The Training and Development Journal*, you would not find that journal indexed in *The Reader's Guide.* Therefore, you would need to ask a librarian to determine which indexing journal would list articles from *The Training and Development Journal.* Following is a <u>small sample</u> of abbreviations listed in the front of *The Reader's Guide.*

Some Abbreviations of Periodicals Used in The Reader's Guide

Nat Wildlife	*National Wildlife*	Sci Digest	*Science Digest*
New Repub	*New Republic*	Sky & Tel	*Sky and Telescope*
Newsweek	*Newsweek*	Society	*Society*
Oceans	*Oceans*	Sports Illus	*Sports Illustrated*
Opera N	*Opera News*	Suc Farm	*Successful Farming*
Parks & Rec	*Parks and Recreation*	Time	*Time*
Phys Today	*Physics Today*	Todays Educ	*Today's Education*
Pop Electr	*Popular Electronics*	Travel	*Travel*
Pop Phot	*Popular Photography*	UN Chron	*UN Chronicle*
Psychol Today	*Psychology Today*	U.S. News	*U.S. News and World Report*
Read Digest	*Reader's Digest*	Vogue	*Vogue*
SLJ	*School Library Journal*	Wilson Lib Bull	*Wilson Library Bulletin*
Sat R	*Saturday Review*	Writer	*Writer*
Sch Arts	*School Arts*	Yale R	*Yale Review*

Exercise G

Look at the entry from The Reader's Guide *below. Then answer the questions that follow.*

> MEDICAL NEWS
> New advances in medicine. L. Glaton. 50 Plus. 18:22 S '92
> see also
> Fertility research, Drugs

1. The subject of the article _____

2. The author of this article _____

3. The title _____

4. The name of the periodical _____

5. The volume _____ The page number _____

6. The date of the issue of the magazine _____

7. Under what headings could you find additional information about this topic?

   _____

Exercise H

Using the information below, which was taken from a page of The Reader's Guide, *answer the questions that follow.*

TSETSE flies
> Taming the TSETSE. W.J. Broad. il Sci News 114:108—110 Ag 12 '92

TUCKER, Frank
> Longet prosecutor has book thrown at him. L. Goldman. por New Times 11:18 Ag 7 '92

TUCKER, Ken
> Pop rock. il Hi Fi 28:138+ Ag '92

TUCKER, William
> Good earth pesticide. il New Times 11:28—30+ Ag 21 '92

TUMOR promoting substances. See Cancer—Causes

TUMORS
> Brain tumors in owl monkeys inoculated with a human polyomavirus (JC virus) W.T. London and others. bibl il Science 201:1246—9 S 29 '92

TURKEY
> See also
> Baths. Public—Turkey
> Istanbul
> Military assistance. American—Turkey
> Opera—Turkey
>> Description and travel

Following Paul in Turkey. J.R.W. Stott. il por Chr Today 22:36—37 Jl 21 '92

TURKEY cookery. SEE Cookery, Turkish

TURTLES

Texas voice of the turtle. il South Liv 13:88 S '92
See also
Tortoises

TUTENKHAMON, King of Egypt

Tomb

Golden Tut. New Yorker 54:28 O 2 '92

TUTORS and tutoring

Tutors: a timeless system for stretching the mind. E.L. Hoover. il Hum and Behav 7:14—15
Ag '92

TWAIN, Mark, pseud.. SEE Clemens, S.L.

TWINS

Double parenthood: HLA typing as paternity test. M. Clark. Newsweek 92:67 S 25 '92
Twins who made their own language: Grace and Virginia Kennedy. D. O'Brien. il Fam Health 10:32 S '92

UFOs

Study challenges sky mirages as a sighting source. D. Berliner. il Sci Digest 84:30—32
Ag '92

U.K. (rock group) SEE Rock groups

1. You are writing a paper about King Tut. What is the title of an article you might find helpful?_____

In what magazine did it appear?_____

When? _____

2. Your professor has suggested that you read an article by William Tucker. What is the title of the article? _____

Where did it appear? _____

When? _____ On what page does it begin? _____

3. You are researching a paper about an opera entitled A Turk in Italy. Where do you need to look in *The Reader's Guide* to find information on this subject?

   _____

4. Mark Twain wrote a book titled Tom Sawyer. Your assignment for an English course is to write a paper about the author. Under what heading do you need to

   look for information? _____

5. You are writing a paper for a genetics class. Write the bibliographic information

   for an article about twins. _____

   _____

6. You are interested in Unidentified Flying Objects (UFOs). What is the title of an

   article that might be useful? _____

   Who wrote it? _____

   In what journal would you find it? _____

7. You need to write a paper on military assistance in Turkey for a political science course. Where should you look in *The Reader's Guide*?

   _____

Computerized Indexing Journals

Many academic libraries have installed **computerized indexing journals**. That is, the information from an indexing journal (or, more likely, several indexing journals) is put onto a computer database. For example, **Info-Trac**, the most widely known of these computer databases, includes all entries from *The Reader's Guide, Business Periodicals Index*, and the *Newspaper Index*.

Like the computerized card catalog, the directions for using the computerized indexing journals appear on the screen of the computer, and users can follow those directions. Usually you will type a descriptor onto the computer, and then push the Return key. Articles about that descriptor will then appear on the screen.

The computerized database has many advantages. First, like the computerized card catalog, it is more efficient than searching many volumes of a paper indexing journal. Second—and very important—if your descriptor is too broad, the computer will suggest sub-headings (that is, other descriptors) that you can use. Therefore, the computer can help you learn to "think like a librarian." Third, you can combine searches by typing more than one descriptor into the computer; as a result, you can find more journal articles specifically about your topic. Fourth, because several indexing journals are included on the database, you will find articles from many more magazines with just the touch of a finger. Finally, computerized indexing journals are often equipped with a printer; by pushing a single key on the computer keyboard, you can print the reference that is on the screen. As a result, you will have all the information necessary to find the article that interests you, and that information will be complete and correct.

NOTE: The computerized indexing journals include articles from every journal in their database. However, your university library probably does not subscribe to every journal. Therefore, when you search Info-Trac (or another computerized indexing journal), remember that some of the articles that interest you will probably not be in the library. Fortunately, many computerized indexing journals will give that information as part of the reference to the article. For example, here are two references from Info-Trac:

America—the environmental dictator? (the effects of the embargo on Venezuelan tuna fishing) James Brooke. *The New York Times,* May 3, 1992 v141 F7 30 col in
Holdings: Current Issues   Newspaper area
1851—   Basement   Microfilm

This reference indicates that the article "America—The Environmental Dictator?" about the effect of the embargo on Venezuelan tuna fishing, was written by James Brooke. It was published in *The New York Times* (a newspaper) on May 3, 1992. The **volume** number of the newspaper is 141; the section of the newspaper in which the article is located is F, and the page number within that section is 7. The article is 30 column inches long. The university "**holds**" this current issue in the Newspaper area. In addition, it has all the issues of The New York Times from 1851 to the present; the dash (—) after 1851 that is followed by a space indicates that the library is still receiving the newspaper. Older issues of *The New York Times* are located on microfilm in the basement of this academic library.

Saving some cetaceans may require breeding in activity. Marcia Hope Ames.
   BioScience, Dec. 1991 v12 n10 p22 (6)
Holdings: 1968—   HF5001   .B89
                Current Year at Circulation Desk

This reference indicates that the article "Saving Some Cetaceans May Require Breeding in Activity," by Marcia Hope Ames, was published in the journal *BioScience* in 1991. The volume number of the journal is 12, and the issue number is 10. The article begins on page 22 and continues for 6 pages. The university has all of the *BioScience* journals since 1968, and the library is still receiving issues of that journal. The call number (that is, where you will find the older "back" issues of B*ioScience* in the library stacks) is HF5001 / B89. However, the current year of the journal is kept at the Circulation Desk in the library, and you will have to ask for new issues there.

Exercise I

Suppose you have been assigned a research paper about <u>dolphins</u> in your environmental issues class. Below are several references to articles about dolphins from Info-Trac. Examine the references. (The references have been numbered for ease of discussion.) Notice that they are listed from newest to oldest because the newest articles may be the most valuable. Then answer the questions that follow.

(1) **Close encounters with dolphins and belugas.** (Cover Story) *National Geographic World,* April 1992 n20 p2(6)
Holdings: 1985—　　　　　2nd Floor, North Wing

(2) **US—Mexico tuna pact would lift import ban: environmentalists attack plan.** John Maggs. *Journal of Commerce and Commercial,* March 5, 1992, v 391 p1A(2)
Holdings: Current issues　　Newspaper area
　　　　　　　 1979—　　　　　Basement　　　　　Microfilm

(3) **Playful genius of the sea.** (dolphins) Per Ola and Emily D'Aulaire. *Reader's Digest,* March 1992 v140 n839 p54(6).
Holdings: 1928—1991　　　AP2 .R255

(4) **Dolphins' day: Japan.** *The Economist,* Nov 30, 1991 v321 n7735 p34(2).
Holdings: 1982　　　　　　Q1 .D56

(5) **Mexico: no threat to dolphins.** (world trade controversy created by United States environmental community and tuna canning industry instigating ban of Mexican tuna) (Editorial) Felipe Charat. *Journal of Commerce and Commercial,* Nov 5, 1991 v390 n27598 p8A(1).
Holdings: Current issues　　Newspaper area
　　　　　　　 1979—　　　　　Basement　　　　　Microfilm

(6) **Dolphin epidemic spreads to Greece.** (virus that kills hundreds of dolphins in the western Mediterranean) Jeremy Webb. *New Scientist,* Sept 7, 1991 v131 n1785 p18(1).
Holdings: 1871—　　　　　Q1 .N52

(7) **Smarts: notes on dolphins' brain powers, communication skills, and social style.** Susan H. Shane. *Sea Frontiers,* March—April 1991 v37 n2 p38(6).

(8) **The new flipperism.** (new studies on dolphins) (column) Will Nixon. *BUZZWORM: The Environmental Journal,* Jan—Feb 1991 v3 n1 p16(1).

    (9) Those smart dolphins. Sergei Zholus. *Soviet Life,* June 1990 n6 p44(3).
    Holdings: 1965   DK 1 .U67

    (10) Swim with the dolphins; tuna fishing will change. *Newsweek,* April 23,
        1990 v115 n17 p76(1)
    Holdings: 1940—   AP 2 .N6772

    **(11) Save-the-dolphin drive to spur Asia tuna imports: some suppliers out
        of stock.** Charles Thurston. *Journal of Commerce and Commercial,* April
        18, 1990 v384 n27209 p1A(2).
    Holdings: Current issues   Newspaper area
               1979—   Basement   Microfilm

1. Where would you go in this university library to locate the first reference? The second?
2. As you examine these references, what possible topics do you think you might write about? That is, what are the environmental issues that might interest your professor?
3. What other ideas about dolphins might you choose to write a paper for another class? Use the titles of references to support your opinion.
4. For the fourth reference, looks at the "Holdings." Will you be able to find issue 321, number 7735, at this academic library?
5. Which other two references on this list are not available in this university library? How do you know?
6. Look at the call numbers for three of the journals listed above. Use the list of the Library of Congress Subject Classifications earlier in this chapter. What major fields are served by the call numbers you are examining?
7. Examine reference 11. How will you read this article?
8. Using reference 5 or reference 9, write a descriptive paragraph (similar to the one just above Exercise I) explaining each part of the reference.

Identifying Magazine (Journal, Periodical) Articles

    When you have found several articles from different magazines about your topic, the next step in this process is locating the actual article. In order to find journal articles, you <u>must</u> have the following information:

- the call number
- the title of the magazine
- the volume number of the magazine
- the title of the article, and
- the page number of the article

Copy this information carefully (or, for Info-Trac, simply print out the reference). If you make a mistake in copying the information, you will have difficulty locating the article. Next, you must (a) discover whether or not the library has each of the journals and (b) locate those journals.

While it is possible to find the call number for journals in the card catalog or computerized card catalog, it is sometimes easier and more efficient to consult the **Serials Record** ("serials" is another name for periodicals), a list of the library's periodicals that also includes exactly what volumes and issues the library has. Some libraries have a small card catalog for their Serials Record. Periodicals are listed alphabetically by title in this small card catalog. A sample card follows:

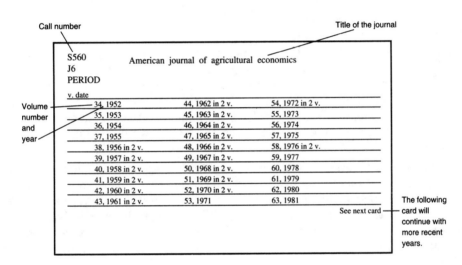

Other libraries have their Serials Record in a notebook instead of (or in addition to) the small card catalog. Still others keep information about their journals on their computerized indexing journals (as in Exercise I above). Ask the librarian at the reference desk to show you where the Serials Record is located, and ask that librarian any other questions that you might have about using periodicals in the library.

Locating Periodicals

If you find the journal you are looking for in the Serials Record, and if the library has the volume and the issue of that journal in the library, the next step is to locate that journal and the article for which you are searching. For journal articles that are current, and for issues from the previous months (about one year for most periodicals), you should look on the **display shelves where current periodicals** are displayed on slanted shelves. Each issue of the magazine (for example, the January issue, the February issue, or, for weekly magazines, the November 4th issue, the November 11th issue) is placed in the **current periodical section** of the library when it arrives. While only the most recent issue of the magazine is visible on the slanted shelf, the slanted shelves lift up (or have shelves immediately beneath them) where slightly older issues of the periodicals are stored. Look through the small stack of issues until you find the appropriate issue, that is, the current month or week; then turn to the page number you copied, and that will be the article.

Magazines older than a year are stored in the **stacks** of the library. Each periodical has a call number, and you can locate this call number in the same way you would find a book in the library. But journals also have **volume numbers**. Once a year the **individual issues** of a journal are bound into a hardback (cloth-bound) **volume**. (For some weekly publications, two volumes a year are bound.) Each volume is numbered, and it is this volume number that you use to find the appropriate volume. Inside the volume, you will find that each issue also has a **number**; that number indicates the order of the issues (for monthly periodicals, issue 1, for example, is probably January; issue 2 is February, etc.). After you have found the correct issue, find the page number in that issue, and you will have found the article itself.

For example, if you wanted to locate number 6 in Exercise I (above), you would go to the place in the library where the QIs are kept, then find QI, N52 in the same way you would locate a book. Then you would notice that many volumes have the same call number, but that in addition each had a <u>volume</u> number. You would find volume 131. Then, inside that volume, you would look for the individual issue numbered 1785. When you found that issue, you would look on page 18 and you would find a one-page article about the dolphin epidemic.

Many academic libraries do not permit periodicals (in particular, current periodicals) to be checked out. If there is a check-out period, it is usually quite short. Therefore, if you find an article that will help you with your topic, you might want to simply read it and take notes about the topic in your journal, or it might be worthwhile to make a photocopy of the article at the machines in the library. The photocopy machines generally cost 10 cents per page. You will need to have the appropriate coins for the machine.

Exercise J

Return to the library. Use The Reader's Guide *or a computerized indexing journal like Info-Trac to identify several recent articles about your topic. Check to see whether or not the library has the journal. Then locate three of those articles. Read each article quickly.* **In your journal**, *take notes about the three articles. Photocopy one of the articles (the most helpful for your topic).*

Writing Assignment 3

Using the information you have gathered, write 2-4 paragraphs about your chosen topic. Your audience for these paragraphs continues to be the small group of classmates who serve as your peer reviewers.

> **Pre-writing and Drafting:** Use the information you have collected, and the Paragraph Planning Guidelines (on the inside front cover of this book) as a

checklist to generate adequate detail, construct point paragraph outlines, and write rough drafts of your multiple paragraphs.

Peer Feedback: With your small group of classmates, read the multiple paragraphs of your peers. Take notes **in your journal** about the following for each set of peer paragraphs:

- the topic, and the 2-4 main ideas of the paragraphs
- one thing you learned from reading that set about the topic
- one thing you learned about good writing from reading that set of paragraphs

On each set of paragraphs:

- mark with an asterisk (*) in the margins of each set of paragraphs the details you find most interesting
- label in the margins of ONE paragraph for each set the techniques of support used by the author
- at the end of each paragraph, write a single question or suggestion that will help the author
- mark any grammar or sentence structure problems you find

Discuss your journal notes and the marks you put on your peers' papers with your classmates. Take notes **in your journal** or on your rough paragraphs drafts about the suggestions your peers make.

In your journal, write a paragraph about the set of paragraphs you read that were most interesting and valuable for you. Use the notes you took **in your journal** as well as your memory to specify why you preferred that set of paragraphs.

Revision: Using (a) what you learned about writing from reading your peers' paragraphs, (b) the advice of your classmates, and (c) the Revision Guidelines (on the inside back cover of this book), make changes in each of your paragraphs that will improve your writing. Then write the final drafts of your multiple paragraphs.

In your journal, write a paragraph about your multiple paragraphs:

- what was easy about writing these paragraphs?
- what was difficult?
- what problems did you have?
- how did you solve those problems?
- what did you learn from writing these paragraphs?

Peer Feedback: With your small group of classmates (your audience), read the final drafts of the sets of paragraphs. Discuss with your peers the ways in which they (and you) revised your paragraphs. In your journal, take some notes about how your classmates' paragraphs changed.

Finally, **in your journal**, write a paragraph about how one of your classmates changed her/his paragraphs. Were the multiple paragraphs improved? In what specific ways? Use the notes your took during your discussion. Below is an example of one student's paragraph about his classmate's revision.

In the revised draft, Alexander takes a stand to convince his reader that punk music is a legitimate form of music. One specific improvement in Alex's revised paper was the use of clearer controlling ideas. In his first draft, he jumped from one idea to another. It was very rough to read. But now the paragraph is clear.

Ahmed Mohamed Ali
(Somalia)

10

Summary Writing

Writing in English is a difficult job for me. I have to find the correct words from my vocabulary to express my ideas, and I have to pay more attention to the grammar which is so far away from the grammar in my language. More terrible, I have to do translation when I think and write.

Qiang Zhang
(People's Republic of China)

We often summarize for different audiences and different purposes. For example, a friend asks us to describe a film we have seen, and we <u>briefly</u> tell that friend what the movie was about. Or we explain to our roommate what a terrible vacation we have had by <u>briefly</u> describing the worst parts of that vacation. Or we tell a friend about a story we have read by <u>briefly</u> describing the main ideas in the story.

Summaries are often written rather than spoken. That is, we write a shortened form of a long article by writing just about the main ideas in that article. In addition, <u>titles</u> are often very brief summaries of the paragraphs, essays, or articles that follow. <u>Newspaper headlines</u> are *short* summaries of the newspaper articles that follow. In academic journals, the title of an article is often followed by an **abstract**, which is an academic summary that briefly tells the readers what the research article is about. The **purpose** of these written summaries is **to inform** the reader about the main ideas in the articles that follow and/or **to persuade** the reader to read the whole article.

In each of these cases, the person who is summarizing does not include all the specific details. Instead, that person states the main ideas of, for instance, the film, the terrible vacation, or the article. The summary does not repeat words or phrases; it does not use many adjectives or introductory phrases. **A summary**, then, is **a brief description of the main ideas** or actions. We summarize for someone who has not read (or seen or experienced) the book, article, film, or terrible vacation, that we have read (or seen or experienced). The general purpose of a summary, then, is to give a limited amount of information to a specific audience.

229

Writing Summaries

Although writing summaries may seem to be an easy task, summary writing is complex. The summary writer must be able:

1. to read the original material well and understand it thoroughly

2. to identify the main ideas

3. to restate these ideas

Moreover, summary writing is both different and similar to the writing you have been practicing in earlier chapters of this book. For example, in some ways, writing summaries is the opposite of drafting an original paragraph. In your own writing, you gather supporting detail and arrange that evidence for your topic sentence. You explain, define, clarify, and illustrate your ideas. In contrast, summary writing contains very little (or no) detail. Instead, you extract the main ideas from someone else's work. However, in one important way, summary writing is similar to writing original paragraphs: summaries are written in your own words. In fact, the most difficult part of writing a summary is accurately stating the main ideas of another person's article without using the exact phrases or sentences of the original material.

Finally, successful summaries are clear and balanced. That is, the reader (or listener) can easily understand the main ideas of the longer material. If the summary is unsuccessful, the reader (or listener) will be confused.

Exercise A

Think of a film you have seen recently. **In your journal**, *write three sentences (25–50 words) that describe the main ideas of the film for a friend who has not seen the film. Then, with a small group of classmates, share your summary. What questions can you ask your group about their summaries? What other information would you like to know about the main ideas of the films they have summarized?*

Journal Assignment

With your classmates, listen to a short lecture by your teacher. As you listen, take notes about the lecture in your journal. After the lecture, write a summary of the lecture for a student who has not heard the lecture. Your summary should be about 100 words in length.

After you have written your summary, share it with a small group of your classmates. As you read your classmates' summaries, take notes in your journal about the differences between your summary and the summaries you are reading.

Finally, discuss the differences with your classmates. Then, with your group, write <u>one</u> *summary that uses the best parts of all the individual summaries.*

Writing Assignment 1

Read the essay below that was written by a student about her grandfather. Then, re-read the essay and <u>underline</u> the main ideas of that essay. In your journal, list the main ideas in your essay for a friend (your **audience**) who has <u>not</u> read the essay. Then write the summary; the **purpose** of the summary is to persuade your friend to read the essay. Make your summary <u>brief</u> (about 50 words).

My Grandfather

Even when I was a small child, I noticed that my grandfather was a very unusual adult. The rest of the adults were serious, and with their air of importance, they were busy with their own problems all the time. But my grandfather didn't "belong." He treated me, not like a child, but like his contemporary, and I enjoyed it. In spite of his age, he was very jolly, kind, and frank. Both he and I liked to talk to each other.

I especially appreciated his telling me the truth. Such sincerity wasn't typical for my other relatives, I always felt that there was something they tried to keep from me or at least to soften it. But my grandfather was a reliable man, and I always trusted him. For example, when I asked my relatives about their school years, they gave me scanty pieces of information about what subjects had been taught. Even those who had finished school with excellent marks and gold medals, and who seemed to have had a good time at school, were very laconic. To fish something really interesting from them was impossible. But when I asked my grandfather questions about his education, he pleased me by telling stories of his school life.

Grandpa's parents were specialists in chemistry. As they were researchers, they had to move from one place to another very often. Grandpapa liked such changes in his life. It wasn't difficult for him to change schools because he accustomed himself to the new requirements very quickly. Although he remembered nothing about his senior years, except that he and his classmates were serious students, he remembered his first several years at school very well.

When Grandpapa was very young, it was a harsh economic and political time for our country and its people. Though my grandfather lived in one of the biggest Russian cities—St. Petersburg—there weren't enough teachers in the schools. Because of the political instability, they came and went, so the headmaster couldn't find decent teachers sometimes. He was glad to give a job to anyone who applied for it. Not all of them stood the test.

For example, the Soviet power had replaced gymnasias with Soviet schools, where pupils were supposed to study everything from the very beginning. But most pupils were prepared for academic education and had very good home education, so they knew the basics of the sciences. However, some of the new "teachers" were persuaded that children should be taught from the beginning with the ABCs. So the children, who already knew Russian literature, had to study the alphabet. One new teacher brought bricks with letters—a new method of teaching to read. It was great fun for my grandfather and his classmates, and the teacher was shocked by the children's quick progress. By the end of the first day, all the children could read fluently and with proper intonation! She realized the state of things a bit later.

Another story that my grandfather told me was about how the children of his class liked to entertain themselves during history lessons. The history teacher was a very old gentleman. He had a very decent personality, and his knowledge was extremely rich in many subjects. He was vivid and passionate while teaching his pupils, but when a student answered a question, the teacher immediately began to doze. Consequently, my grandfather and his classmates asked questions frequently. Then, as the teacher snored, the pupils often devoted that "spare time" to games and talk.

The geography teacher was also unsuccessful, but for a different reason. He was very stout and took great care about his meals and food. He used every opportunity, every second, to tell the pupils something concerning food. He spoke often of his past, when there were a lot of restaurants, canteens, and cafes. He described many meals that he had eaten in great detail. And he knew every public house, and the name of every bar owner in St. Petersburg. That's why the children were good at physics and math, but they easily mixed up countries and their capitals.

According to Grandpapa, however, one teacher made a positive change in the students. For example, the students found biology boring and tedious, and no biology teacher could get through to them. When the headmaster introduced the new young teacher, they were sure that in a month or so she would leave the school. But in spite of themselves, they fell in love with her, this fragile young lady who was beautiful and clever. And she seemed to cast a spell on them. They listened to her with great interest, read different books about *papilionaceous* plants and *Labiatae*, learned long Latin names by heart, drew pistils and tendrils, and never complained. They were delighted with her lessons. Unfortunately, their teacher fell ill, and her disease was very dangerous and complicated. The doctors could do nothing, and she died. For many of the children, including my grandfather, that was the first loss in their lives, and they had fits of depression. She was a fairy forever in their minds.

Despite the disadvantages of my grandfather's education, he said that his younger school years were happy. It was his good fortune, he said, to meet so many different kinds of human beings, and Grandpapa expressed his gratitude for that.

Tatyana Donets
(Siberia)

Exercise B

*Share your summary with a small group of classmates. As you read your classmates' summaries, take notes **in your journal** about what you found that might improve your summary. Discuss the information used in the group's summaries with your classmates. Then, using the best parts from your classmate's summaries, write one summary for the group.*

When you have finished, break into "fragmented groups" (by assigning a single number—1, 2, 3, 4—to group members and then having all 1s form a new group, all 2s, and so forth), and share the group's summary. Finally, in the new "fragmented group," answer the questions below.

1. The sources for this essay were (a) observation, (b) personal experience, and (c) interview. With your fragmented group, write the assignment that this student might have received for this writing task.

2. With your group, underline the sentences of observation and personal experience. Circle the connectors that introduce parts of the interview.

3. What questions might you and your group ask this author about this essay? That is, what other information would you find interesting?

4. What vocabulary words were difficult for you? Ask members of your group to help you define those words.

Academic Summaries

Summarizing is an essential academic skill. Usually, academic summaries are brief written descriptions of other written materials. For example, students:

- summarize lecture notes so that they can study a smaller amount of material,

- summarize an article for a professor who has not read the article

- summarize written material in the introduction to a paragraph or essay that will evaluate that material

- summarize material that they have learned in class on a test so that the professor will know that they understand that material

The length of any summary depends on the assignment, the audience, and the available material. Sometimes the assignment for a summary is a single sentence; sometimes it is a paragraph or even longer. A summary for an **audience** that has already read an article (and so needs only to be reminded of the main ideas), for example, will be shorter than a summary for an audience that has not read the article. The amount of information given in a summary also depends on the length of the original **material**; an article of one page will usually have a shorter summary than an article of twenty pages.

Like most writing, constructing a successful academic summary is a **process**. Reading and re-reading the material is the first step. As you reread the material, read with a pencil. Underlining the main ideas will help you gather the necessary information for the summary, and making notes about those ideas in the margin will make further rereading easier and quicker. Often these main ideas will be the topic sentences in the paragraphs. Therefore, rereading the first and the last sentences of paragraphs will also help you identify the main idea(s) of that paragraph. And rereading the introduction and the conclusion of a multiple paragraph article will help you identify the main ideas of the article. The example below shows how students read and identified the main ideas of an article. After you finish reading and rereading this article, cover the article with a piece of paper. Then study the **NOTES** the students made (in italics) in the wide right margin about the main ideas.* As the students began to write their summaries, they used (a) the notes they made and (b) their memories of the article.

Business and Education in America

One of the oldest axioms in America is the saying, "To get a good job, get a good education." During the 1980s, however, a curious trend in education reversed that time-honored logic. Now, students in high school and college think they must get a job while they are in school. <u>Because jobs no longer teach the value of the dollar and the importance of responsibility, however, students' part-time employment is now a major cause for America's crisis in education.</u> Recent studies of the effects of students' jobs on their education show a depressing reality: As students' working hours increase, both their grade point averages and their academic ambitions decrease. When we analyze the problems, we discover that <u>the real culprits are the lax child labor laws and the unethical business practices</u> that promote quick profits and immediate self-gratification. If America is to solve its crisis in education, therefore, it must reform its business practices and dramatically restrict students' working hours.

Several studies of the effects of part-time employment on educational achievement paint an alarming picture of America's youth working 20 and 30 hours a week in order to buy themselves unnecessary luxuries. Rather than teaching the value of money, <u>jobs take time away from studies and encourage students to spend their money frivolously.</u> Last year, 13 to 19 year-olds spent $56 billion on themselves. The effect of these "part-time" jobs on education can be devastating. One student admitted that, after working from 3 p.m. to 11 p.m., he was too tired to study: "By the time I got home, I really didn't do any homework. I did what I had to do to get by."

The statistics about working students show exactly how <u>employment undermines education</u>. Recent studies show that three-fourths of all students have part-time jobs, and a quarter of those working students spend more time on the job than in school. Moreover, one study showed that the mean GPA (grade point average) for working students was

NOTES

Students' part-time jobs cause decrease in education.

causes: poor child labor laws and unethical business practices

Jobs provide money for luxuries but take time from studies.

---

* My thanks to Carolyn Spencer and Beverly Arbon, who teach at the English Language Center at Brigham Young University, for their paper at Intermountain TESOL (Provo, 1991), "Myths Underlying Writing Tasks," for the origin of the split-page summary-planning idea used in this chapter.

1.92 while the GPA for non-working students was 2.24. The bottom line is that <u>part-time jobs distract students from classes and homework and encourage students to spend their wages on frivolous self-gratification.</u>

  <u>The students themselves, however, are not to blame for this crisis: America's unethical business practices are.</u> It is no coincidence that the1980s saw a dramatic increase in white collar crime. As television producer Norman Lear says, "America has become a game show. Winning is all that matters. Cash prizes. Get rich quick. We are the captive of a culture that celebrates instant gratification and individual success no matter the larger costs." <u>Instant gratification—</u> which is the only lesson students learn from their part-time jobs—<u>is diametrically opposed to goals of education which stress personal fulfillment, learning, and long-term commitment to society and to the environment.</u>

  <u>The solutions for the current crisis in education are to make business practices more ethical and to revise our current child labor laws.</u> White collar criminals should receive prison sentences, not just a slap on the wrists. College curriculum should be revised to require all students to take <u>courses in business ethics.</u> Flashy <u>advertising for those luxury items</u> that teenagers buy, such as clothes, alcohol, music, and cars, <u>should be taken off television.</u> Finally, our child labor laws must become far more strict. Currently, some state laws permit students to work as many as 46 hours per week while attending school. <u>All high school students should be restricted to working 10 or fewer hours a week,</u> and college students should not be able to enroll in classes if they are working more than 10 hours a per week. Once <u>education is restored to a position of importance,</u> work can once again teach the virtues of self-discipline and responsibility. Education, not jobs at McDonald's, should have the highest priority. If American doesn't change its priorities soon, America's educational prize may be as worthless as last week's losing lottery ticket.

Dudley Erskine Devlin
Colorado State University

Students concentrate on making money

Reason for the problem is unethical business practices which focus on goals of instant gratification.

Solutions: reform child labor laws to maximum of 10 hours/week, Work to improve business ethics. Make education the first priority.

Below are three summaries written by students about the article above. Then do the Exercise that follows. Notice that while the students use some of the vocabulary from the article, they use their own phrases and sentences in their summaries. That is, they do not copy the sentences of the author of the original article. Instead, they use the notes (in the wide right margin), and details that they remember from the article to construct their summaries.

I

"Business and Education in America," an essay by Dudley Erskine Devlin, attributes the downfall in America's educational achievement to the increase in high school and college students who hold part-time jobs. Mr. Devlin believes that, beginning in the 1980s, there has developed a crisis of unethical business practices, encouraging young people to place more value on money and profit than on the benefits of education. As a solution, Devlin suggests limiting the hours which a student can spend at his or her job to 10, imprisoning white collar criminals, requiring courses in business ethics, and removing advertising from television for items which appeal to young consumers such as alcohol, music, and cars. Implementing these solutions will "'restore education to a position of importance," and only then can we "once again teach the virtues of self-discipline and responsibility."

II

Dudley Erskine Devlin, in his essay entitled "Business and Education in America," blames lax child labor laws and unethical business practices for the decline in America's education endeavors. He states that, for high school and college students, jobs and education are not compatible. He demonstrates that not only does student employment detract from the students' overall academic performance, but the money earned from these jobs is spent with a blatant disregard for financial planning. Devlin states several solutions to these problems, including improving business practices and revising the current child labor laws. Finally, he states that students should work less and make education a higher priority than money.

III

Dudley Erskine Devlin's "Business and Education in America" explores the theory of how our capitalistic society is slowly destroying the education values of our youth. Devlin suggests that a student's increasing work hours and decreasing grade point average are directly related. In his own words, "... as students' working hours increase, both their grade point averages and their academic ambitions decrease." Devlin also states that the money earned in these jobs is spent on frivolity—fast food, clothes, entertainment. Furthermore, he concludes that the decline in the American educational system may be traced to unethical business practices and lax child labor laws. Devlin's solution? No more than 10 hours of work per week for all high school and college students, along with stricter penalties for white collar crime.

Exercise C

1. With a small group of classmates, examine how each paragraph of summary follows the guidelines for writing summaries. Identify the introduction, the body, and the conclusion of each summary.

2. Circle the connectors used in each paragraph. How do these connectors help the reader?

3. With your group, discuss the direct quotations ("...") used by students in paragraphs I and III. Why did these students choose to use phrases from the original article?

4. Which of the summaries do you think is the most successful? Why? Use specific detail from the original article and the student summaries to support your opinion.

Organization of Summaries

Like most academic writing, summaries have a beginning, a middle, and an end. The **introduction** of the summary must contain the <u>kind</u> (that is, an article? a book? a film? a report?), the <u>title</u>, and the <u>author</u> of the written material. In that way, the audience knows what is being summarized and where the material originated. Below are some examples of introductory summary sentences. The essential information that introduces the article to the reader is **boldfaced**.

- In an **article** entitled **"Summer's Bloodsuckers," Hendrik Hertzberg** describes the reason why mosquitoes whine.

- In **Sophfronia Scott Gregory's article, "Teaching Young Fathers the Ropes,"** she presents the problem of helping unmarried black fathers the skills they need for fatherhood.

- **"You Just Play Through It,"** an **article** by **Richard Hoffer,** narrates the story of Heather Farr, a rising golf star, as she battles cancer.

In addition, the introduction to the summary should state the main point of the original article. That is, after reading the first sentence, the reader should know, in general, the single main point of the article.

The middle of the academic summary, the **body**, contains the main ideas of the article <u>in the same order</u> that they appeared in the article You should not simply copy the words, phrases, and sentences of the author of the article. Instead, you must use your own sentences to summarize (although some of the words will, of course, be the same as those in the article). In order to use your own sentences and vocabulary, rather than copying the words and phrases from the original article, you might use just your notes— not the article itself—to write the rough draft of your summary. Then refer to the article as you revise your first draft.

<u>NOTE:</u> Sometimes, as you write a summary, you will use a phrase or sentence directly from the article. Then you must use quotation marks ["..."] to show the reader that the phrase or sentence belongs to the author of the original article and not to the

summary writer (see Example II below).

The body of the summary will be a miniature version of the original article. You will use appropriate connectors to help your reader. Furthermore, it is important for the <u>reader</u> of the summary to understand that the information you are writing comes from the original source. In a similar way to identifying the person you might interview, it is necessary to refer to the author of the original material in the body of the summary. Possible introductory phrases include

According to Hoffer, ...	Ms. Gregory believes that ...
Hertzberg describes ...	The author presented ...

The **conclusion** of the summary should briefly relate the conclusion of the author of the original article. In the same way as you have summarized the rest of the article, the conclusion should <u>not</u> contain your judgments or conclusions (for example, "This wonderful article," or "I hated this article" or "The conclusion in this article is right/wrong"). That is, your summary should be <u>objective</u>; you should report just the main ideas.

Exercise D

Below are two summaries, each about 100 words in length, written about the articles that are introduced above. Note the introduction, body, and conclusion sections of each paragraph of summary. Then answer the questions that follow.

I

In an article entitled "Summer's Bloodsuckers," Hendrik Hertzberg describes the reason why mosquitoes whine. According to Hertzberg, the answer is sex: male mosquitoes whine to attract the female. The article also describes the life span of the mosquito and the process the female uses to feed her young—that is, extracting blood during a "mosquito bite." Finally, Hertzberg presents the research being done at the Mosquito and Fly Research Unit of the U.S. Department of Agriculture in Gainesville, Florida to control mosquitoes with both chemical agents and, more recently, genetic engineering that will prevent breeding. (96 words)

II

In Sophfronia Scott Gregory's article, "Teaching Young Fathers the Ropes," she presents the problem of helping unmarried black fathers learn the skills they need for fatherhood. According to Ms. Gregory, new programs like The Responsive Fathers Program in Philadelphia help "young unmarried men become better fathers, providers and mates through counseling services" and job preparation. The article explains that the program, sponsored by Public/Private Ventures, believes in long-term solutions. Because so many black children grow up without fathers, the program targets unemployed young black males. For three to six years, participants work to become responsible, self-sufficient productive citizens. (100 words)

1. Underline the introductory phrases that help the reader identify the parts of each summary that distinguish between the author of the original article and the summary writer.

2. How does the second sentence of each summary help direct the reader?

3. What questions could you ask the authors of each of these summaries? That is, what summary points seem confusing or incomplete?

4. Which of the two articles would you prefer to read? Why?

Exercise E

With a partner, choose three of the paragraphs from previous chapters in this book from the list below. Write a single sentence of summary (25 words or fewer) for each of those paragraphs. Your audience is a student who has not read the paragraph. Be sure to identify the <u>kind</u>, <u>title</u>, and <u>author</u> of each paragraph in your summary.

Then join another set of partners (so you will be in a small group of 2 sets of partners, 4 people). In your group, share your summary. If you have questions about the other summary, ask the summary writers.

Paragraphs:

Chapter 2	The Cold Front	p. 42
Chapter 3	Indonesia's Transmigration Program	p. 66
Chapter 3	Java Wedding	p. 68-69
Chapter 4	The Student Center	p. 91
Chapter 5	How to Fail a Big Test	p. 118
Chapter 5	Routine	p. 122
Chapter 7	Solar Cell Energy	p. 167

Writing Assignment 2

Read the article below. Your audience is a person who has not read this article. Then write a single paragraph of summary, following the guidelines above. First, re-read the article. Underline the main ideas in each paragraph. Make notes about the main ideas in the wide right margin. Then, cover the original article. Use the notes you made and your memories of the article as you write your paragraph of summary.

<u>Note:</u> Some sentences in the article have been omitted; the omissions are indicated by ellipses, that is, three dots [...].

Women in the Driver's Seat*

What would a car look like if it had been designed by a woman? Seat belts would not wrinkle clothes or smash breasts. Shoe heels would not be worn out by pedal pushing. And there would definitely be a place to put a purse.

Today's cars reflect their makers: men. For the most part, they are designed by men, for men. They have been customized for men's comfort, men's fascination with technology, men's need to speed. "In the past, any car for a woman came in the form of tokenism," says Joseph Molina, spokesman for the Greater Los Angeles Motor Car Dealers Association, referring to the Dodge La Femme and Ms. Mustang of the '60s. "But cars were designed primarily with men in mind."

Slowly but surely, however, women are infiltrating the field of car design—they are even being pursued by car makers offering scholarships to study automotive design. As a result, future cars may have an entirely new look. "I approach design from a woman's point of view," says Amy Hiroshige, a 31-year-old senior designer at Mitsubishi Motors in Cypress, California. "It should be easier for women to operate switches with long nails, and easier for women to get out of a car in skirts."

Although some of these inconveniences might seem trivial, they are not so to women. Nor are they to a car industry whose best efforts to accommodate women in the past was to paint a car pink and put in an extra-large makeup mirror. Chelsea Lau, a transportation design student at Art Center College of Design in Pasadena, says she brings a different approach to her designs. To her, car design is comparable to fashion design and gives her an opportunity to incorporate her style and personality. "I pay a lot of attention to detail," says Lau, 25, who moved to Pasadena three years ago from Hong Kong. "I think about daily life, try to solve problems, try to think of needs as a female, consider grocery shopping, dry-cleaning, how operating a car could be easier for a woman." ...

According to research, women make up about half of the car-buying public (although luxury cars still are bought mostly by men). And although car companies say they are now taking women into consideration more than ever when designing cars, there are some things, most women would agree, that just haven't gotten it right. "The seat belts always

* Heiman, Andrea. 1992. "Women in the Driver's Seat," Los Angeles Times, reprinted in the Fort Collins Coloradoan, August 14, 1992, B1. Reprinted by permission.

wrinkle my clothes," complains Vicki Karlan, 25, a health educator. "I also wish there was more light inside a car. At night I always check to make sure no one is in the car, but there is not a lot of light, and it's dangerous." Says Mary Larkin, a 28-year-old concierge: "The headrests come to the wrong place. The seats move forward and backward, not up and down to compensate for the smaller size."...

Not only have women's comfort and convenience been ignored, but women have been left out of many safety considerations. For example, federal regulations require injury testing only on male dummies, which means safety systems in cars are designed to protect healthy young males, says Brien O'Neill, president of the Insurance Institute for Highway Safety, a non-profit research institute funded by automobile insurers. As a result, companies design their safety features, including safety belts and air bags, for males rather than for females (although many auto companies do their own independent testing with female dummies). "If a dummy were a female, there would be differences in dimensions," O'Neill says. "There is a lack of tolerance in females. All the research on injury has been done on males."

In both its testing and its designs, the industry is making efforts to cater more to women's comfort and safety... "Companies want women to have input in their designs, so the ideas that male executives put forward that have pitfalls can be identified," says Carl Olsen, chairman of transportation for the Center for Creative Studies in Detroit. "They're also discovering women can be as creative as men when it comes to cars, and they see what an asset they are." ... Truman Pollard, chief designer at Mazda Research and Development of North America Inc., says the industry is working on adjustable seat belts that would fit more comfortably as well as on making controls easier to use. "Things have to work for women and men," Pollard says. ...

Andrea Heiman*
Los Angeles Times
August 14, 1992 B1

Peer Feedback: Discuss with your group the main ideas of the article below, and answer the following questions about the article.

1. Underline the topic sentences and circle the controlling ideas in at least three of the body paragraphs.
2. Locate the resources used by the author: observation, interview, library research. Underline with wavy lines (~~) the introductory phrases to four of these resources.

3. Identify the techniques of support used by the author of this article. Label those techniques in the margins.

4. What other design changes might you make for women if you designed the inside of a car?

Pre-Writing and Drafting: Now, make the necessary notes in the wide right margin of the article that will help you gather the information necessary to write a single paragraph of summary. Then write a draft of the summary. Be sure to include an introduction, a body, and a conclusion. Use your own words and sentences. Be careful to distinguish the author's ideas by using appropriate introductory phrases.

Peer Feedback: Share your summary with a partner. Does the introduction contain the essential information about the kind, title, and author of the original article? Does the body of the summary make the distinction between the author of the article and the writer of the summary? Does the conclusion parallel the conclusion in the essay? Discuss your findings with your partner.

Revision: Using the advice from your partner (and what you learned from reading your partner's summary), make changes that will improve your summary. Then write the final draft of your summary.

Exercise F

*Read the article below. With a small group of classmates, discuss the article. Use the questions below to begin your discussion. As you talk with your classmates, take notes **in your journal** about the discussion.*

1. What is the purpose of the article? Be specific. Find details in the article to support your opinion.

2. Who is the audience for this article? Discuss the age, education, background, and interests of this audience. In what way(s) are the audience and the purpose of this article integrated?

3. Are you persuaded by the article? Why or why not? Use specific detail from the article to support your opinion.

4. How do the main ideas in this article differ from an article about this topic in your country? In what ways would the article be similar?

Furry and Feathery Therapists*

... An estimated 52 million dogs reside in U.S. homes. also 56 million cats, 45 million birds, 250 million fish and 125 other assorted creatures ... "Animals are so taken for granted," says Alan Beck, director of the University of Pennsylvania's Center for the Interaction of Animals and Society. "We have a gut feeling they're good for you, but how they're good and what can be done with that, we don't know."

Now things are beginning to change. A variety of health professionals have started to assess rigorously pets' impact on physical and mental health. Meanwhile, the beneficiaries of programs in prisons, hospitals and nursing homes do not much care about cool science but are warmly grateful for what amounts to animal therapy. A groundbreaking study came in 1980, when researchers from the Universities of Maryland and Pennsylvania reported on the survival rate of 92 patients with serious heart trouble. Of the 39 without pets, eleven were dead within a year. The remaining 53 had animals ranging from an iguana and Bantams to the typical cats, dogs, and fish; just three of those patients died. The results were not due to increased exercise, like walking a dog. Even owning fish proved a boon. Later research provided a partial explanation: an animal's presence helps lower blood pressure and reduce stress.

More recent studies suggest other pluses. In a 1984 Philadelphia study of patients about to undergo dental surgery, some were hypnotized, others were told to look at an aquarium full of fish, and the rest sat quietly for 20 minutes. The first two groups experienced the least discomfort. Surprisingly, watching fish was as effective as being hypnotized. Why animals are so soothing is still a mystery. Psychiatrist Aaron Katcher of the University of Pennsylvania speculates that stroking animals and talking to them stimulates the brain's production of its own pleasure chemicals, the endorphins.

Psychological benefits have also been documented. Troubled teenagers, for example, are more likely to open up when a therapist brings a dog along. Carol Antoinette Peacock, a psychologist in Watertown, Massachusetts, starts treatment of new adolescent patients with an introduction to her dog Toffy. "It helps them to trust me," says Peacock, who finds that patients sometimes express their feelings through the animal. "They'll say, 'Your dog looks pretty sad,' meaning 'I'm pretty sad.'" ...In Lima, Ohio, at a facility for mentally ill [prisoners], part of the courtyard resembles a barnyard. Sheep, goats, ducks, rabbits—even deer—roam around. "We're finding the prisoners who have pets are less violent," says Psychiatric Social Worker David Lee. In a double bonus, women inmates in Gig Harbor, Washington, are training special dogs to aid the handicapped. ...

Hospitals are finding that animals ease patient isolation as well as anxiety and distress. Three of the most popular visitors to elderly patients at Beth Abraham Hospital in New York City come from the A.S.P.C.A: Jake, a bull mastiff; Boris, a 50-pound Samoyed; and Regina, a tortoise shell cat. At Children's Hospital in Denver, staff members and volunteers bring in their dogs, cleanly clad in smocks or T-shirts, and make rounds of wards. Retirement and nursing homes are welcoming pets too. The Tacoma Lutheran Home in Washington boasts a menagerie of furry and feathery live-ins. A stroke patient who had lost motor control groomed an Angora rabbit; another worked on speech problems by talking to a cockatiel...

Pets are no cure-all, of course. "If you feel sick, you can't just pet your dog and call the doctor in the morning," says Veterinarian Larry Glickman of the University of Pennsylvania. Moreover, they require care, can bite and cause allergies. But what they bring can be hard to improve on. New Yorker Reuben Selnick, 61, is a recovering alcoholic who adopted a cat named Oliver. 'I was at a very low ebb when I met Oliver," he says. "Now I have something to live for."

Anastasia Toufexis
Time
March 30, 1987

Writing Assignment 3

Reread the article. Underline the main ideas, and make notes about those ideas in the wide right margin. Then, cover the original article. Using the notes you made and your memories of the article, write a paragraph of summary about this article. Your audience is a friend in your country who has not read the article.

Pre-Writing and Drafting: Follow the guidelines for the introduction, the body, and the conclusion of summaries (on page 237). Consider your audience as you begin drafting your summary.

Peer Feedback: Share your summary draft with a small group of classmates. As you read your classmates' summaries, take notes in your journal about the best parts of each summary. Then discuss the best parts of each student's summary. Using the best parts of each summary, write a <u>single</u> summary for the group.

Exercise G

Use the article above to answer the following questions.

1. Find the ellipses […] that indicate sentences have been omitted from this article. Why might someone use ellipses?

2. Underline examples of the resources (observation, interview, library research) in this article. Circle introductory phrases that introduce four of these resources.

3. Find examples of *facts, examples, experience,* and *description* in this article. Which details did you find the most interesting and valuable? Why?

4. What concluding technique(s) does this author use?

Citation of Articles

Readers of summaries may want to read the entire article. Therefore, you may want to **cite the source** of the article so that readers can go to the library and find the article. There are many forms of citation (also called **references**). Below is a common form. Notice the **order of information**, the **capitalization**, and the **punctuation** of the citation.

EXAMPLE:

Last, First. 19__. "Title of Article." *Title of Journal*   vol(issue):pages.

Below is a list of references of the articles used in this chapter. The list is arranged alphabetically by the last name of the author (Last, First). Examine the form of these citations.

References

Gregory, Sophfronia. 1992. "Teaching Young Fathers the Ropes." *Time* 140(6):49.

Heiman, Andrea. 1992. "Women in the Designer's Seat." *Los Angeles Times* reprinted in *The Fort Collins Coloradoan*, August 14, 1992, B1.

Hertzberg, Hendrik. 1992. "Summer's Bloodsuckers." *Time* 140(6): 46–47.

Hoffer, Richard. 1992. "You Just Play Through It." *Sports Illustrated* 77(8): 52–54, 56.

Toufexis, Anastasia. 1987. "Furry and Feathery Therapists." *Time* 135(4):74.

Exercise H

Below are sentences containing citation information for articles from several magazines. Using the citation format in the Example on the previous page, alphabetize the references by last name of the author, and then write a reference list, using all of the citations.

1. "Cambodia: Can Women Survive the New 'Peace'?" by Chanthou Boua was published in *Ms.* The article was in Volume 3, Number 1 in September, 1992, on pages 19 to 21.

2. *The Utne Reader*, Vol. 53, in 1992, had an interesting article by Marjorie Kelly entitled "Are You Too Rich if Others are Poor?" The article was on pages 67 to 70.

3. Tony Oswald wrote an article published in *Fly Fishing* entitled "Belize, Please." It was in volume 12, No. 5, (January-February, 1990), on pages 4–5, and 22–23.

4. In the June 3, 1991 issue of *The New Yorker*, (volume X, pages 37–40), Edward Allen wrote a story entitled "More Songs About the Titanic."

5. In 1992, Karen A. Schriver wrote "Teaching Writers to Anticipate Readers' Needs" A Classroom-Evaluated Pedagogy." She published it in *Written Communication*, volume 9, number 2, on pages 179–208.

Writing Assignment 4

Reread an article that you located in the academic library and then used for your multiple paragraph assignment in the last chapter. (Or read another article from a magazine or a textbook.) Using the guidelines for summaries (above), write a clear summary of 125–225 words for a classmate who has not read that article.

> **Pre-Writing and Drafting:** As you reread the article, underline the main ideas and take notes about those ideas **in your journal**. Then organize the main ideas and draft the summary. Use appropriate introductory phrases. Try to make your summary clear and complete for your audience. Bring the original article to class, as well as the rough draft of your summary.
>
> **Peer Feedback:** Exchange original articles and summary drafts with a partner. As you read your partner's summary:
>
> - Circle the **introductory** material. Does it give the kind, title, and author of the article? If not, write a question about the necessary information.
> - Is the **body** of the summary complete? Does your partner distinguish the ideas of the author with appropriate introductory phrases? At the end of the summary, ask 1–2 questions (or make 1–2 suggestions) to help your partner improve the summary.
> - Is the conclusion of the summary clear? If not, write a question asking about the necessary information.
> - Read the original article. Have all the main ideas been included in the summary? If not, list the main ideas you think should be added at the end of your partner's summary.

- Has the writer of the summary used her/his own words? If the writer has used words from the original article, has she/he used quotation marks?
- Help your partner by marking any grammar or sentence structure problems that you see.
- Discuss your suggestions and marks with your partner.

Revision: Using your partner's advice (and what your learned from reading your partner's summary), make changes in your summary to improve it. Write a final draft of your summary. Then, **in your journal**, write a paragraph about the process you used as you revised your summary. What was easy? Difficult? What did you learn? Finally, write a citation for that article. Use the form on page 245.

Journal Assignment

Write a paragraph evaluating the learning experiences you have had in this chapter. What did you learn? How will what you learned help you in future academic classes?

Sentence Combining Assignment

The jokes below are written with short, choppy sentences, and some of the information is repeated. Combine some of the sentences so that the jokes flow more smoothly. You will eliminate some of the words in order to combine the sentences effectively. Use appropriate connectors when necessary.

I

One day a man went by a restaurant. He was poor. He was hungry. He could not resist the smell. It was meat. It was delicious. It came from inside the restaurant. He went in. The price of meat was extremely expensive. He looked at the meat. With a poor smile, he turned to leave. The boss of the restaurant suddenly appeared. He held the poor man. He held him by the sleeve. He said, "What? You are going without paying?" The poor man said, "I had nothing." The boss replied, "You smelled the meat, that's a part of the meat, so you should pay part of the fee!" The poor man was silent. He took out his billfold. The boss secretly smiled. The poor man showed his billfold. He showed it to the boss. Then he waved the billfold back and forth. "Did you hear some money in there?" he asked the boss. "Yes!" the boss replied. The poor man said, "Good. The sound is part of the money, so you've been paid already!"

Pan Jianxiang
(People's Republic of China)

II

One day a student took a test. The test was full of true-false questions. The student completed the test. He sat in his desk. He took a coin. The coin was in his pocket. He began playing. He was playing "flip the coin." Another student spoke. She asked him a question. She said, "Why are you flipping that coin?" The student replied. He said, "I'm checking my answers."

Issam Al-Azzawe
(Iraq)

III

The teacher assigned a task. He assigned it to a student. The assignment was to draw a car. The student drew two lines. The teacher asked, "Where is the car?" The student answered. He said, "The car left. The two lines are the street."

Ala Khalaf
(Jordon)

Appendix A

Diagnosing Your Language Strengths and Weaknesses

When you <u>speak</u> in English (or in your native language), the listener understands the difference between a statement and a question from your intonation—that is, the "music" of your voice. If, for example, you raise your voice at the end of a sentence, the sentence may be a question. In addition, you will use facial expressions (for example, raised eyebrows or a down-turned mouth) and body language (for example, a pointed finger or a hand on your hip) to indicate your feelings about what you are saying.

However, when you present your ideas in writing, these elements of communication are not available to you. Still, you must help your audience to understand your ideas. Punctuation and capitalization rules help you express your ideas clearly in writing. The exercises below will help you to diagnose your strengths and weaknesses in capitalization and punctuation. If you need to learn more about the language elements below, use your grammar book.

Exercise A: Capitalization Diagnostic

Write the following sentences, using capital letters where they are needed. Be prepared to explain to a small group of classmates why you capitalized each letter.

1. tomas villaroel is a good student.

2. the classes he enjoys are american history and organic chemistry.

3. he is also a good athlete, and he plays soccer every friday at alfred packer memorial gymnasium.

4. tomas' soccer team is named the allison eagles.

5. their coach, dr. rodney stephens, is responsible for the team's improvement.

6. in fact, the team is playing in the championships next april in miami, florida.

7. tomas also wants to visit many places he has read about like philadelphia, baltimore, and washington, d.c.

8. tomas' roommate, ali, comes from libya.

9. his major is business management, so most of his classes are in the clark building.

10. tomas and ali often go to movies together; last week they saw"batman returns."

Exercise B

Write five sentences that use capital letters, but do not use capital letters. Exchange papers with a partner. Capitalize your partner's paper correctly. Then give the paper back to your classmate, and check to see whether or not you capitalized correctly.

Punctuation

In written English, the period and the comma are the most widely used forms of punctuation. Question marks (?) are sometimes used, and semi-colons (;) are also used frequently; see Chapter 1 for information on the use of semi-colons. Below are some general rules for punctuation.

Periods (.)

1. Use a period at the end of a sentence.

2. Use a period after an abbreviation:

Mr.	lb.	Jan.	Mon.	N.Y.
Mrs.	oz.	Feb.	Tues.	U.S.A.
Ms. (but not after Miss)	ft.	Nov.	Wed.	U.A.E.
Dr.	in.	Dec.	Sun.	D.C.

Question Marks

1. Use a question mark after a direct question.
   A. Where are you going?
   B. What classes are you taking this semester?
   C. He did? (In spoken language, intonation would signal that this was a question.)

2. Do not use a question mark after a reported question or an indirect question.
   A. He asked where the post office is.
   B. I wonder what time it is.

Commas

1. Use a comma to separate items (words, phrases, or clauses) in a series.
   A. The colors of our flag are red, white, and green.
   B. He looked for the missing money in the desk, under the bookcase, and between the chairs, but he couldn't find it.
   C. Today students are using computers when they study, when they work, and when they play.

NOTE: the comma before the "and" that connects the last two items is optional.

2. Do not use a comma if every item in the series is joined by a connector.
   A. He ate bacon and eggs and toast and jam for breakfast.
   B. The Joneses will buy a Ford or a Chevrolet or a Honda.

3. Use a comma to separate the items in an address or date.
   A. On July 4, 1776, the Declaration of Independence was signed in Philadelphia, Pennsylvania.
   B. Syracuse, New York is the site of several old salt mines.

NOTE: Use the comma only if there is more than one item in the address or date.
   A. Syracuse is also the location of Syracuse University.
   B. The War of 1812 was fought between the Americans and the British.

3. Use a comma after a long introductory phrase or clause.
   A. After he listened to tapes in the Language Laboratory, Carlos went to the Student Center.
   B. In most situations, Carlos can communicate very well.
   C. As a consequence, he has made many friends.

4. Use commas to set off **appositives**. An appositive is a word or phrase that provides *extra* information about a noun. It always directly follows the noun, and it is set off by commas if the meaning of the sentence is clear without it (that is, it is extra information, not necessary information).
   A. Pizza, **an American food**, is easy to prepare. (Extra information)
   B. Mr. Stacey, **my teacher**, speaks ten languages. (Extra information)
   C. Chao, **who is from China**, is a Physics major. (Extra information)
   Appositives are often used during sentence combining.
   A. Perlini is a young woman from India. She wants to become an engineer.
   Perlini, **a young woman from India,** wants to become an engineer.
   B. Mountain Lakes is my hometown. It is very quiet there on Saturday nights.
   Mountain Lakes, **my hometown,** is very quiet on Saturday nights.

Exercise C: Punctuation Diagnostic

Punctuate the following sentences correctly. Use commas, periods, and question marks. Be ready to state why you used each mark of punctuation.

1. Subhi who lives in Morocco arrived in the U S on June 26 1992

2. For several months he lived at 104 Princeton Avenue in Dallas Texas

3. Now he lives with his parents grandparents and three cousins in St Louis Missouri

4. Is he happy there

5. He likes it a lot because his friend whose name is Mike lives there

6. In addition St Louis has shopping malls an opera and a famous baseball team

7. Does Subhi eat often at McDonald's

8. He prefers French Mexican or Arabic food to American food

9. Subhi says that he is going to begin school at St Louis University which is in the city next fall

10. He hopes to live in the dormitory meet many American students and have a good time while he is there

Exercise D

Write 10 sentences that require commas. Do not insert the commas or other forms of punctuation (periods, question marks). Exchange papers with a classmate. Insert the necessary punctuation. Then discuss with your classmate your reasons for inserting each punctuation mark.

Exercise E: Appositive Diagnostic

Combine the following sentences, using appositives.

1. My friend is Rafia. She is from Sudan.

2. She lives in Cambridge House. It is the large apartment building on the west side of the campus.

3. Rafia's roommate is Paula Wang. Paula is majoring in Electrical Engineering.

4. Paula is the president of the Chinese Student Association. The CSA is one of many student associations on the campus.

5. When she is finished with her studies, Paula will return to Taiwan. Taiwan is her home.

6. Her brothers are Kenny and Jeff Wang. They are also studying engineering.

Exercise F

Read the following paragraph. Then, with a small group of classmates, insert the correct capitalization and punctuation. The slashes (/) indicate the end of each sentence.

the people of northwestern argentina the coyas adore a goddess called *pacha mama* / she is considered the goddess that gives fertility to the land / she has black shiny hair dark brown eyes and a big mouth with thick lips that are always smiling / perhaps her smiling mouth is the major attraction in her face / like her beautiful eyes and hair her complexion is dark / she wears a brightly colored poncho a typical native dress / her costume is similar to the ponchos worn by the northwestern indians / in fact she looks similar to those people /

Ani Sala
(Argentina)

Apostrophes (')

1. Use apostrophes to show possession or ownership. Usually, persons or living things can possess or own.

   With singular nouns:

   A. A mother's love is precious

   B. My brother-in-law's car is a Porsche.

   C. He never likes anyone else's ideas.

   D. Ali will receive his master's degree in June.

   With plural nouns that do not end in s :

   A. All the women's papers were completed on schedule.

   B. The children's parents were able to come to the meeting.

   C. I will see you again at the salesmen's conference.

2. Use an apostrophe (without s) to show possession:

   With plural nouns that end in s :

   A. All the students' reports were excellent.

   B. The dogs' ferocious growling terrified the child.

   C. For two cents' worth, he could cut your throat.

   With singular nouns that end in s (the s is optional):

   A. Charles' new car is a Fiat. (OR Charles's new car is a Fiat.)

   B. The waitress' tip was small. (OR The waitress's tip was small.)

3. Use an apostrophe to replace an omitted letter or letters. These shortened forms are called contractions. Notice that the apostrophe goes in the exact place where the letters were omitted, and the two words are joined as one.

A.	do not	⟶	don't
B.	did not	⟶	didn't
C.	would not	⟶	wouldn't
D. (EXCEPTION)	will not	⟶	won't

Exercise G: Apostrophe Diagnostic

Write the following groups of words, using apostrophes to show possession. Then use what you have written to write complete sentences.

1. an essay by Natalia _____

2. the complaints of the student _____

3. the problems of the students _____

4. the twins born to Yusmary _____

5. the oil well owned by Shen _____

6. the toy of the child _____

7. the delight of the people _____

8. the ideas of everyone _____

9. the capital of my country _____

10. the example of Naser _____

Colons (:)

1. Use a colon to introduce a list at the end of a sentence.
   A. He loves only three things: his car, his boat, and himself.
   B. I like three kinds of sandwiches: peanut butter and jelly, turkey, and cream cheese.

2. Use a colon after the salutation (that is, the greeting) in a formal business letter.
   A. Dear Professor Latief:
   B. Dear Sirs:

The Hyphen   (-)

1. Use a hyphen with compound numbers.

    forty-seven   twenty-three   eighty-eight

2. Use a hyphen for compound words when your dictionary indicates that the hyphen is necessary for correct spelling.

    sons-in-law   hide-and-seek   hide-out   so-so

3. Use a hyphen to divide a word at the end of a typed or written line. Your dictionary will show you how to divide English words. Use the following guidelines.

    A. divide only at syllable boundaries

iden-tify	not	ide-ntify
infor-mation	not	info-rmation

    B. do not divide a one-syllable word

    C. do not divide a contraction

    D. do not divide numbers written in numerical terms

    7, 400, 000   not   7, 400 - 000

Exercise H: Hyphen Diagnostic

Divide the words below as you would at the end of a line. If you are not certain of the syllable division, use your dictionary.

1. paragraph _____

2. sentence _____

3. word _____

4. writing _____

5. written _____

6. does _____

7. dictionary _____

8. punctuation _____

9. capitalization _____

10. nineteenth _____

Exercise I

Read the paragraph below. With a partner, insert correct capitalization and punctuation. The slashes (/) indicate the ends of sentences.

Taxis in Taipei

consider your life and health / dont take a taxi in taipei / in a typical example i took a taxi that nearly killed me several times on the way to my friends house / first i raised my hand to stop a taxi but another taxi saw me so the driver increased his speed / he cut across the center line drove up on the curb where i was standing and nearly ran over me / being scared made me jump back about one meter / i got in the taxi and gave him my friends address on taichung street and the driver immediately drove off without signaling / the car behind us almost hit us going sixty mph / the driver didn't pay attention to red traffic lights other cars or pedestrians / i told him i wasnt in a hurry but he told me not to worry and continued to break all the traffic rules / suddenly there was a crash as the driver who was trying to avoid a bicyclist ran onto the sidewalk and into a post / the driver jumped out to examine his taxi and said "its ok / lets go / i said no and told him that li my friend lived nearby / i paid him the money and he drove away just like nothing had happened / i felt lucky to be alive and i decided i would never take a taxi in taipei again /

Kenny Wang
(Taiwan

Appendix B

Taking an Essay Examination or Short-Answer Test

Writing a good response to a short-answer or an essay test answer requires the same skills as writing a good paragraph or essay. First, you must understand the test question: what does the **audience** expect? what will the **purpose of your response** be? Next, you must **gather adequate material, organize it appropriately**, and **write the response**.

Analyzing the Question

Since the topic for an essay-test answer is determined by the question, it is important to understand exactly what the question is asking. Interpreting the question correctly (that is, determining the purpose of the question) and communicating the answer are essential skills for success in taking an essay exam.

Breaking an essay question into parts is the first step. Look for the **controlling ideas** in the questions that clarify and limit what your answer (your response to the question) should include. Also, look for the words that direct the focus (that is, the <u>form</u>) of the response. Below are four essay test questions; their controlling ideas have been circled. Notice that key words describing the <u>form</u> of the response are **boldfaced**.

1. **Explain** three significant events or inventions that make our milk today the best ever.

2. **Discuss** the **process** involved in testing pollution that is caused by carbon monoxide.

3. **Give three reasons** why the "infrastructure crisis" is so apparent in the U.S. highway system.

4. **Analyze** the relationship of fatty acids and/or cholesterol to heart disease.

Identifying the Focus

Many questions on essay (or short-answer) tests include words that direct the writer (or give directions) about the focus, or the form, of the expected response. In the assignments above, those key words were boldfaced. They tell the writer how to arrange (that is, organize) the material for the response.

When you read the essay task, does it ask you to describe a process, compare and/or contrast two ideas, analyze the causes of an effect, and/or explain an answer to a question? Look for key words; notice in the list below that some key words can mean different things.

Key Word	**Additional Meanings**
Compare	Contrast, OR Compare and Contrast
Contrast	
Define	Simple (1-2 sentences) definition OR Complex (a paragraph with details)
Relate	Compare OR Discuss Causes/Effects
Trace	Chronological Order (First, Second)

Some key words are more general. They may indicate one or more of the following meanings. You will have to read the test question carefully to determine the actual meaning of the general key words below.

Key Words	**Possible Interpretations**
	Reasons AND/OR Results
Describe	Causes AND/OR Effects
Discuss	Types OR Kinds
Explain	Differences AND/OR Similarities
	Process
	Complex Definition
	Answer to a Question

Many test questions require that your answer include your opinion. Remember to make your opinion clear. Your topic sentence will be a **statement of opinion**. The key words below direct the writer to state and support an opinion.

Analyze	Criticize (or Critique)
Evaluate	Interpret
Justify	Prove

Some test questions will not require an opinion. In these questions, your answer should include a **topic sentence of intent,** a sentence that makes a clear statement of purpose. The key words below ask writers to explain without giving an opinion.

Outline   Review

State   Summarize

Demonstrate   Show

Exercise A

<u>Read</u> *the academic short-answer or essay test assignments below. With a small group of classmates,* <u>circle</u> *the controlling ideas in each task. Then* <u>underline</u> *the key words that direct the writer about the form of the response.* <u>Discuss</u> *whether or not an opinion is required.* <u>Describe</u> *the expectations of the academic audience. Finally, discuss possible organization and detail for the answers to the questions.*

1. Compare two types of management performance review, and discuss which you think is preferable.

2. During World War II, what effect did the bombing of Pearl Harbor have on American public opinion of the Japanese and World War II?

3. Define four of the following terms in 1 or 2 sentences:
   A. fixed input
   B. pure profit
   C. elasticity of supply
   D. variable cost
   E. marginal product

4. Should current federal and private proposals for protecting the nation's waterfowl population be improved?

Planning Your Time

The amount of time and/or the number of points given for a question can help you decide how long your answer should be. For example, if the short-answer (or essay) test consists of three questions to be answered in 50 minutes, you will probably have time for only one-paragraph answers. And you will have approximately 15 minutes for each question. In contrast, if the test consists of two essay tasks, one that counts 80 points, and the other that counts 20 points, and you have an hour to complete the test, 80 per cent of your time might be spent on the first question, and 20 per cent on the second.*

<u>Read the entire test before you begin to answer the questions.</u> That way, you can efficiently plan your time. How many questions are there? Are some questions more important than others? How much time should you spend with each question in order to

---

* NOTE: Many professors expect the test to be completed; you will be penalized if you do not complete all the answers.

complete the test? In addition, quickly reading the test before beginning to answer the questions will allow you to find the questions that will be easy and quick to answer. That may leave more time to answer more difficult questions.

As you plan your time, be aware that the time you have for each answer will determine not only what information you must include but also what information you cannot include in your answer. That is, if your time is limited, you will have to select the most important information to write for your audience.

Exercise B

With a small group of classmates, read the academic essay-test assignment below. The time allotted for each question is given in italics. Discuss the differences between the answer you would give in the time indicated, and the answer you would write if you had only half that time (for example, 50 minutes OR 25 minutes).

1. You are the only doctor in a small, rural town. People of all ages begin coming into your clinic with the following symptoms:

   headache   fever of 102 degrees Fahrenheit

   aches in joints   swelling in the abdomen

   The people in the village are not familiar with the germ theory of disease, and they are very frightened. Write an explanation of the disease process for these people. (*1 hour*)

2. Should the National Park Service continue its "let burn" policy when natural fires occur within park boundaries? Why or why not? (*30 minutes*)

3. Is the role of women in the development of underdeveloped countries an equity issue or a productivity issue? (*50 minutes*)

4. What is a sumptuary excise tax? Give an example to show the circumstances and the objective of using this task. (*20 minutes*)

Organizing Material for the Response

A written response to a test question, like paragraphs or essays, has a beginning, a middle, and an end. So although your time is limited, it is important to plan and to organize before you write. You might only make a few notes, perhaps even one or two words, for your main points and supporting detail. You will also consider an overall pattern of organization (chronological, most-to-least important or vice versa, or equal points). As you write, **think about your audience**.

Finally, as you plan your response, save a few minutes to re-read your answers before turning in your essay examination. Remember, some grammar mistakes can alter the meaning of your sentences or make your meaning unclear.

Exercise C

Read the academic assignments below. With a small group of classmates, circle the controlling ideas and underline the key words in each writing task. Discuss whether or not an opinion is required. Describe the expectations of the academic audience. Finally, discuss possible organization and detail for the answers to the questions.

1. As a manager of a cattle operation, you have found Brucellosis in your herd. Define the means of eradicating this disease and preventing its recurrence. Explain how each of these is effective.

2. Property tax is often considered a bad tax. Do you agree or disagree? Present your argument (for or against) on equity and efficiency grounds.

3. Describe the wheat rust cycle.

4. Are natural pest management techniques in agriculture as effective and efficient as petrochemical methods?

5. Is it feasible to make the Russian ruble a convertible currency? Why or why not?

6. If you were in charge of the armed forces, how would you handle the role of women in the military? Support your opinions with research.

20 Test-Taking Guidelines

1. Begin your study for an examination early. Do not wait until the night before the exam to begin studying.

2. Try to get an adequate amount of sleep the night before an exam.

3. Give yourself time in the morning of the exam to go through your regular routine (for example, shower, exercise, etc.).

4. Eat a good nutritious breakfast to help your body prepare for the test.

5. Plan your day before the exam. Include strategies for studying and for dealing with tension (anxiety) during the day.

6. Give yourself positive self-statements (for example, "You can do it," "Just do your best") throughout the day. Avoid making yourself doubt your own abilities.

7. Try to avoid other anxious students before the exam. They will only make you more anxious.

8. Stop studying at least a half hour before the test. Then, do something relaxing or pleasant for yourself right before the exam.

9. Avoid getting to class too early. Time just before examinations is usually spent engaging in worry.

10. Be aware of your own signs of developing anxiety. Use strategies to keep your tension at a manageable level (for example, breathe deeply, or imagine that you are in a pleasant relaxing place like the beach).

11. Be prepared: Have the right books, sharpened pencils, pens, paper. Also, bring a watch so that you can watch your time.

12. Sit in the seat you occupy during regular class sessions unless you will be easily distracted there. If you feel you may be distracted, move to a more isolated location in the room.

13. Do not reopen your books after you enter the exam room. That will only make you more anxious.

14. When you receive the test, identify which questions have more points.

15. Read each question twice, slowly. Underline key words and phrases.

16. If a question is confusing, try to reword it in a way that is clear for you.

17. Answer easier questions first. Then move on to more difficult ones.

18. If you cannot answer a question, go on to the next one. Return to that question only when you have completed answering all the questions you know.

19. One you have decided on an answer, do not alter your response.

20. Try to complete the exam a few minutes before the end of the test period. Look over the test to make sure you have answered all the questions completely.

INDEX

A

Academic libraries
    card catalog, 205-206
    computerized card catalog, 209-210
    Reference section, 211
    Reader's Guide, The, 217-218
Academic summary
    definition, 233
    organization, 237-238
Alternative point outline, 138
Apostrophes, use of, 255-256
Appositives, use of, 253-254
Audience
    definition, 4-5
    Guidelines for (inside front cover)

B

Basic point outline
    definition, 86-87
    format, 141
    Guidelines for, 88
Business letters
    of complaint, 17
    of informing and requesting, 13
    of invitation, 19

C

Call numbers (library), 205
Capitalization, use of, 251-252
Card catalog (library), 205-206
Cause-effect paragraphs
    connectors, 162
    definition, 157-158
    developing, 170-172, 175-178
    exercises, 162-166
Chronological connectors, 110
Citation, 245
Clarification paragraphs
    connectors, 125
    definition, 122
Clauses
    combining independent, 22-23
    combining dependent, 26
    dependent, 25-26
    independent, 21-23
    review of 27
Clustering, 3
Coherence
    definition, 82
    exercises, 83-84
Colons, use of, 256
Commas, use of, 253
Comparison/contrast paragraphs

alternative point outline, 138, 142
basic point outline, 141
connectors, 143-144
overall organization of, 150-151
using parallel structures in, 153
Computerized card catalog (library), 209-210
Computerized indexing journals (library), 221-222
Conjunctive adverbs, 24
Connectors
cause-effect, 162
chronological, 110
comparison-contrast, 143-144
definition, 125
for coherence, 82
for second sentences, 57
middle paragraph, 125, 143-144
Controlling ideas, 38-39
Contrast paragraphs (see comparison/contrast paragraphs)
Coordinate conjunctions, 22

D

Definition paragraphs
definition, 122
connectors, 125
Dependent clauses, 25-26
Description, Physical (technique of support), 67
Descriptors (library), 205
Dewey Decimal System (library), 213
Drafting paragraphs (see each Writing Assignment)

E

Ellipses, 239
Encyclopedias (library), 211
Envelopes, addressing, 9
Essay
definition, 189
introduction to, 196-197
overall topic sentence (thesis statement), 184
Example (technique of support), 66
Expanded point outline, 186-187
Explanation paragraphs
connectors, 125
definition/clarification, 122
process, 109-110

F

Facts (technique of support), 63

G

General reference section (library), 211
Guidelines
for defining the audience (inside front cover)
for modifying topic sentences, 95
for drafting point paragraph outlines, 88
for constructing second sentences, 61
for paragraph planning (inside front cover)
for revising (inside back cover)
for test-taking, 263-264

H

Hyphens, use of, 257

I

Indexing journals (library)
computerized, 221-222
definition, 215-216
Info-Trac, 221-222
Reader's Guide, The, 217-218
Info-Trac, 221-222
Intent, statement of (topic sentence), 36-37, 39
Interviews
definition, 170
samples, 171-172
reporting the results of, 172

J

Journals
definition, 6-7
(see also each Journal Assignment)
Journals (library) (see Periodicals)

L

LC (see Library of Congress)
Library of Congress (LC) System
definition, 211-212
subject classifications, 212

Letters
business, 12
envelopes, 9
personal, 7-8
"Long words" (conjunctive adverbs), 24

M

Middle paragraph connectors, 125, 143-144
Multiple paragraphs
definition, 183
developing, 183-184
expanding, 186-188, 190-193
overall topic sentence, 184

O

Opinion, statement of (topic sentence), 36
Organization of
cause-effect paragraphs, 158-159
comparison/contrast paragraphs, 137-138
overall paragraphs, 150-151
Outline
alternative point paragraphs, 138
basic point paragraphs, 86-87
expanded point paragraphs, 102-103
Overall organization
least to most important, 151
most to least important, 150
points of equal importance, 151
Overall topic sentence (thesis statement), 184

P

Paragraph, planning the
coherence, 82
concluding sentences, 42
controlling ideas, 38-39
format, 29
organization, 81
support, 63
topic sentence, 36-37
unity, 75
Paragraph planning Guidelines (inside front cover)
Parallelism, 153
Passive Voice
definition, 114-115
reducing use of, 117
Peer feedback (see each Writing Assignment)

Periodical indexing journals (see indexing journals)
Periodicals (journals)
identifying, 224-225
locating, 225-226
Periods, use of, 252
Personal experience (technique of support), 69-70
Personal letters, 7-8
Physical description (technique of support), 167
Point paragraph outlines
alternative, 138
alternative format, 142
basic format, 141
definition, 86-87
expanding, 102-102
format, 87
Guidelines, 88
Pre-writing
definition, 30, 35
brainstorming, 34
clustering, 31
listing, 30
looping, 34
review, 35
trees, 32
Primary sources, 201
Process paragraphs
definition, 109-110
problems with, 120
Punctuation
apostrophes, 255-256
colons, 256
commas, 253
diagnostic, 254
hyphens, 257
periods, 252
Purpose, 2 (see also each Writing Assignment)

Q

Question marks, use of, 252

R

Reader's Guide, The
definition, 216
abbreviations in, 217
abbreviations of periodicals, 218

Reference Section (library), 211
References (citation), 245
Revision
    definition, 78
    examples, 186-188
    Guidelines (inside back cover)
    modifying the topic sentence, 94-95
    (see also each Writing Assignment)

S

Scrambled paragraphs, 85-86
Second sentences
    connectors, 57
    definition, 55
    Guidelines, 61
    inappropriate, 59
Secondary sources, 201
Semi-colons, 24
Sentence combining
    dependent clauses, 25
    exercises, 28, 52-53, 79, 106, 107,
133-134, 154-155, 181-182, 199-200, 247-
248
    independent clauses, 21-23
Serials Record (library), 225
"Short words" (coordinate conjunctions, 22
Statement of intent, 36-37, 39
Statement of opinion, 36
Subordinating words, 26
Subject classification, Library of Congress,
212
Summary
    academic, 233
    definition, 229-230
    organization of, 237-238
    writing, 230
Support, paragraph (see Techniques of
support)
Surveys
    definition, 175-178
    samples, 176-178

T

Techniques of support
    examples, 66
    facts, 63
    multiple techniques, 71
    personal experience, 69-70
    physical description, 67

Thesis statement, 189
Titles, 41-42
Topic sentence
    controlling ideas, 38-39
    definition, 36-37, 94
    Guidelines, 95
    modifying, 94
    statement of intent, 36-37, 39
    statement of opinion, 36
Topic
    choosing, 30
    narrowing, 30-33

U

Unity, paragraph, 75

W

Writing-reading connection, 1-2